# GREEN MOUNTAIN CINEMA I
## Green Mountain Boys

# GREEN MOUNTAIN CINEMA I

A Journal of Vermont and New England Film and Video

Green Mountain Boys:
Election-Year Special

Created and edited by

Stephen R. Bissette

Packaged by
Evergreen Images
and
SpiderBaby Grafix & Publications

A Black Coat Press Book

This one is for William Hunter.

**Acknowledgements:** To those who blazed the trail—Barry Snyder, Susan Green, and Kenneth Peck; and to Frank Manchel.

Special thanks to Marjory Bissette, Joe Citro, Diane E. Foulds, Carl Hoglund (thanks for the years of access to stills, pressbooks, and treasures, Carl!), Nora Jacobson, Jean-Marc and Randy Lofficier, Michel and Linda Moyse, Alan Goldstein and the folks at First Run Video for undying support.

Additional thanks to Photofest for use of their photographs and http://www.grsites.com for the fonts.

Along with the filmmakers cited herein, the various contributors to this issue, and the sources noted at the end of each article, the editor also thanks 2nd Look Books, Joe Bookchin, Booksmart, Booksphere, Becky Cline, Alan Dater, Art Donahue, David Dudey, Michael Hanish, Arlene and Brian Hanson, Charles Horomanski, Josh Joy, Scott MacQueen, Lisa Merton, Michel and Linda Moyse, Chris Nixon, Roz Payne, Phil Pochoda, Robert Richardson, Steve Cutcliffe and the folks at MovieGoods, Inc., Drina Vurbic, Rick Winston, Norman Witty, George Woodard and Xochi's Bookstore & Gallery.

Text and package Copyright © 2004 by Stephen R. Bissette; all articles © 2004 by their respective authors.
Cover: *Fred Tuttle*, photograph Copyright © 2004 by Jack Rowell.
Back Cover: *The 4th of July*, photograph Copyright © 2004 by John Douglas.
All other illustrations Copyright © 2004 by their respective proprietors and/or studios.

Visit our website at www.blackcoatpress.com

ISBN 1-932983-29-5. First Printing. November 2004. Published by Black Coat Press, an imprint of Hollywood Comics.com, LLC, P.O. Box 17270, Encino, CA 91416. All rights reserved. Except for review purposes, no part of this book may be reproduced or transmitted in any form or by any means, electronic or mechanical, including photocopying, recording, or by any information storage and retrieval system, without permission in writing from the publisher. The stories and characters depicted in this book are entirely fictional. Printed in the United States of America.

Fred Tuttle
(*photo by Jack Rowell*)

Jay Craven, Henry Gibson and Fred Willard
on the set of *The Year That Trembled* (2002)

# Table of Contents

Roots, Reasons, Ramblings: Ye Editor's Intro .................................................... 9
Farewell, Fred .......................................................................................................... 17
The Tuttle Papers .................................................................................................... 31
Rusty DeWees: Lovin' The Logger ....................................................................... 37
Brigette Blood: "Learning How To See" ............................................................. 49
*Da Speech*: An International Project .................................................................... 63
    A talk with Simon Stockhausen ........................................................................ 89
    Haven't Seen Da Speech...? ............................................................................. 101
Reviews ................................................................................................................. 111
    Recently Released to DVD ............................................................................ 111
    Hard Choices: Pursuing Happiness ............................................................. 121
    A Brick in the Wall: Talking To The Wall ................................................ 127
        "I don't expect to win, I only expect to fight..." ................................ 133
    Jonathan Brandis: The Year That Trembled ............................................. 137
        *Remembering Jonathan Brandis...* ....................................................... 147
        The 'Other' Kent State Film ................................................................. 153
A Look Back... ..................................................................................................... 157
    Walter Ungerer's And All This Madness ................................................... 157
    Nora Jacobson's My Mother's Early Lovers ............................................. 167
In Production/Recently Completed .................................................................. 175
End Papers ............................................................................................................ 209
    Screening Vermont Films ............................................................................... 209
    Bob Keeshan: A Final Tip of the Cap to the Captain .............................. 213

Alfred Hitchcock filming *The Trouble With Harry* (1955)
in Craftsbury Common, VT.
(*source: Photofest*)

# Roots, Reasons, Ramblings: Ye Editor's Intro
by Stephen R. Bissette

*A fellow died one day and found himself waiting in the long line of judgment. As he stood there, he noticed that some souls were allowed to march right through the pearly gates into Heaven. Others, though, were led over to Satan who threw them into the burning pit. But every so often, instead of hurling a poor soul into the fire, Satan would toss a soul off to one side into a pile. After watching Satan do this several times, the fellow's curiosity got the best of him. So he strolled over and asked Satan what he was doing.*

*"Excuse me, Prince of Darkness," he said. "I'm waiting in line for judgment, but I couldn't help wondering, why are you tossing those people aside instead of flinging them into the Fires of Hell with the others?"*

*"Ah, those..." Satan said with a groan. "They're all from Vermont. They're still too cold and wet to burn."*

When I began work in 1999 on a dream project I'd nurtured for a number of years—a book on Vermont films and filmmakers—I had no idea how expansive that canvas would prove to be. The running joke I fielded whenever the subject came up was (in a variety of deliveries and wordings), essentially:

"Hmmmm, interesting. What will you put after page three?"

Vermont is, after all, a mere "speck of a state" [1] and hardly seems a mecca of regional filmmaking and videography.

I say, open your eyes. Wide.

Vermonters with long memories tend to recall the handful of films made by major studios—Alfred Hitchcock's *The Trouble With Harry*, the Disney feature *Those Calloways!*, maybe even D. W. Griffith's *Way Down East*—and thanks to Fred Tuttle's much-publicized grass-roots Senate race, celebrity, and more recent passing, John O'Brien's *Man With A Plan* still holds a place in many hearts and minds.

Folks tend to recall the films that were shot in their respective neck of the woods. Impressions are left by the persistent drum-beatings and road-shows mounted by self-motivated entrepreneurs/educators like Jay Craven (*Where the Rivers Run North, Stranger in the Kingdom, The Year That Trembled*) and Bess O'Brien (*Here Today*)—collectively, Kingdom County Productions—mount

---

[1] "Is Dean for Real?", *Time*, August 11, 2003, Vol. 162, No. 6, pg. 22.

with every current production. Only time will tell how long those impressions will remain.

But there's little conscious sense of a shared history, much less a legacy, of filmmaking in and about the state, and only fleeting glimpses that there might be a new generation of filmmakers and videographers at work as you read this.

The fact is Vermont does have a cinematic legacy—a legacy that extends far beyond (and beneath) that shaped by Hollywood with the occasional films they chose to set and/or film in the Green Mountain State.

Lillian Gish and Richard Barthelmess
in D.W. Griffith's *Way Down East* (1921)

It appears that the first films made in Vermont (over a century ago) chronicled military maneuvers. Those that followed were, by and large, products of industry: echoes of the quarries, run-off from the sugaring firms, romances culminating in tours of industrialized baking and bread factories, tourism travelogues charting the state's most alluring landmarks and portable charms. There were also home movies, many long-lost and never-to-be-recovered, while a precious few now reside in a marvelous movie museum in Bucksport, Maine.

On the Burlington side of Lake Champlain, famed French cinema pioneers the Lumière Brothers opened a plant in 1902; it changed hands to the Eastman Company, and was abandoned in 1911. The following year, the celebrated silent comedy mogul Mack Sennett formed the production company Keystone with two partners, one of whom was Adam Kessel, Jr., whose Kessel Park estate on the New York side of the lake reportedly housed guests like Charlie Chaplin. The Vermont Progressive Party—such as it was in 1915—produced a skewed romantic feature that urged orphaned lasses to spurn the lovesick farmer down the road (even if he gives his last dollar in aid), find a rich man, and marry.

In a frigid barn where W.A. "Snowflake" Bentley photographed his beloved crystals, Bentley himself fleetingly demonstrated a firmer grasp of the principles of filmmaking than did his camera-toting visitors; the short film was later exhibited at Burlington's Majestic Theatre. There was a pair of feature-length morality plays written, directed, and produced by an earnest, adventurous woman named Margery Wilson, who summered in Randolph; though she'd appeared in many features made in California (in and around what would become Hollywood) and even turned down a marriage proposal from one of America's leading movie stars, she chose Randolph as the ideal place to make her films.

A decade or so later, a very different nomadic female filmmaker wandered all of New England (and, possibly, many other states in the Union), currying favor and funding from local businesses to produce and promote her rapid-fire "Movie Queen" featurettes. She shot and completed her featurettes in a little over a week, reaping whatever boxoffice exhibition of the rough-and-ready finished product might earn from the locals eager to see themselves and their neighbors on the big screen at the local town hall or opera house, only to hurry off to another remote village to do it all over again.

There was also the celebrated arrival of the silent era's greatest director, who was sorely in need of success to recharge his flagging career and thus dared to place one of America's most beloved actresses afloat on a cake of ice in thawing March waters.

Long after D.W. Griffith shouted down irksome Dartmouth students who dared to disrupt his filming along the White River; after a weather-wearied Alfred Hitchcock ordered fallen autumn colors packed into crates to follow his cast and crew back to Hollywood after heavy October winds and rain had caused more trouble than dear dead Harry ever would; even after documentary pioneer Robert Flaherty set down his wayward roots in Dummerston dirt and completed his last productions here before his final breath, leaving it to his wife Frances, family and friends to carry on via their Center and annual workshop, a generation of young urban underground filmmakers came north to create their own lively breed of cinema.

These films were, by turns, playful, angry, poetic, political, ambitious, enigmatic, kinetic, contemplative. Adolfas Mekas, John Douglas, Walter Ungerer, and others came and left their mark—and were marked themselves by the rocky soil and wintry mountains. Some chose to stay, founding communes and communities (most all, at one time or another, also were teachers, opening eyes/minds/doors for new generations), but whether they stayed or left, their personal/imaginative/cinematic landscapes were reshaped by that of Vermont, as their films demonstrate. Homegrown filmmakers like Bob Campbell, Herb DiGioia and David Hancock, quite apart from this movement, carved out their own brand of regional cinema.

Hollywood returned now and again, peopling their films with characters that seemed far afield from those who actually live here, but a true regional filmmaking scene emerged from the 1960s and its growth can be measured as surely as that of a tree splitting a rock, determined to make its way however unyielding the apparent obstacle.

There remains no deterministic form or formula inherent to this regional filmmaking scene: the films and videos themselves were (and are) as individual as the people who made them. There is and was no coherent template or genre, nor should there be or have been; the growth was organic and uncontrolled, wherever fertile opportunity and hard work took root. The films range from the narrative to the anecdotal, from documentaries (of all stripes), somber dramas, antic comedies, and heartfelt coming-of-age tales to animated fantasies, dreamy absurdities, nightmarish horrors, and meditative visions.

Some were made in Vermont by non-Vermonters; others were made in faraway lands by Vermonters opening eyes/lenses/hearts to the world, bringing home, shaping, and sharing their paths for all to see.

Despite the inherent obstacles of funding, support, resources, and distribution, films of remarkable depth and scope were completed; in each and every case, too, it seemed the filmmakers were forced to "reinvent the wheel" to distribute their work, reaching audiences more often than not by road showing their creations themselves.

That remains as true today as it was in the 1960s, when the Newsreel Group (partially based in Vermont) would project their completed works on any available building face, gym or classroom wall, or tacked-up sheet to bring their message to the people; in the 1970s, as Walter Ungerer, David Ehrlich, and others personally toured the state and the globe with their latest creations; in the 1980s, as filmmakers tapped every available venue, from film festivals to educational distributor catalogs to Vermont Public Television, to get their work seen by anyone, everyone within reach.

By the 1990s, the scene shifted, expanded, and changed. Throughout the decade, a Rutland local built a studio facility dedicated in part to packaging and producing genre features for various foreign and domestic markets; meanwhile, in southern Vermont, a veteran industry professional who had worked with America's stellar filmmakers (including Woody Allen and Brian DePalma) chose to shift gears toward making his own artistic works and, with his wife, co-found a center dedicated to teaching and expanding filmmaking, videography, and digital art. In Montpelier and Charlotte, prohibitive costs and the evaporation of arts funding prompted two of the state's most seasoned active filmmakers to separately embrace emerging digital technologies and thus explore fresh vistas, within and without. A Marlboro couple documented the artists and communities around them, all the while keeping eyes and lenses open to the world at large (eventually traveling with a Tibetan transplant back to his homeland), while a neighbor and former collaborator in Guilford documented the gay activist movement, before and after the famous Stonewall riots. An earnest young man in Northern Vermont lovingly sired a brood of evocative short fantasies; on the heels of completing an intimate portrait of urban displacement in New Jersey, a Norwich filmmaker adapted her neighbor's unpublished semi-autobiographical novel into her first narrative dramatic feature.

A sheep-farming prodigal son launched what would become the "Tunbridge Trilogy" (and, initially by accident, a satiric Senate political campaign), while a native Waterbury Center farmer somehow juggled endless chores with an impressive body of character and lead roles in regional and mainstream films, long and short. At the same time, a lanky red-haired actor from Stowe expanded a skit he'd debuted in his farmer friend's traveling "Ground Hog Opry" into a touring one-man-show, *The Logger*, which revved into a one-man merchandizing machine (that included not one but two videos and a DVD) preserving his best performances for all to see.

And all the while, animators scattered throughout the state continued to bring their visions to life; documentarians lovingly crafted portraits, by turns intimate and expansive, of their households, their neighbors, their world, the world around them; and from Brattleboro to Burlington, student filmmaking programs blossomed at all education levels, spawning the first diverse generation of digital filmmakers who heed no limits on the horizon, save those imposed by means and ambition.

The only question for many of them now is: "Should I stay, or should I go?" Either option is ripe with opportunity, risks, perils, possibilities, and pitfalls.

Self-distribution is an integral part of the Green Mountain Cinema legacy, and one sorely in need of study, analysis, and innovative thought and action if we are to free future filmmakers and videographers from the constant 'reinventing of the wheel' every new production seems to require. Vermont has come a long way from the days of Margery Wilson debuting *Insinuation* at the Randolph Opera House.

Throughout this past year, evidence of that legacy was all around me. In a single research trip this spring, I passed through Randolph while researching Margery Wilson's self-produced and self-distributed silent features, only to find Jay Craven's self-distributed *The Year That Trembled* playing at the local playhouse; after interviewing a number of filmmakers in their homes and visiting Edgewood Studios en route north, I lucked into an opening-week matinee of John O'Brien's self-distributed *Nosey Parker* at a recently-renovated downtown Burlington theater.

With the arrival of the new millennium, we already have a few local youths who've made good, and in doing so have embraced an innovative new model for self-distribution that is both selfless (non-profit) and selfish (spreading their featurette and names across the state practically overnight).

With the emergence of new digital filmmaking and videography technologies, there has been a literal explosion of creative work in every corner of Vermont. It is astounding how much new work—much of it inventive, ingenious, insightful, and of great value—has and is being completed.

And it is to that explosion, and the firm foundation it is building upon, that this magazine project is dedicated.

As work continues on my book proper on Vermont films, filmmakers, and video, the fruits of that labor has yielded this periodical chronicle dedicated to Vermont and New England film, video, and the people who pour their creative lives into their production.

It is my humble hope that this publication will provide some collective focus for information about the Vermont and New England filmmaking and video scene. Each volume will feature at least one retrospective essay on past films and videos, the bedrock the current generation is (often unknowingly) building upon, along with interviews, reviews, and updates on current productions and just-completed features and shorts.

It is also my hope that this venture will provide some catalyst for the necessary building and broadening of the creative filmmaking community in and around my home state—looking forward, looking back.

Adolfas Mekas's *Hallelujah the Hills* (1963)

Which brings me to a final promise, and possible word of caution:

Reflecting the remarkable diversity of Vermont and New England films, videos, and creators, essentially anything goes here.

This publication will reflect my own absolutely omnivorous appetite for all manner of cinema and video, from the most fragile of experimental films to the most ambitious of big-studio productions, from the most obsessive documentaries to the most tasteless exploitation fodder. That appetite has forever driven those near and dear to me nuts, and I have no doubt it will eventually rub some of you the wrong way, so I'd best get all this out in the open from the outset.

I have no qualms about accommodating, enjoying, and embracing the virtues of *Way Down East* alongside *Hallelujah the Hills*, Alfred Hitchcock beside

Michael Hanish, the greenest of student films alongside the most top-heavy of big-budget Hollywood features, idiosyncratic experimental creations in tandem with a *Newhart* retrospective. You may find family-tailored mainstream fare like *The Trapp Family* and *Those Calloways!* lovingly analyzed alongside articles discussing disaster films, Canada's 'maple syrup porn' films, or the blood-bong-smoking night stalkers of *Vampire Vermont*. Mr. Deeds goes to Salem's Lot and the Northeast Kingdom prostitution rings make the trouble with Harry seem barely scandalous. Just as Rudy Vallee, M. Emmet Walsh, and George Woodard are native sons, Bob Keeshan, Charles Bronson, Micheal J. Fox, David Mamet, and Whoopi Goldberg (among others) chose Vermont as their adopted 'second-home away from home.' We'll be finding all kinds of odd neighbors, woodchucks and flatlanders, rubbing shoulders and sharing fences between these covers.

Young love: Linda Evans as Bridie, Brandon deWilde as Bucky Calloway in *Those Calloways* (1965)

Regional mavericks and Hollywood hucksters interest me equally, as do films and TV programs that claim to be set in, but were not shot in, our neck of the woods: they still reveal how others perceive us, and that is of interest, too. High art, low art, crass commercial product, idiosyncratic personal visions—though I hasten to add that it's not "all the same to me," I will not erect and perpetuate false boundaries on content.

All elements of Vermont and New England film and video history will remain fair game. It's all Green Mountain Cinema to me.

As I hope this maiden voyage demonstrates, all perspectives and points of view can and will be welcome. Fred Tuttle and Simon Stockhausen, Brigette Blood and Walt Disney, John Douglas and Edgewood Films, Kent State and Captain Kangaroo: as in our beloved state, art and commerce can and do co-exist herein.

The mix will forever be as lively, engaging, informative, entertaining, and provocative as possible.

Welcome, one and all.

This is only the beginning.

Stephen R. Bissette

# Farewell, Fred...
A remembrance of Fred Tuttle by Peter Miller
photos by Jack Rowell

*A few lucky folks knew Fred Tuttle all their lives, among them Fred's Tunbridge neighbor, John O'Brien. It was through John that most of the rest of us met Fred, along with his wife Dorothy and (then 93-year-old) father, Joe, in* Vermont is for Lovers *(1992). We met Fred onscreen, giving directions to a hapless fellow. Fred thereafter described his World War II experiences (including his eight trips to Paris) and shared an intimate moment with Dorothy discussing the virtues of marriage. Later in the film, laying in the grass, Fred explained the arcane pre-Columbian archeology of the old stones and Indian markers on his property ("one place to make you well, one to make you sick").*

*Recognizing star potential, John made Fred the center of his next "anthropological comedy," the satiric* Man With a Plan *(1996). The rest is history. In the film, armed with a campaign budget of $16, Fred defeated an incumbent Congressman by a single vote; in life, at age 77, Fred became a local hero and* *a national celebrity, joining Jay Leno and Conan O'Brien on late-night television and gracing the front page of the* New York Times.[2] Life *magazine declared Fred "perhaps New England's most beloved political figure since JFK himself."*[3] *In 1998, Fred really did campaign against Jack McMullen in the Senate Republican Primary; after a series of amusing debates, the wry old man of Tunbridge defeated McMullen. Fred thereafter endorsed Democratic candidate Senator Patrick Leahy, retiring from politics to return to his hillside home.*

*He appeared in one more film for John,* Nosey Parker *(2003), and my wife and I were fortunate enough to see Fred in all his glory at the Brattleboro, VT premiere of* Nosey Parker *at the Latchis Theater. John and Fred introduced the film to a sell-out house, and enjoyed a lively Q&A session afterwards. Though he needed help getting up and down the theater's steep stairs, Fred was clearly enjoying himself, and the audience thoroughly enjoyed his company. His spirits were visibly high, and he answered questions with characteristic enthusiasm and candor (including my own, whether Democratic Presidential hopeful and former Vermont Governor Howard Dean had approached Fred for sage political advice; he had, and Fred shared a hilarious anecdote). It was his final public appearance.*

*Fred Tuttle, dairy farmer, actor, politician and Vermont's most beloved citizen, died of a heart attack on October 4, 2003, in Tunbridge, Vermont. He was 84.*

*Thanks to John's films, we all felt we knew Fred a bit, but only a lucky few really knew Fred the man. The following essay was written by one of those folks, Peter Miller, and it is reprinted here with his kind permission. Peter came to know and love Fred, Dorothy, and Joe Tuttle, and his affection for them informs every word that follows. Peter also photographed and interviewed Fred and his father Joe, and both appear side by side in the pages of the new edition of Peter's exquisite book,* Vermont People. *—SRB.*

---

[2] Friday, November 8, 1996.
[3] October 1997 issue.

On a mountain top in Tunbridge, Vermont,
Fred Tuttle and Nancy Wires behind-the-scenes
making John O'Brien's *Man With a Plan*.

**Peter Miller on Fred Tuttle:**

It was one of those soft Indian Summer days. The early morning fog lifted to bare blue-hazed mountains under a sky unblemished with clouds. The temperature climbed slowly into the high seventies but the shade was fresh as spring water. It was a day to live easy, but this Thursday, the ninth day of October, Vermont's most benevolent and beautiful month, was Fred Tuttle's funeral.

I had put on my only suit, which I hadn't worn for a decade, my black shoes, a pale pink shirt and a muted paisley tie left over from a time past. Tunbridge, Fred's home town, is about 40 miles from Waterbury, where I live. I drove to Randolph and took the short cut, over the mountain, past some rolling fields of corn stalks being chopped into silage, then into the woods and down past a landscape of farms into Tunbridge.

The Tunbridge Congregational Church is typical of most small villages that were never wealthy. A simple steeple punctuated the center of town. The interior was plain with graceful discipline. Judy Lewis—it's always a woman at these funerals— was playing the organ that had a deep voice that was constant, solemn but respectful as attendants ushered in the mourners. On the left aisle were seated friends of Fred. Among them was Senator Patrick Leahy, who defeated Fred in the 1987 Senatorial campaign (well, Fred, after he won the primary, deferred to the Senator, on the advice of his wife Dottie—"THERE IS NO WAY YOU ARE GOING TO WASHINGTON!", she once screamed at him when he was toying with the idea as we sat at the dining room table. He gave me a sly smile and I could see he liked, in his own way, to have Dottie lecture him). Also seated in the church, in the pew in front of Senator Leahy, was John O'Brien, who had the brilliance to recognize that his neighbor down the road was just the right person to star in his film *Man With a Plan*. Next to him was Jack Rowell, associate producer to *Man With a Plan*, woodchuck photographer and fly fisherman, whose photographs sparkle with warmth and humor, and who traveled and documented Fred's years as a performance artist.

Filling the right side of the aisle were members of the family. There were more elderly women then men; their husbands had already died. A few men had the bronzed healthy look of farmers who spent the last month on their tractors, haying and chopping. Others were white faced, their bodies crumpled, waiting out their time, and they walked with difficulty. A few wore open collar shirts with suspenders, as Fred dressed. One elderly man had on high patent leather shoes, the creases in the toe of the shoe coated with dust collected from years in a closet. Two wore mismatched coats and trousers. In the front row was seated Fred's wife Dottie and Fred's children, some of them adopted, some direct descendents, but all part of the fabric of the Tuttle family which is thick in these parts.

Fred Tuttle as a young man with a younger Bessie Roberts.
(*photo courtesy of Bessie Roberts*)

In 1798, the first Tuttles settled in Tunbridge. In 1872, Fred Herman Tuttle, Fred's grandfather, bought the Tuttle hillside farm, which still remains in the family. Two hundred and five years is sure enough time to spread the Tuttle roots.

*Fred had two great moments in his 84-year life. The first was as a soldier in World War II. Attached to a combat engineering company, he landed in Normandy on D-Day plus seven and was sent to Le Mans when the Germans were just vacating it; Fred could still smell cabbage soup. His unit constructed a bridge in 36 hours ("How long does it take them in Vermont to put up a bridge? A year?") but he found time and the directions to visit a house of pleasure. Downstairs, he left his helmet and cartridge belt and rifle ("I shouldn't had done that") walked upstairs and made love for the first time.*

*"Guess what, Peter?" and he leaned forward, the glint gleamed in his eyes, the famous Tuttle smile began to crease his face, as he held up his hand with the thumb and forefinger about three inches apart. "For one cigarette! That's all! One cigarette!" and he sat back and his face expanded into a huge Cheshire Cat smile.*

*Fred first visited Paris the day after its liberation and was overwhelmed with his reception, so much so that he volunteered to patrol a section of pipeline that lay north of the city and through which flowed fuel for the tanks and trucks on the front line. He was there until the war ended, and his trips to the City of Light were numerous.*

*"Peter, The Paris women. They were... beautiful. Beautiful! There was red carpet on the floor, long bars, they served us drinks, we sat in sofas." He was referring to his hangouts on Boulevard Clichy, which he knew as Pigalle.*

*Fred returned from France not being shot at, and not shooting at others, but seeing too many dead bodies and almost drowning while returning to the States on a troop ship that was caught in a storm. The hold was full of water and Fred kept his head and that of a stow-away dog above water. He always liked animals.*

*When he was discharged, Fred rode the train to Randolph, the nearest train station to Tunbridge. "There were two pretty women in the station, when I got off," remembered Fred, "and they didn't even look at me." That night, Fred milked the cows, as he did daily for the next 40 years.*

David Wolfe, the church's minister, climbed the pulpit and gave a humorous but compassionate portrait of Fred as "perhaps my most reluctant parishioner." Fred's son recalled his younger years and how he liked to hunt without killing anything and the importance of Fred as a father to his natural and adopted children. John O'Brien described Fred's natural talent as an actor and mentioned some of the funnier moments he spent with Fred. After years of anonymity and nights and mornings looking at the hind end of cows, days of reaping and sowing and the never ending job of cutting and splitting fire wood, Fred savored stardom as he did ice cream.

Forty-five thousand videos of *Man With a Plan*, about a farmer who decided to run for Congress on the slogan, "I've spent my whole life in the barn, now I just want to spend a little time in the House," were sold. In the movie, Fred's character won by one vote and stole the hearts of all who saw the movie. The movie was whimsical, gently satirical and so very, very Vermont. Fred became the icon of a Vermont farmer—he had an accent that almost needed translation, an honest mind, an ability to express himself with as few words as possible, sweetness in his affability. There was no pretense in Fred and he said what he thought. He was just... Fred.

At the service, Maria Lamson sang *Simple Gifts*, in a sweet voice and Priscilla Farnham gave an stirring rendition of *Amazing Grace*. Fred lay in an open casket at the front of the church. His glasses were in place and he looked peaceful, his eyes closed, as if he was remembering something from the past, and would suddenly open them and start telling a story. His hands were clasped together and on his belly lay his cap with FRED spelled on it. (As he said in the movie, it is an acronym : F for friendly, R for renewable, E for extraterrestrial, D for dinky.)

At the end of the service, I walked up the aisle to say good-bye to Fred and I thought of the last time I saw him, a few weeks before. I was camped on his property as I attended the Tunbridge Fair. I brought him a copy of a revised edition of *Vermont People* with photos and stories on him and Joe, his father. When I left Fred, he was standing in the doorway in his striped pajamas, hand on the half opened door, peering out at me, through his thick glasses, like an owl. He flipped his hand up and waggled it in a short wave. It was one of those photographs I never took, but an image that will stay with me all my life.

Up way past his bedtime: actress Hallie Eisenberg, Fred Tuttle, and Jay Leno on *The Tonight Show with Jay Leno*.

*In 1989, I first met Fred when I came over to photograph his father Joe, who was then 93. At the same time, I photographed Fred as he leaned on his cane and gave me a penetrating glance through his big glasses. We didn't talk much but he reminded me of a Mr. Magoo. His father's photograph and story appeared next year in the book. Every so often I would visit Tunbridge and drop in to see Fred and Joe and, after Joe died, I visited with Fred and Dottie.*

*When I was updating* Vermont People *in 1998, I photographed Fred in the same pose as I photographed his father, holding his father's photograph who was holding his father's photograph. The photograph was taken in front of the Tuttle barn that was about to fall down in the movie* Man with a Plan. *It really did fall down and needed to be reconstructed.*

*John O'Brien asked Fred to run in the Senate GOP primary against a Massachusetts millionaire and Fred, never bashful, agreed. His opponent was Jack McMullen who had moved to Vermont from Massachusetts because, we assumed, he had political ambitions. Everyone called him a carpetbagger and the election and the debate drew howls of laughter and nationwide political coverage. Fred appeared on* The Tonight Show *and shared laughs with Jay Leno. He met beautiful women in Hollywood and New York and kissed them all with the same gusto that he kissed babies while campaigning.*

*The most famous debate between Tuttle and McMullen hinged on one question Fred asked Jack McMullen and it had nothing to do with politics.*

*"How many teats does a cow have?"*

*"Six," answered McMullen.*

He lost the election to a farmer who milked by hand and who campaigned with a few dollars and won 54% of the vote. He supported his opponent, Senator Leahy, in the senatorial campaign and capped his campaign fund at $251, representing a dollar from each Vermont town. He went over the fund when Vermonters, mostly children, donated $600. His biggest expense was for renting two portable johns at a fund raising dinner at his farm. At the end of the campaign he donated his PAC money to the Lincoln Library, which was damaged by flood, and the Tunbridge Library. Even after endorsing Senator Leahy, he still won 24% of the vote.

Fred and Dottie lived in a small white house a few hundred yards from the farm, where his daughter Debra and Sean now live. The front door opened into a shed, that usually had in the corner a basket of vegetables Fred had pulled from the garden. Another door opened into the kitchen. Dottie kept her house neat and prim, with flowers in the windowsill. The cats had taken over the sofa. The dining room table was in front of the stove and sink. On the table were bottles of pills Fred was taking for his heart, his eyes, his diabetes, rheumatism. We sat and talked. Fred would fire up his accent, thicker than grade-B commercial grade maple syrup.

"How come people don't visit anymore? I don't know anyone in town. Why does everyone go so fast? Isn't it just a mess in Washington? Look at our taxes, why, we used to pay taxes with our maple syrup sales! What's happening to our state, Peter? Everything is going to hell, ain't it?"

Tuttle on the Town: actress Elizabeth Berkley, Fred Tuttle, and Conan O'Brien on *Late Night With Conan O'Brien*.

*We digressed onto the origin of the stone huts on his property, which may be Celtic, and moved on to farming.*

"I sold the cows in 1984," Fred remembered, looking up at the ceiling. "On Friday, they picked up the cows and on Monday, I had prostate surgery. Worst thing can happen to anybody is when they have to sell their cows, you know."

But, most of all, Fred remembered the political campaign, the interviews and appearances and people he met, and the debates and campaigning he did in the 1998 primary. He peered at me over his glasses and those blue eyes gleamed and that wide, wide smile lit up and he confided, almost in a whisper.

"Peter, you know... these have been the happiest years of my life. The happiest!"

At 77 years, Fred changed lanes from a retired dairy farmer to a performance artist who crossed the reality barrier to become a politician and Vermont's leading citizen.

This past summer, I had a booth at six Vermont county fairs, promoting my books Vermont People *and* Vermont Farm Women. *I had made a poster of the photograph I used in the book—Fred holding the family photos—and displayed on an easel. Almost everyone who walked by, it didn't matter which fair, looked at the photos, smiled, and said "Fred! There's Fred!" Then, they would ask me how he was. Fred Tuttle is Vermont's most recognizable citizen, outside of presidential candidate Howard Dean, but much more popular than the ex-governor.*

After the funeral, we walked a few yards to the town hall for a reception. On one table were newspaper clippings, posters, old and new family shots and other mementos of Fred Tuttle as a young man, a farmer, father, actor and politician. We sat on long tables. Baloney and cheese and egg salad sandwiches filled a large platter beside bowls and plates of pickles and some dips, squares of Cabot cheese, five flavors of Ben & Jerry's ice cream and fresh, home made cookies. A big punch bowl had a label stuck on it that read "Fred's Punch." I suspect it was vanilla ice cream, milk and ginger ale swirled together. We renewed acquaintances and told stories about Fred.

It was a good funeral—Fred had a fast passing after a long life of hard work with all the desserts at the end. He won our hearts and always, when I think of him I smile and say to myself... Frrredddd... the word drawn out and flowing as sweet as honey. I enjoyed so much visiting with him, sitting at the table, having a coffee and a chat, listening to Dottie's rants to keep him in control, or going to a nickel-a-plate fund raiser at the Tuttle farm with all his neighbors. Fred was fun. He was witty without knowing it. He had a plastic face and such a glint in his eye. He had no guile. He was, and I say this as a great compliment, a simple Vermonter with a wonderful smile and compelling charisma.

I left the funeral reception early and drove my car through the covered bridge that was rebuilt after the flood a few years back washed it downstream, and headed up the mountain. On the left, not a mile from the bridge and overlooking the valley is the cemetery where Fred is buried. An iron fence surrounds it. Fred was buried in a private, family burial while we were enjoying the warm afternoon sun and munching baloney sandwiches.

A backhoe sat idle in the cemetery as two men shoveled dirt into Fred's grave. Dottie was then at the reception, seated at a long table with friends and relatives. Daughter Debra was just beginning to retain her tears. I wondered, as I drove slowly past the cemetery and up the mountain, on this clear, beautiful Indian Summer day, if we were not only burying Fred but also the character that made Vermont what it was, what we have cherished and loved.

*Peter Miller is a photographer and writer, author of* People of the Great Plains, The First Time I Saw Paris *(a memoir of photographs and text of the years Peter spent in Paris as a US Army Signal Corps photographer), and the award-winning* Vermont People, *which includes a profile and photograph of Fred and Joe Tuttle. Peter's new book is* Vermont Farm Women, *now in book shops and also available from Peter's website. The book took almost four years to complete, profiling in text and photographs 44 Vermont farm women, illuminating what Peter refers to as "the revolution that is spreading from Vermont to Maine, Pennsylvania to the West Coast. Women are now the majority who are buying and operating small farms." The foreward is by Gert Lepine. The books may be viewed and purchased from http://www.silverprintpress.com. If you'd like a peek at Peter Miller's photographs, go to his online gallery at:*
*http://www.yankeeimage.com.*

Fred Tuttle with John O'Brien

# The Tuttle Papers
by John O'Brien
photos by Jack Rowell

Sweeten the current election year with memories
of Fred Tuttle's famous 1998 Senate race,
punctuated as it was by these profundities.

*Thanks to John O'Brien, writer/director/editor of* Vermont is for Lovers, Man With a Plan *and* Nosey Parker, Green Mountain Cinema *offers this archival record of Fred Tuttle's key speeches from his whirlwind Senatorial race.*

*Fred entered the 1998 Republican primary opposing only one prominent candidate, wealthy businessman Jack McMullen, who had recently moved to the state. The opening and closing speeches framed the memorable Thursday, September 3, 1998 Vermont Public Radio debate Fred participated in (a highlight of the campaign, which Peter Miller mentions in his loving memoir); the Victory Speeches were scribed for the Tuesday, September 8, 1998 Primary.*

*Fred easily defeated McMullen, thereafter endorsed Democratic Senator Patrick Leahy for the general election and in fact campaigned with Leahy.*[4]

*John authored these historic speeches for his beloved neighbor, friend and star, proof that another lucrative career beckons if he wearies of either filmmaking or sheep-farming. John recalls,* "Fred could never memorize any lines (the 'but the people called collect, and I accepted the charges' line in the film took about sixteen takes) but he read these speeches beautifully. This was a change for me—I got to hear an actor perform something I'd written!" *And what a performance. Needless to add, the following should be read keeping Fred's distinctive delivery and thick Vermont accent in close recall.*

*In closing, John offers this sage observation:* "My objective for Fred's speeches: Keep it simple. Make it funny. Print it in really large type." *John, we hear ya, and we obey.*

---

[4] Note that McMullen is the leading Republican candidate for this upcoming 2004 election, at the time of this writing facing Peter Moss of Fairfax and Westminster West's Benjamin L. Mitchell in the September primary—or, should I say, not facing them, as he has refused to engage in any form of public debate; I do not know if McMullen has visited the Tunbridge World Fair between '98 and today. SRB.

# Opening Speech

The U.S. Senate is full of millionaires and lawyers.
I am not a millionaire.
I am not a lawyer.
I am a senior citizen, and I want to help senior citizens.
I am a farmer, and I want to help farmers.
I am a veteran, and I want to help veterans.
I live on social security, and I know what that means.
I am a 10th grade drop-out, but my granddaughters graduated from Middlebury, UVM, and Johnson State College. I want drop-outs to be able to send their granddaughters to college.
I am a Vermonter.
My father was a Vermonter.
My grandfather was a Vermonter.
My great grandfather was a flatlander.
I'm a man with a plan, and I plan to stand for Vermonters.

## Closing Speech

In 1832, my Great Grandfather, Joe Tuttle, a flatlander from Boston, moved to Vermont. He wanted to be a U.S. Senator, but the natives told him to wait a while.

"Get to know Vermont first," they told him.

So Joe waited.

In 1857, Joe had a son Fred.

Fred wanted to be a U.S. Senator, but the natives told him to wait a while.

"Get to know Vermont first," they told him.

So Fred waited.

In 1897, Fred had a son Joe.

Joe wanted to be a U.S. Senator, but the natives told him to wait a while.

"Get to know Vermont first," they told him.

So Joe waited.

In 1919, Joe had a son Fred.

I am that boy.

And now the natives tell me, "Why not Fred?"

I say, "If the people lead, I will follow."

## Victory Speech - Part One

I like Vermont. I really like Vermont.

I don't know of another place where a farmer can beat a lawyer;

Where a poor man can beat a millionaire;

Where a 10th grade drop-out can beat a Harvard man;

Where $16 buys more than four hundred thousand dollars.

I like Jack McMullen.

He's friendly.

He's a gentleman.

And he's a hard worker.

But history was not on Jack's side in this race.

It is a fact that Vermont has never elected a U.S. Senator who has not been to the Tunbridge World's Fair first!

Don't mess with tradition!

## Victory Speech - Part Two

I like Senator Leahy too.
He's friendly.
He's a gentleman.
And he's a hard worker.
But this Fall I will stay on the ballot.
I will run a positive race against Senator Leahy.
I will listen to all Vermonters.
Remember, if the people lead, I will follow.
And now let's have some fun.
So thank you Vermont.
You called collect, and I accepted the charges!

# Rusty DeWees: Lovin' The Logger
## Part One
### by Stephen R. Bissette

Or,
*How a Rowdy Red-Headed Lad from Stowe Done Made Good and Built a New England Stage, Screen, and Multi-Media Phenomenon.*

In a remarkably short period of time, Rusty DeWees carved a distinctive niche as a feature film and television character actor. He is currently Vermont's most prominent and visible star. Regionally, Rusty made his mark with his hilarious one-man stage show *The Logger*. He has acted in many films and TV shows, but he's also the producer, director, writer, co-editor, packager and distributor of the video production of *The Logger* (1999) and its sequel, *The Logger Visits New York City* (2000).

Rusty has justifiably become a local hero. "I just want to entertain Vermonters," he enthuses. "I want to entertain all people, but I'm from up here, and want to entertain my own neighbors." An actor's life can be a tough row to hoe, but Rusty's made a steady effort and distinguished himself in theater, regional films and big-budget Hollywood productions as a player to reckon with.

While many fine actors have based their careers on the kinds of character roles Rusty continues to score, he's gone a step further and taken the bull by the horns, so to speak, establishing *The Logger* as his own distinct trademark.

Indeed, Rusty has self-merchandised his character of *The Logger* into a one-man franchise. Not only has *The Logger* stage show firmly placed Rusty's take on a venerable New England archetype in the local pop culture, Rusty has also self-packaged, self-promoted, and self-distributed a line of *Logger* products: videos, audio tapes, CDs, a calender, and more. He's made *The Logger* his own vehicle, laying bedrock for future endeavors most actors only dream about.

This do-it-yourself entrepreneurial savvy strikes as deep a chord in fellow Yankee spirits as Rusty's amusing Vermont character does. Rusty was born in November of 1960 in Philadelphia, Pennsylvania. "My folks moved us to Stowe, Vermont, when I was seven," Rusty recalls. Arriving in June of 1968, Rusty grew up in Northern Vermont's prime ski town. He first took to the stage in high school, appearing in the school musicals and local community theater. During this period, Rusty's bond with fellow Vermont actor and musician George Woodard grew from the friendship they'd nurtured as neighbors to a shared interest in pursuing acting as a profession. They remain friends to this day, and often appear together on stage and screen.

The flames were fanned further after Rusty attended Champlain College in Burlington, Vermont. "I got involved in a really good group called Vermont Repertory Theater in Burlington," Rusty explains. "That's where you might say that I caught the bug." From 1984 to 1987, Rusty worked with the famed Burlington theatrical group under director Robert R. Ringer. "We toured and I learned a lot from Robert," he said. Rusty particularly distinguished himself in the Repertory's touring production of *Judevine* by David Budbill. It remains a vital turning point in DeWees life; you can hear its import in his voice when he mentions its title, referring to the play numerous times as a personal touchstone.

Poet and playwright David Budbill moved to Wolcott, VT., in 1969, and in his poetry anthology *The Chain Saw Dance* (1977), introduced the fictional village of Judevine ("the ugliest town in northern Vermont, except maybe East Judevine! Disheveled, wretched, Judevine...") and its inhabitants, the "Judevine uglies," earning critical kudos and local ire. For the play *Judevine*, Budbill incorporated components from his anthology *From Down to the Village* and verse play *Pulp Cutters' Nativity*, creating an anecdotal series of vignettes fueled entirely by the characters, including "uglies" like Antoine LaMotte. Vermont Repertory's director Ringer considered *Judevine* ideal for his actors, and began working with the cast in December of 1985, as the company was on the brink of fiscal ruin. With each of the half-dozen performers playing multiple roles, Ringer cast Rusty as the French-Canadian alcoholic Antoine and as Conrad, Judevine's tipsy mechanic. Though DeWees was physically unlike the Antoine Budbill delineated in *The Chain Saw Dance*, he won the role, and Rusty's life forever changed.

Breakthrough role: Tom Blachly, Rusty DeWeens on stage in *Judevine* (1986) (*photo by Fred C. Hill from Vermont Life*)

At the time, Rusty was still working construction. Cabot writer R.D. Eno then wrote of Rusty's involvement in *Judevine*: "Though he's a fine actor, DeWees expresses no desire to make a life in the theatre. In fact, he is the only member of the cast you might actually meet in a place like Judevine. This winter, when there are no construction jobs, he is working at a local gas station," but acknowledged Rusty was clearly "the lynchpin of the production," citing the young actor's gift for improvisation and rapport with his fellow performers and the audience.[5] Even the regional resentment some had harbored toward Budbill's original poems for almost a decade softened, as the play and its cast (which also included Kelly Andrews, Deborah Freeman, Tom Blachly, and Patti Quinn) breathed fresh, recognizable life into its characters. *Judevine* rescued the Repertory's season, praised by the regional press and selling out every performance of its initial run, having to turn away a crowd even after an extra weekend was added. By popular demand, the production returned to the stage the following

---

[5] "*Judevine*," *Vermont Life*, Winter 1986, pg. 54.

September, then toured Vermont and New Hampshire.

For Rusty, life had irrevocably changed—for the better.

Another key creative figure in Rusty's budding career is filmmaker Jay Craven. "Jay cast me in *Ethan Frome*, which was my first film role," Rusty continues. "Jay didn't direct the film,[6] but he was involved in the casting." Rusty delivered two lines as a bearded local who gives the crippled Ethan (Liam Neeson) wide berth in the Starkfield post office. Jay later cast Rusty in his own feature films. In Jay's stout adaptation of Howard Frank Mosher's novel *Where the Rivers Flow North* (1993), Rusty played circuit chain-fighter Bennie "The Champ," who is beaten in the ring by the one-handed logger Noel Lourdes (Rip Torn). "That was the role where I really became interested in doing more film work."

In Jay's and Kingdom County Production's subsequent Mosher adaptation, *A Stranger in the Kingdom* (1998), Rusty lent an edge to the proceedings as the racist, cock-fighting filling-station proprietor Harlan Kittredge, a minor character in the novel fleshed-out for the film by incorporating elements of Mosher characters like Bumper Stevens. As ring-leader of a makeshift backwoods "girlie show," Harlan fans the flames of perdition in Kingdom County. Rusty also lent his talents to Jay Craven's Kingdom County Productions' Fledgling Films Institute, a hands-on filmmaking workshop for teenagers, appearing in their feature film *In Jest* (1999) as Smelton, Vermont's taxi-driving deputy and eccentric farmer Leroy Crumb. He has also played supporting roles in many student and amateur film productions, selflessly lending his big-screen experience and credentials to a new generation of young filmmakers whenever time allows.

During this period, Rusty moved to New York City for a stretch, finding green pastures in the cement jungle. "I did spend 11 years in NYC," Rusty recalls, "the final five I drove home every weekend." That kept him juggling acting jobs from 1987 through 1998, including his gigs with Kingdom County Productions, among many others. "I was doing a lot of TV commercials, soap operas, and TV shows. I've done tons of commercials for Chevy, Coke, Wendy's, and so on. In the soaps, I appeared in *As The World Turns, All My Children, The Guiding Light, One Life to Live*... I didn't have contract parts, I wasn't on all year, but I had good character roles." Rusty also landed parts on series like *Law and Order* and *Saturday Night Live*, among others. These roles traded on Rusty's look and sound—not just the stereotypical Vermonter embodied by *The Logger*.

"There are several things I sell," Rusty explains. "You have to learn that as an actor, what you can 'sell.' A lot of what I 'sell' is my 'physicality,' of course, and my presence. Farmer, cop, the country boyfriend—for Citroën, the French car commercials, I played a real fancy bank robber with the nice clothes and glasses. But my strengths are with the more rural types."

---

[6] The director was John Madden. SRB.

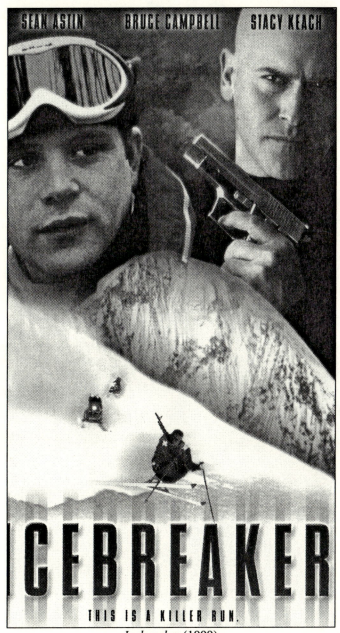
*Icebreaker* (1999)

As Rusty's film parts continued, one could see the actor's repertoire grow. Most of his film work remained rooted in Vermont: Rutland-based action director David Giancola cast Rusty as a New York City cop, gunned down in the opening minutes of the jewelry-heist thriller *Diamond Run* (1997); in Giancola's *Pressure Point* (1997), Rusty was one of the loud-mouthed locals eager to pick a fight with the film's hero in a feed-and-grocery store. In Giancola's recent *Icebreaker* (1999), Rusty's turn as an overly-talkative contract killer aboard a plane revels in such a nasty streak that the pilot deliberately sends the aircraft crashing into a Killington peak; Rusty survives just long enough to spill the beans to the film's cueball villain Bruce Campbell, kicking off the film's action (before Campbell kicks Rusty's character to his death from a helicopter).

Rusty also graced the medium-budget Patrick Swayze trucker-action film *Black Dog* (1998), playing a laconic truck-yard grease-monkey named Junior, sidekick to the film's lethal Bible-thumping gun runner villain (Meat Loaf). Junior buys the farm trying to take out Swayze during one of the film's many startling setpieces, but with a cocky look and an improvised jab of his finger, Rusty registers with his first shot of the film. "Patrick Swayze loved that, you know," Rusty chuckles. "When you get to a level where you're able to get work in movies and TV, you're trusted. The director hires you because they trust you, trust what you can do, and they see you in that character. So when I was there, we just played it—and what I did, that was it, they were all laughing about that finger-pointing thing. [Director] Kevin Hooks just loved that."

Rusty DeWees as Tom in Nora Jacobson's *My Mother's Early Lovers* (1999)
(*photo by William Stetson*)

As he matured as a screen performer, Rusty's roles reflected a greater breadth and depth of characterization. Rusty played the "strange and beautiful soldier" Louise (Molly Hickok) makes out with on the bus in Nora Jacobson's *My Mother's Early Lovers* (1998), and co-starred as Tom, a Gulf War veteran ("I get back here and it's a video game") whom Maple (Sue Ball) is drawn to later in the film. In Anthony Hall, Rob Lewbell, and Ed Fillian's *Mud Season* (1998), Rusty scored his first screen leading role as a stoic hermit whose life is irrevocably changed when he finds a young Asian woman (Linda Shing) shivering in his home after her escape from enforced prostitution. *Mud Season* proved Rusty's ability to carry a film; the tender chemistry between Rusty and Linda Shing becomes profoundly moving, demonstrating a warmth and depth few of Rusty's previous roles even hinted at. [7]

When asked about the difference between working on high-ticket items like *Black Dog* and regional indy films, Rusty ponders for a moment. "The difference comes down to simply the money," Rusty explains. "Things can be pretty tense when someone's got just two million to spend, as opposed to a $50 million movie like *Black Dog* where they can afford whatever. But really, there's no difference between a big Hollywood set and a small independent film. There's more fancy things going on, you get a bigger trailer with a large budget—but with the actual work you're doing, when the camera rolls, it's the same. When the camera rolls, the work is the same. That's the way I look at it, but other people might tell you different."

*The Logger* grew out of a character Rusty created for George Woodard's stage variety shows. "George has a theater group called The Woodchuck Theater Company," Rusty elaborates, "and every other winter or so around Groundhog

---

[7] Those who jeered at the film's premise of an Asian prostitution ring in the Kingdom should note the summer 2004 busts of just such a ring in northern Vermont, linked to similar busts as far north as Maine. SRB.

Day he does kind of a Grand Ol' Opry show called *Ground Hog Opry*, where he plays music with his friends and does old-time *Hee-Haw*-type skits. I had written a couple of these Logger stories in my own head while I was living in New York. I called George up, thinking the *Ground Hog Opry* would be a good place to try these skits; he said 'Ya, come on up,' and he let me try those little stories—about twelve or fifteen minutes—and people like it."

That was in 1997, and those two bits are still fixtures of *The Logger* show (the deer-jacking story ending with the sheriff's "stop or slow down" punch line, and the tale of his wife freezing on the treadmill). "So I just continued to work on them. I knew people would be entertained by them, and I was entertained by doing them and enjoyed putting them together, and saw ahead that I could entertain a large group of people, and pushed it in earnest." Rusty wrote the second act on the set of *Black Dog* ("right in the middle of Georgia, in my little apartment there").

*The Logger* soon evolved into Rusty's first state-wide stage tour (launched in 1998) and two-volume video set, filmed at the Vergennes Opera House in Vergennes, Vermont, accommodating the complete two-act show as two videos. *The Logger* (1999) became a regional hit, self-produced, packaged, and distributed to the tune of over 18,000 copies sold in its first year. Thanks to hard work, the support network of friends and family, the constant tie-in with his touring stage show, and an avid and ever-growing audience, *The Logger* has become a one-man cottage industry. "Believe it or not, counting the DVDs, I've sold to date around 40,000 *Logger 1*s and about 25,000 *Logger 2*s," Rusty told me in August of this year. "Add in calendars, CDs, t-shirts, hats, and stuff, and *Logger* products sold tally somewhere around 90,000 pieces."

*The Logger Visits New York City* (2000)

Rusty DeWees and Rip Torn in
*Where the Rivers Flow North* (1993)

The tone and tenor of *The Logger Visits New York City* (2000) was markedly different from the first volume, bringing the second act of *The Logger* stage show to the home screen. Laughter still fueled the show, but the characters Rusty brought to life on stage dig a little deeper, plucking less comfortable chords. Reflecting this shift, the video incorporates on-the-street interviews with a diverse group of Big Apple residents: a transplanted fellow Stowe native now working as a venture capital investor; the employees at the William Doyle Galleries; a heartbreaking dialogue with a homeless man; an extended, somewhat furtive interview with a stripper. Rusty has self-rated both volumes of *The Logger* 'SC': "Some Cussin; material may be inappropriate for some children." Of the two, *The Logger Visits New York City* incorporates more mature material. Both videos feature occasionally strong language, but Vol. 2's NYC trip proffers more adult content during its strip show sequence and Rusty's interview with exotic dancer Amber Paul.

"There's a bit more to chew on, I try to say a little bit more with this video," Rusty said to me back in 2000, just before the release of the second *Logger* video. "I'll be interested to see how people like it. I'm not nervous, really, but you want to see how people take it; the payoffs and laughs don't come as rapidly as they do in the first video. So I have been worried if the core audience won't find it as funny—but they haven't, people say they're getting it. You've got to trust your audience."

Trusting his audience—and his own instincts—has served Rusty pretty well thus far.

*Part Two of "Rusty DeWees: Lovin' The Logger" will appear in our spring 2005 issue.*

---

**Sources:**
Phone interview with Rusty DeWees, November 2000.
Followup 2004 emails with Rusty DeWees, August 24, 13:30:15; August 27, 15:27:04, and August 28, 00:28:30.
Phone interview with George Woodard, November 2000.
Eno, R.D., "*Judevine*," *Vermont Life*, Winter 1986, Vol. XLI, No. 2, pp. 53-55.

The Yellow Chair from *The Yellow Chair* (2001)
(*photo Brigette Blood*)

# Brigette Blood: "Learning How To See"
by Stephen R. Bissette
photos by Brigette Blood

An introduction to the filmmaker and her recent film,
*i went home last fall and found the place
where i could remember learning how to see.*

"I am an experimental filmmaker who is a Vermonter," Brigette says. "My 16mm film work lyrically meditates on rural Vermont themes and images." With only a handful of short films to her credit, Brigette has already carved a vital niche for herself among her generation; significantly, she has (with one notable exception, cited below) avoided digital media to embrace true film as her medium of choice. Apologizing for the inadequacies of the video transfers of her work, she notes, "it is best to view the films on actual 16mm film in order to appreciate the subtleties of the image and frame—after all isn't that what experimental film is all about?"

Brigette's cinematic lyricism arguably owes its contemporary roots to one of the classics of the American underground cinema, which also happens to be a keystone of Vermont's movie legacy: "I am most familiar with Adolfas Mekas's film work (Hallelujah the Hills) as I have known him for five years now," she explains.[8] "He was one of my film professors at Bard College where I obtained a BA in film in 2002. I worked closely with him my senior year as he served as one of the members of my senior board critiquing my senior film. I see Adolfas often as I currently work at Bard. What a brilliant, hilarious, unpredictable man!"

For this initial interview, Brigette and I chose to focus on her recent work, i went home last fall and found the place where i could remember learning how to see (2002). "It is my most refined film and most Vermont-centric," she explains. It is difficult to describe the film itself; hopefully, the following interview will offer some meaningful impressions.

Brigette prefaced our conversation saying, "I feel obligated to insert a disclaimer: I am a filmmaker for a reason—I work and think in images, not words." As we got into our conversation, she added, "How odd it is to be answering questions about my life and influences.... I am a filmmaker so I feel most comfortable and articulate in images. It is with images that I answer my own questions of identity and influence.... but then again, I did make a film called i went home last fall and found the place where i could remember learning how to see, so I guess I set my self up for it." Despite her concerns, she proved to be an articulate and engaging conversationalist.

This interview was conducted via email in June and July, 2003. At that time, Brigette's next project depended in part upon a grant which was under consideration by the Vermont Arts Council; sadly, at the time of this writing Brigette reported, "I was denied funding from the VAC and was told there is no place for experimental film in Vermont."

This decision is most unfortunate, and not only for Brigette. As we shall demonstrate time and again in this periodical, underground and experimental films—which paradoxically demand, yet defy, analysis—are absolutely central to the state's cinematic legacy. Brigette is among the movement's most vital contemporary practitioners; with or without the sanctions of such institutions, I've no doubt Brigette will find the means to continue on her path, and I for one greatly look forward to what she will create next.—SRB.

**Stephen R. Bissette**: *Where were you born and raised?*
**Brigette Blood**: A dirty little secret of mine is that I was born in Laconia, New Hampshire, but I moved to Vermont before I turned three. My great grandparents lived in Jeffersonville, and the Bloods/Seeleys are long-time locals in Cam-

---

[8] Mekas's *Hallelujah the Hills* (1963) was filmed in and around Westminster West and Dummerston, VT. SRB.

bridge and Jeffersonville. So I consider myself a Vermonter. I was raised in Jeffersonville; graduated from Cambridge Elementary School in Jeffersonville, Vermont, and Lamoille Union High School. My great great grandfather, Lyman James Seeley of Jeffersonville, fought for the North in the Civil War; he wrote home about the war and the daily rituals of his company of soldiers. His letters were published regularly and are still referenced by Civil War scholars, as they are a rare source for details on the life of Yankee Civil War soldiers. But that is another story... so yeah, I'm a Vermonter.

**SB**: *What first fired your creative spark?*

**BB**: What fed my creative life? Well I suppose it was more a question of absence rather than presence. By this, I mean that growing up in Jeffersonville in the 1980s/1990s meant a beautiful absence of external influence. There was no cable TV on Route 108—not that my parents would have bought it anyway— which means I grew up in the mountains with no TV reception. On a good day we'd get CBS and a few Canadian channels. I lived in a "giant" log cabin that was/is my parents' restaurant, the Three Mountain Lodge. We lived above the kitchen. It was great; I grew up with both my mom and dad always around. It was like having two stay-at-home parents,
who also worked. My sister Jessica is two years older than I, and we spent our days in the woods behind our restaurant. We built tree forts, rafts, and trails; we'd have adventures with our neighbors "the boys."

At night, we would spy on customers at the restaurant. We would laugh when the out-of-state tourists would marvel at the "real wood" that the log cabin was/is made of. My mother always fostered my interest in crafts. I would sew, knit, weave, bead; anything "hands-on" and tactile appealed to me. That is *one* of the reasons that film first appealed to me as it continued this obsession with the tangible. And of course with my father, a chef, food was always a source for creativity and celebration. I was literally fed creativity.

*SB*: When do you first remember wanting to be involved with making films?
**BB**: Before I knew I was a filmmaker, I knew that I liked watching; spying on the customers—shall we say 'observing?' it sounds less menacing—at the restaurant was great fun. We could make up stories for each one; why they were limping, why their shirt had a wrinkle in the back. The visual inspired a narrative when I was young and later in my film work the visual became its own narrative; the visual drove the work rather than a narrative driving the film. As I mentioned before, I grew up with little pop culture influence. Movie theatres are scarce in Northern Vermont, expensive for, at the time, poor restauranteurs and frugal yankees, and for restaurant people who work every night, going to an evening movie is not an option. But my father liked films. I remember when we got our first VCR—my parents still use the same one. My mother bought us *Little Audry* cartoons, Shirley Temple movies, and *Our Gang*. My father bought classics: *Gone With the Wind, Dr. Zhivago, It's A Mad Mad Mad Mad World, Now Voyager*, etc. Both loved musicals. I grew up watching Gene Kelly, Frank Sinatra, Judy Garland, James Cagney, Vera Ellen—while these movies are very different from the films of experimental cinema, their impact on my idea of cinema is undeniable. Because of our lovely rural isolation, these films provided my first glimpse of times and places outside of my small Jeffersonville, VT; film and film viewing was rare and exciting and always an event. The magic of film/cinema hooked me.

*SB*: In hindsight, what experiences, films, or works have had the greatest impact upon you creatively?
**BB**: Without copping out, I think that every experience impacts me "creatively;" I think most artists would agree. If there is no regular impact, what are you, as the artist, responding to in your work? As a filmmaker, I am visually oriented. As I can't help being inundated with images every moment, I feel continually impacted by these visual experiences. I guess the question then becomes what constitutes an experience—I'll leave that one alone though! Among the films that had the greatest impact on me as filmmaker are those by Stan Brakhage: *Moth Light, Water for Maya, Dog Star Man, Anticipation of the Night*. I was so jealous when I first saw *Moth Light*, I was angry that he beat me to it. Such a simple idea, such a simple film but impossible to take your eyes off. Like a moth to light, I could not look away. That was it. I would make films. Stan Brakhage freed cinema from traditional forms; he showed me that I could make my own images and take them outside narrative structures; that images had a life of their own; a life that was ripe for expression.

Maya Deren: *Rituals in Transfigured Time, Meshes of the Afternoon*—from her, I learned that visual symbols exist and are available for manipulation. She was among the first and she was a woman. Her independence and clear, strong, unique film intentions/theories have undeniable impact on every experimental filmmaker.

Stan Brakhage (left)
Maya Deren in *Meshes of the Afternoon* (1943) (right)

Michael Snow: *Wavelength, La Région Central*—Michael Snow showed me that in all the heavy conceptual art world mumbo-jumbo there could still be humor and there could be playfulness. Snow allowed for a lightness that Brakhage did not. His direct, experiential approach to film inspires in me a fresh excitement for film and film viewing. Every time a film is viewed, it is a new experience and a new space of viewing and presence is created in which that film now exists. His filmic explorations and manipulations of space and presence are inspiring, beautiful, brilliant, and highly impact my own filmwork (intentions) and my theories on the film medium and the film viewing experience.

Jonas Mekas: *Diaries, Notes and Sketches*; *Lost, Lost, Lost*; *As I Was Moving Ahead Occasionally I Saw Brief Glimpses of Beauty*—Jonas Mekas also made me jealous. This man makes beauty and great swells of emotion from breakfast, rain, a cat, a house plant, and his living room. Now that is power. His pace is slower than Brakhage, allowing the viewer to settle into his images and familiarize themselves with the faces and places that continually reemerge in his films. We become part of his memories as he shares them with us. This gentle attempt to maintain/sustain identity and presence in fleeting and long past memories in a fast-moving life is admirable. His treatment of these everyday events impact my views on film, film making, and the purpose of film.

Adolfas Mekas: *Going Home, Hallelujah the Hills*—Adolfas, what a character. His vocal admiration of Vermont drew me immediately to him. It is a rare quality for a non-Vermonter to understand the subtle beauties of our state. His film *Going Home* and its mastery of memory on film plays in my mind constantly.

John O'Brien: *Man With a Plan*, the first film to portray Vermont and Vermonters in believable positions; the dignity, grace, and humor with which O'Brien portrays Vermont is admirable and something I strive for in my own work. Further, his unconventional timing underscores the strikingly non-

Hollywood, Vermont-particular aesthetic of his work.

Nathanial Dorskey and Jenn Reeves are other experimental filmmakers whose work and drive I admire.

Adolfas and Jonas Mekas in 1955

*SB*: *When did you first work with a camera?*
**BB**: I had tried my hand at photography as a child and a highschooler, but the medium lacked depth and range for me. I felt frustrated by its singularity; I'm sure my ignorance, naivety, and lack of experience was to blame for my frustrations with the form. I somehow knew I wanted to make films, and not Hollywood films; there had to be more to the film medium. Though I had never seen an "experimental film," had never heard the term, and did not really know they existed, I found Bard, which happily is where one goes if one wants to make and study experimental film. My sophomore year I took film production with Peggy Ahwesh. Our first day we loaded and shot 16mm film with a Bolex. A hand-cranked camera; the camera of choice amongst experimental filmmakers. I loved it. I felt at home. I had found it. No question. If there was not this certainty, I would never have worked so hard and sacrificed through four years to pay for tuition and film and obtain a "useless" degree that did not "prepare" me for a career—rather it provided me with some of the necessary technical equipment, a productive working environment of creative, intelligent, and motivated individuals and working experimental filmmakers.

*SB*: *You worked with the Vermont Film Commission for a time...*
**BB**: I had a summer internship with the commission; John O'Brien pointed me in their direction. It was a good experience. It cemented my commitment to

Vermont and further convinced me that I would make films and make them without production companies.

***SB***: *If it's not too much trouble, could you describe your studies at Bard College? Who did you study under there?*

**BB**: John Pruitt taught the first film class I took at Bard: a survey "history of film" class beginning with Lumière and Pathé newsreels and continued through early American avante-garde. John Pruitt became my "advisor" at Bard. His extensive knowledge of the humanities and all genres of film made his film insights beautifully precise, yet allowed the film to open up itself for further interpretation. For this reason, studying with him was a very valuable and enriching experience. His questioning of method and practice, both of studied films and of student films, forced students/filmmakers to exhaust all creative possibilities resulting in films or a reading of a film that solidly, dramatically, purposefully and entirely expressed emotion and intent. He forced me to think in new terms, helped me develop my filmic vocabulary and expected me to make films whose conceptual existence was reflected in its visual existence. As an experimental filmmaker, this is one of the/my great goals.

***SB***: *Your resume also cites professor Jenn Reeves?*

**BB**: Jenn Reeves: before I ever met her, I heard of her; "Jenn Reeves the superstar." She teaches at Bard, but also went to Bard, where she received her BA. Her junior film is shown at other colleges in their film classes and was in festivals winning awards when she was still an undergraduate. Bard professors spoke of her and her work with respect and admiration. Later, I met her and took classes from her. Above all, the creative force, intricate filmmaking, and mastery of technique present in her work is admirable. While her films are very different from mine, often dark or violent, confronting social and sexuality or gender issues, her profound and layered editing, personal drive, and creative conviction are all elements I admire and hope to achieve in my own work. As a professor, not only did Jenn provide valuable technical and practical advice on film issues, her critiques of student films were biting and insightful. She gave honest, insightful readings and criticism; something that is invaluable, as often one looses perspective on one's own film as it exists complete in your heart and head, but communicating that vision to others often proves difficult. Not only did she give constructive feedback, she expected you to give it as well. She helped us all learn how to see a film, or a film-in-progress, and respond to it in helpful ways for the filmmaker. She helped her students develop a language with which to discuss experimental film—something that is not easy considering films are after all visual and emotional experiences, not linguistic ones.

***SB***: *Before we get into your latest film, could you tell me a bit about your earlier works,* Puja Film *(2000) and* Yellow Chair *(2001)?*

**BB**: *Yellow Chair* is a video—my only complete video work. Later, it evolved into a film project as John Pruitt had, upon seeing the video and accompanying polaroids, asked me to continue the project as a film. It began as a video sketch, but I ended up delving into heavy conceptual and theoretical issues of frame, perception, space, the viewing experience. These issues are really meant to be explored in film as that medium is where these issues are heavily in play; being issues of filmic language. I shot most of the film for the project but got bogged down by academic work. The film was put on hold, and I have yet to find the time or money to return to it. The video was inspired by/is a comment on/conceptual response to Michael Snow's *La Région Central* and *Wavelength*. The piece meditates on space, collapses viewing space, explores the conceptual viewing space in which it—the film—exists. Simply: a yellow chair (of *Wavelength*) viewed from every conceivable angle; at the end we realize both the chair and the camera are upside down, unbalancing the perceived space in which the film had existed up until the moment where visual space and depth are allowed to open up—very conceptual.

Michael Snow's *Wavelength* (1967)

**SB**: *And* Puja Film?
**BB**: *Puja Film*: a filmic interpretation of the hindu act/ritual of *Puja*. This film is abstract and optically printed. It is a Hindu belief that deities exist within their images. *Puja* is the process of worshiping, dressing, sacrificing to these god images. For this film, I made my own film emulsion. I used clear film leader and through a long process I adhered parts of the Hindu images to the film strip. I made a film loop of flower petals and I layered the two images, though there are times in the fim where each element exists independent of the other. For the sound track, I combined several traditional Hindu *Puja* chants with live sounds: water, breathing, etc. The film may be seen silent or with the sound. I think it best to see it silent first, then with sound. The sound track is very strong and sometime runs over the image that is very subtle and rich, requiring little distraction. The sound does however re-inforce the image at moments and allows

for a more compete interepretation/reading of *Puja*. The film was shot on reversal for monetary reasons, so I have but one, very fragile copy of the film. The film is rich with color, texture, light and energy.

Where it all happens: Brigette Blood's work station.

**SB**: *Let's talk about* i went home last fall and found the place where i could remember learning how to see. *The film opens with a most primal image: the ceiling of a room, the very one that was above, I assume, the crib or bed you first remember looking up from; and your, now adult, hands, flexing, forming a fist, reaching. Was this indeed the springboard for the film?*
**BB**: The image of my hand, like all images in a lyrical film, serve multiple purposes: literal, figurative, lyrical, formal... I like your take on the image. Metaphorically/lyrically, the image of my reaching hand is meant to represent first moments of vision, primary memories, but literally the image was not taken from my first ceiling, as mentioned before I moved from my birth home. The film touches on the "handmade" as a theme throughout; literally, the image is me "seeing what my hands could do." The film, being my first real film, was partially about seeing what my hands could do; it was my hands that made the film—in every sense, as I shot and edited it all, I cut my own negative, hot spliced and A&B-rolled the film. Furthermore, this image underscores the power and presence of the hand of the filmmaker; often a forgotten or ignored element of film, but in my film my hand/my eye is ever present.
**SB**: *Almost as primary are images of water, specifically from and, later, of the ferry on Lake Champlain. What are your specific orientations to this area, the ferry, and the lake itself?*
**BB**: Again, water is metaphorically/lyrically meant to serve as another primary image or primary form. Water, babies, yeast, land, hands, wood, are all primary images, primary elements. The primary elements of my vision. Growing up in rural Vermont meant for me, as noted before, little access or influence from the rest of the country/world. The ferry was a major fixture in my childhood—it continues to be so—as we would travel a few times a year to New York State on it. Traveling on the ferry highlighted the physical isolation of my rural child-

hood; in order to "get away" from rural isolation, a serious journey must be made across a great lake on a big boat. Additionally, the image serves as a reminder of travel for the film whose themes include travel, distance, and return—a ferry makes a very specific route and always returns. Lake Champlain is a formative element in my view of Vermont, with its tainted beauty, its rich and influential place in history, and its role in the geographical seclusion of our state.

*SB: Cut wood, and the patterns of stacked wood, also re-occur. Again, what is your orientation to this imagery, and the primal importance of wood—as a heat source, as an object, as a texture—in your memories and the film?*

**BB**: Yes, texture, pattern, image, heat source and more serve as the primal significance of wood in my film. Again, living in a wood-heated log cabin in rural Vermont meant living with a certain kinship to wood/fire wood. While some grow up surrounded by skyscrapers and side walks or McDonald's and manicured lawns, I grew up in the woods, surrounded by wood. Wood's objectness and its image serve to frame and drive the lives of rural Vermonters. Frames—all peoples have frames through which they view the world—these frames are cultural/social/economic/gender specific constructions; in my film and in my life, I chose wood/wood piles to serve as a visual metaphor for my own rural frame of reference, frame of mind, frame of thought, while they serve to focus a viewer to certain aspects of the visual, they also serve to restrict ones view of the whole. Throughout the film I refer back to wood; reminding me/the viewer of the frame through which I/the rural see. Part of the beauty of the rural Vermonter's frame of viewing is the functionality and raw handmade quality of wood/wood piles; functionality, practicality, and the raw/handmade are important themes in my film and themes in the life of the Vermonter.

*SB: Images and elements of the kitchen—the package of yeast, the making of bread dough, the baking and frosting of cupcakes, etc.—thread throughout the film. The most leisurely, lingering view we are given of any single location or process is directed to the frosting of the cupcakes, appropriately enough, given the childhood orientation of the 'seeing' throughout, which becomes a truly anticipatory and sensual experience. Why did you focus so on this process?*

**BB**: Again, the theme of the handmade comes through with the image of the cupcakes. More than that, I felt that cupcakes served well as an additional metaphor for the film medium—there are other filmic references/visual film metaphors throughout. With the cupcakes, you are watching something being crafted before your eyes, just as with the film you are seeing something crafted before your eyes—the film-viewing experience is an important element of the film—all experimental film—itself. The film comes alive through the viewing of it. The space in which the film is viewed is created as you watch it; just as the cupcakes/bread are created as you watch. The film takes the viewer to a new space where this film can be viewed and experienced. The film takes the viewer from his frame into mine; as though through the eyes of a child, the viewer's vision is reborn in the film: you start with primary images and elements of vision—water, wood, hands, yeast—and build more complex visual themes from there—bread, visual rhymes, visual narrative, cupcakes.

I like and am glad you find the cupcakes as an appropriate mirror to the 'childhood seeing' theme of the film. There is definitely something nostalgic and childlike in the anticipation of the cupcakes—and in the leftover bowl of frosting; it is this same feeling of anticipation, nostalgia, and comfort that I hope to convey through my film and my love of film. Additionally, the cupcake is an individual, self-contained moment, as is each frame of film. With my film, each frame was crafted and "frosted" with care, just as the cupcakes. In the end we can see all the cupcakes together—we can see all the film frames together. While I have described some of the primary functions of these images, it is important to note that in addition to these narrative-like purposes, the images also serve lyrically as vessels for emotion and formally as shapes, color, and texture that lend themselves to the overall movement and tension of the film.

*SB: And—following that line of thought—do you consider this a maternal and gender-specific orientation to formative experiences and images? That is, a male filmmaker embracing the identical theme might, or would, not focus on the kitchen as a primary orientation to learning 'seeing' and about the world?*

**BB**: Undoubtedly, gender issues come into play in my film as they are an active element of modern society and culture; my film captures segments of this society and this culture and therefore captures the issues and constructions of said society/culture. However, it is important to note that my father is a chef, so it is not my intention to feminize the kitchen. The kitchen is most definitely the center for most family activity and therefore the center for most "formative experiences;" maybe more so for me coming from a restaurant family, a father chef, and living above a restaurant kitchen while growing up. More than wishing to express social/gender issues, I chose the kitchen as I liked the idea of process, the idea of creating in a familiar comfortable setting—home kitchen; I feel this is something/an idea that transcends culture/gender/race/economics—the emotion that is produced from the comfortable image of "home" and cooking is fairly "unanimous"—or in the words of Fred Tuttle, "world wide."

*SB*: *Seasonal images—the bright autumn leaves, pumpkins, etc.—also anchor the visual tapestry you weave. Is there a reason you chose the fall, other than it was the time of your visit—that is, did your birth date mean the autumn assumed a developmental importance in your own life?*

**BB**: Fall is an important time in Vermont. It is the season where the roads are filled with flatlanders coming to soak in the beauty of our state. They come for the day, a weekend, or a few weeks and go home with their "VT" bumper sticker telling their friends and co-workers "I love Vermont." Well, it is easy to love Vermont when she is at the peak of her ostentatious beauty. While I appreciate that view, I resent that superficial love of Vermont; if you can't love her for mud season on back roads, for her non-photo license, her lack of infrastructure, her lack of industry, her stubborn quiet people, her isolation, her long cold dark winters, than you can not (in my opinion) claim to "love Vermont;" because without experiencing and accepting all of the idiosyncrasies and "backward" culture of our state, how can you begin to really love it? Fall is maybe the easiest time of year to love Vermont; albeit a shallow, incomplete love. There is a hint of this superficial/naive love in the film, though I feel I did not lapse into a clichéd romanticized view of Vermont. I did play off this common attitude and view—"Moonlight in Vermont" is the ultimate cliché/superficial, inaccurate view of Vermont, and it plays through radio 'fuzz' in the film—so anyway, I chose Fall. Fall has traditionally served to represent the near-end, the last life of beauty before the cold end of winter, but happily everything begins again with spring. My return home was my last shot at seeing and remembering home the way it was when I was a child. "You can't go home again (Thomas Wolff?)"—as I live away from Vermont and educate myself, I begin to loose the innocence of my childhood vision; this end of innocence and beauty is mirrored by the autumn landscape.

*SB*: *There are two forms of literal screens that appear: the decomposing drive-in screen, seen from a distance and from the drive-in lot, and television and computer monitor screens. What did the former mean to you—and where, pray tell, is that particular drive-in?—and how did its importance in your own 'learning how to see' differ from the latter? Being born in 1955, computers were not part of my childhood; I'm curious how central they were to your own.*

**BB**: The drive-in is in St. Albans, Vermont—I think there may be a shot of the drive-in sign in the film that identifies it as St. Albans. I am fairly sure there are no TVs in my film, though there is most definitely a computer screen that says "Fox Kids," maybe causing you to read it as a TV screen?

*SB*: *Yes, that's what prompted me to read it as such...*

**BB**: The image of the drive in screen is given such specialized treatment; whenever it is seen, there is great release and visual celebration. The film asks that the viewer love the screen just as the filmmaker does; the serenity and joy that I purposefully put with that image serve to influence and remind the viewer of the film medium and the viewing of film. Computers were not central to my child-

hood; I am fairly well versed in computers now. We had a computer, since I was ten or eleven, anyway, as my parents had their own business and needed one, but on the whole my life was fairly devoid of screens, though never devoid of frames. As the film shows, computers are central to the lives of children nowadays. I remember the image of the computer screen nicely frames the image of the boys—my nephews. This new frame comes toward the end of the film and suggests a shift/modernization as most of the other images are fairly timeless— in terms of recent history—these visual, literal, "traditional" frames juxtaposed with the metaphoric frames of wood—create a tension mirroring the end of my innocent vision.
*SB: Thank you, Brigette. I look forward to your next film!*

---

**Brigette Blood: Filmography:**

*Untitled (Puja Film)* (7 min., 16mm, color, sound/silent, 2000)
*Yellow Chair* (5 min., single channel video, 2001)
*i went home last fall and found the place where i could remember learning how to see* (17 min., 16mm, color, sound, 2002)

# *Da Speech*: **An International Project**
by Stephen R. Bissette
photos courtesy of John Douglas

A Bomb in Charlotte's Web:
Creating/Collaborating on the
Music/Animation/Agitprop Masterpiece in Cyberspace

*John Douglas's video* Da Speech *won the 2003 James Goldstone Vermont Filmmakers Award—But what is* Da Speech? *Just one thread in a vast collaborative international music and filmmaking venture spawned by 9/11 and a particular Presidential speech that continues to send shock waves around the globe.*

The images fade in, already shifting in the darkness, shuffling into one another, as the introduction to President Bush's September 20, 2001 address to Congress and the Nation begins: "I have the high privilege, the distinct honor, of presenting to you the President of the United States..."

*The face comes into full view; high-contrast video black and white close-ups of President George W. Bush stutter, almost subliminally punctuated by an alarming red-and-yellow image with bared teeth ("Warning: Bad Dog"), and a barrage of familiar portraits and photos of Osama Bin Laden flash with accelerating ferocity.*

The music swells as excerpts of Bush's September 20 speech overlap one another, transforming into a throbbing, ritualistic mantra:

*"Osama bin Laden/the Egyptian Islamic Jihad/Osama bin Laden/the giving of blood/Osama bin Laden/who attacked our country?/Osama bin Laden/known as al-Qaeda/Osama bin Laden/killed Christians and Jews—"*

*The rapid-fire shots of Osama bin Laden—some inscribed in circles within circles, now targets—flicker over news images of a smiling President Bush striding across the White House lawn. The vertical 'Alert' chart imposes itself, color-coding national 'Terror Attacks' status, as the pulse-like mantra continues,—the Egyptian Islamic Jihad/Osama bin Laden/the giving of blood/the saying of prayers/(known as al-Qaeda)/kill all Americans—"*

Thus begins John Douglas' *Da Speech* (approx. 8 minutes, 2003), part of an extensive/intensive international project which is, by its very nature, provocatively political, highly critical of the Bush Administration's foreign policies and the war on Iraq, and angrily subversive. John Douglas's *Da Speech* is also by nature a living—as in vital, ever-growing, and still changing—multi-media collage, a single thread in a multi-national tapestry weaved by a collective of music, video, and cinema artists.

While John Douglas created his short in his home studio in Charlotte, Vermont, the other members of the collective reflected their respective countries via their own individual and cultural interpretations of Bush's incendiary post-9/11 speech—or, to be more precise, the unusual synthesized/sampler musical piece that historic September 20 speech inspired: *Da Speech*.

The piece of music was created by German composer Simon Stockhausen,

who is now 37 years-old.[9] Stockhausen has been studying and performing music since the age of five; from 1986-96, he toured with his father Karlheinz and the Stockhausen ensemble through the world, and co-produced electronic scores for two of Karlheinz's operas. He frequently collaborates with his brother Markus and has done so for two decades, yielding many CDs and two compositions for the Cologne philharmonic, all the while composing and arranging music for many recitals, various ensembles: chamber music, 'big band,' brass ensemble, jazz, German theaters, performance artists, etc. Stockhausen has scored many short films and documentaries, and has worked with filmmaker Amos Gitai, and

---

[9] born June 5, 1967.

has his own band, MIR (with Manos Tsangaris). Throughout his illustrious career, Stockhausen believed "that music and politics should be strictly divided because the wonder of music and sound should not be spoiled by the poor and twisted ways people on this planet treat each other."

But all that changed—as did the lives of everyone on the planet—after September 11, 2001.

"After the attacks happened on September 11," Stockhausen explains,[10] "I was sitting in front of my TV for many days videotaping everything I could find about it, because for the first time in my life I felt obliged to use my music as a tool for expressing my attitude towards the way, terror and politics determine the destiny of our world and humanity as a whole."

Stockhausen's struggle to compose a heartfelt creative response to the tragedy went through a number of stages. "First I did a piece called 'September 11' in which I tried to use all the sounds from the collapse of the WTC, the shouting and mourning and the terrible sound of the collapse itself—but this piece of 'music' turned out to be so dark and shocking that I never published it."

The catalyst unexpectedly arrived via President George W. Bush's famous—and infamous— internationally-broadcast September 20, 2001, address to Congress and the Nation on terrorism.

Stockhausen recalls, "after three or four sentences of it, I noticed the astonishing rhythmical structure of those dark and threatening words—'either you´re with us or you´re with the terrorists' and so on—the way he uttered his speech was similar to things I had heard from Martin Luther King and other activists and preachers and there was an omnipresent rhythm to it. Then, there was a memorial service for the victims in the Yankee stadium in New York where many preachers and politicians from all over the world expressed their grief, which was very moving but also very frightening because the purpose of this memorial service was evident—war and revenge—and again, there was the same rhythm in almost all the speeches and prayers... Even the soldiers parading during the service were marching and shouting in the same beat George W. had used two weeks earlier... Towards the end of the service, a black preacher was manipulating the crowd in exactly that rhythm: 'harder yet may be the fight and right may often yield to might... we'll get through it...' "

Among the dense layering of speech, music, and sound that constitutes *Da Speech*, one phrase that seemed almost innocuous in the context of the first paragraphs of President Bush's September 20 speech—"the giving of blood"—takes on religious, almost mystical, significance. In Bush's speech, the phrase was presented and delivered pragmatically, in his typically oblique manner; clearly, for Bush and most of the country, it was a reference to the rush of American citizens donating blood for 9/11 rescue purposes. Recontextualized in *Da Speech*, the phrase instead becomes a central pulse in a blood ritual, taking

---

[10] in a May 31, 2003, statement posted on *Da Speech* website; see *Sources*.

on more ominous and unsettling connotations. The Christian context and metaphor is unmistakable—and absolutely appropriate to the Bush presidency, with its overtly Christian rhetoric and agendas—but the music emphasizes the sacrificial aspects of Bush's phrase in a more primordial religious, even Dionysian, frame of reference. The subtext throbs into a primal, almost occult 'beat' throughout *Da Speech*; it becomes a central metaphor, in and of itself, a relentless demand for the shedding and spilling of blood. Thus, the importance of Stockhausen's *Da Speech*: by having the ear for such turns of phrase in a political speech, and recontextualizing such phrases in the broader arena of the true actions (war) that followed, the composer opens the listener's ears and heart to something urgent, primal, and terrifying.

Stockhausen's *Da Speech* came together relatively quickly once he had recognized and become attuned to this ominous, shared threnody. "I started to put all the collected sounds and speeches together, deriving the tempo and rhythm of my piece from the rhythm of *Da Speech*, later adding saxophone and percussion... after four days in my studio, the piece was finished and so was I."

Ah, but the life of *Da Speech* was just beginning, though the powers-that-be tried to act quickly to silence the composer. Stockhausen recalls, "I uploaded the piece to my MP3 site and there were many hundred downloads just in a few days until the Internet company running my site erased the piece, closed my site for a week telling me that I was abusing the copyright of the American government. I thought I was living in a free country but that was just an illusion and it took weeks until my moral was restored."

Having raised his 'voice,' so to speak, only to be silenced, Stockhausen was reinvigorated by one of those who had heard *Da Speech*, and by the birth of a new venue—many venues, as events gained momentum—for his composition.

*"—the Egyptian Islamic Jihad/Osama bin Laden/the giving of blood/the saying of prayers/known as al-Qaeda/who attacked our country?—"*

*The images of President Bush continue to crosscut with images of Osama bin Laden. Superimposed over this staccato weave of Bush/bin Laden/Bush is a denser crosscutting of faces, slogans, images: (Warning: Bad Dog); key members of the Bush Administration and associates (Secretary of Defense Donald Rumsfeld, National Security Advisor Dr. Condoleeza Rice, Assistant Secretary of Defense Richard Perle, Attorney General John Ashcroft, grinning sibling and Florida Governor Jeb Bush, snarling Vice-President Dick Cheney, Dr. Henry Kissinger, etc.); horribly emblematic news footage of the World Trade Center towers, smoking, flaming, exploding, collapsing...*

*"—Osama bin Laden/who attacked our country?/Osama bin Laden/known as al-Qaeda/Osama bin Laden/killed Christians and Jews/(the giving of blood/the saying of prayers)—"*

The alchemical agent of transformation was a filmmaker from Japan named Toshi Fujiwara. Born in Yokohama, Japan in 1970, raised in Tokyo and Paris, educated in Tokyo and Los Angeles, Fujiwara's transition into the world of cinema began in 1994 via his work as a writer: reviewing films for various Japanese magazines, translating books dedicated to films and filmmakers, subtitling films, and teaching film and film criticism at the Art and Architecture School of Waseda University in Tokyo. Fujiwara began making his own films in 2001, completing the award-winning feature-length documentary *Independence* (2002). He has since directed feature-length portraits of Japanese documentary filmmakers Noriaki Tsuchimoto (2003) and Kazuo Hara (in progress). Amid this remarkable activity, Fujiwara and Simon Stockhausen met via email and the internet [11] and Stockhausen gave Fujiwara a CD copy of *Da Speech*. They subsequently collaborated on an experimental short film entitled *Walk* (2003).

In his statement on the *Da Speech* website, Fujiwara details what occurred, noting the ban of Stockhausen's website presentation of his composition "on the pretense that *Da Speech* is invading the copyrights of the government of the United States"—a dubious legal interpretation frighteningly in synch with the Bush Administration's veiled record to date. "So Simon sent me a CD," Fujiwara writes, "and I got the idea of making a video clip of this music, and Simon found the idea interesting." Stockhausen confirms this on the *Da Speech* website, writing, "...Toshi Fujiwara came in to my life asking me for the permission to do a video to my music, which I found a fantastic idea—I had already given up—and so this video-project got started."

Thus was born Toshi Fujiwara's *DaSpeech, or How 9/11 Changed My Country and Helped Me Setting the U.S. Against the World* (2002), citing Jerusalem and Tokyo as the creative bases, "featuring George W. Bush, his Honorable the President of the United States," which incorporated footage Fujiwara "shot in New York City during the war on Iraq."

Inspired to continue expanding on the potential and urgent relevance he believed Stockhausen's composition harbored, Fujiwara ached to expand the canvas. He continues, "this idea of ours developed into... 'Why not ask other people to do the same, and have multiple points of views?' "

With Stockhausen's blessing, Fujiwara first extended the invitation to create videos from *Da Speech* to his students. First to respond creatively were Satoshi Kubota and Jin Otagiri, who Fujiwara felt "came up with very original and beautiful approaches." Having 'acted locally,' Fujiwara still felt the need to expand the tapestry to a truly international scale—just as the ripples of the notori-

---

[11] See interview with Stockhausen, pg. 94. SRB.

ous George W. Bush speech spun into unprecedented revisions of US foreign policy and active warfare.

"Then the ambition became greater," Fujiwara writes, "like, 'why not have an international variation of points of views?' As the Bush administration was cooking up their plan of attacking Iraq, friends joined."

Among those who responded to Fujiwara's invitation and Stockhausen's composition were Malaysian director Amir Muhammad, Pascale Feghali of Lebanon, Jean-Baptiste Duez of Belgium, Mohamed-Hashim Elkareem of Canada and Maya Puig, working in Stockhausen's native country of Germany.

Canada's Mohamed-Hashim Elkareem, filmmaker and one of the organizers of the Toronto African Film Festival, created *DaSPEECH: Umm, the Interhumane Order* (2003). On the *Da Speech* website, he describes his perception of the total project as a "human testament in memory against the monument of history... A relational aesthetic which is most reliable as a way to understand the different modalities and functions of contemporary art and history, finding another way of communicating through the efforts of international filmmakers from different cultures and backgrounds working together...." For Elkareem, the process of the project is vital to its function: "These relational shifts, or pieces of *DaSPEECH*, evolve and mutate in accordance with historical and social contexts, to create a relationship between different people and worlds, may imply an intimate, minimalist approach in music and film to reality, as well as to language in *DaSPEECH*. These relational issues are perceived by the shifts in terms of strict or unstrict [sic] necessities: for the artist today is above all a 'mediator,' who through his own actions and projects and collectives, is able to produce an 'added value SPEECH' of an ethical and political nature."

Within this framework and dynamic, West-Berlin native Maya Puig [12] took a different approach than that of Fujiwara and his students, reflecting her 'world citizen' perspective, having lived abroad most of her life; she had only recently returned to Berlin in 2000 to study filmmaking. Since her return, Puig co-created the independent film school the FilmArche e.V., became a board member of the European association of young filmmakers NISI MASA, and has directed a number of short films and videos, including *Da Speech*; her latest is *Uber Den Schatten* (*Over the Shadow*).

One of the most novel approaches to *Da Speech* was forged by Amir Muhammad,[13] who had been writing professionally since his teenage years, earned a legal degree, labored in theater and television, scripted and directed Malaysia's first digital video feature *Lips to Lips* (2000), half-a-dozen video shorts (*Lost, Friday, Mona, Checkpoint, Kamunting, Pangyau*, all 2002), and completed a second feature, *The Big Durian* (2003); he is currently working on *Tokyo Magic Hour* (2004). For Muhammad, his video rendition of *Da Speech*

---

[12] b. 1981.

[13] born 1972 in Kuala Lumpur.

"will always have a space in my jagged little heart because it is the first thing I edited myself. You wouldn't think it by looking at it, but the thing took me days."

Unlike others, Muhammad eschewed any footage of President Bush (or the other speakers) in his video, choosing instead to cull interview footage from his docudrama *The Big Durian*, "which talks about a different, local, instance in which a political juggernaut plowed through regardless of public opinion. But couldn't these Malaysians just as easily be talking about a different, more global, controversy?... Some seem thoughtful, outraged, wistful, even amused, but their words are erased by the booming voice on the track—the way the voices of non-players are so easily sidelined when corporate-military interests are at stake."

Writing on the *Da Speech* website about his decision, Muhammad notes, "I knew I wouldn't want any images of the notorious protagonists of this well-known drama, since Simon's excellent track would have already conjured them. I wanted something of a Tower of Babel feel, but with the paradox that you can't actually hear what any of my characters are saying... When the salaryman on the Tokyo subway finally wakes up, what will he remember of the multiplicity of silent voices, or the imagery of things getting hotter? Or will he dismiss it all as a bad dream, as unreliable as any soap opera? The notion that ordinary citizens in a country like Malaysia can say anything impactful about the course of an international conflict may strike some as absurd. But things do connect, in ways that can seem almost dream-like."

Still, Fujiwara felt it crucial to involve American filmmakers in the process; in fact, the American filmmaker he approached was among the first to respond—and with a completed video. Fujiwara writes, again on the *Da Speech* website, "since it was very important to have a US point of view, I asked a friend of my old friend and mentor who has now passed away, Robert Kramer..."

Thus, the invitation went out to John Douglas, who had long ago earned international renown for his collaborative work with Kramer. "John Douglas was a member of Newsreel with Robert, and they co-directed *Milestones*," Fujiwara recalls. "He certainly should have a very strong point of view of his own about what the present government of his own country has been trying to do since the September 11 incident."

Indeed.

*"—Osama bin Laden/(the Egyptian Islamic Jihad)/Osama bin Laden/(the giving of blood)/Osama bin Laden/(who attacked our country?)—"*

*The flurry of faces—Bush/bin Laden/Kissinger/bin Laden/Secretary of State Colin Powell/Bush/CIA Director George J. Tenet, etc.—seem to swell with the rhythms of the chant, the music. Agitprop text flashes by, barely registering; satiric (USA Terrorist Hunting Permit—No Bag Limit—Tagging* **Not**

*Required), succinct (W=War), sardonic (Vapid Petulance), merging and fusing with the flicker of visages (Bush pouting/Vapid Petulance)*

*"—of blood)/Osama bin Laden/(known as al-Qaeda)/Osama bin Laden/(kill all Americans)/ They follow in the path of fascism and Nazism and Totalitarianism and they will follow that path—"*

*Now bin Laden—within circles, the target—is juxtaposed with the Third Reich's seal (the golden circle framing the eagle grasping the swastika, the slogan Gott Mit Uns) as still-smiling President Bush crosses the White House lawn/a montage of historic photos and footage of Adolf Hitler superimposed uber all—*

*"—all the way to where it ends—"*

*President Bush's face (Warning: Bad Dog) strobed by increasingly extreme/absurdist agitprop imagery/text fragments/frames (Hitler to the left, Bush to the right: "When History Repeats/Do We Notice?"/Steve Reeves to the left, Bush to the right: "The Bush Who Started It All—HERCU-BUSH"/colorful campaign image of Bush with a swastika blazing behind his face) as Bush turns and waves as he and First Lady Laura Bush mount the stairs to their transport/New Yorkers flee as the Towers twist/burn/fall—*

*"—in history's unmarked grave of discarded lies—(Osama bin Laden)/known as al-Qaeda/(the giving of blood)—"*

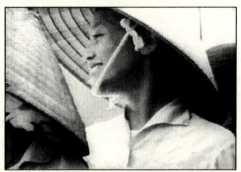

*People's War*

John Douglas moved to Vermont in the late 1960s; initially based in Putney, he is now living in Charlotte, after ten years (1973-83) in New York's Chinatown. He is still known and revered in many international film circles for his 1960s and early '70s collaborative work with the innovative activist documentary filmmakers the Newsreel Group, and with his friends and creative associates Robert Kramer and Norm Fruchter, co-directing the documentary *People's War* (1969), filmed in North Vietnam, and the epic narrative feature *Milestones* (1975) and editing Kramer's *Route One* (1988). He may live and create in Vermont, but he is very much a 'citizen of the world,' and his personal and political, as expressed in his films and videos, reflect that worldview with clarity, integrity, and vigor.

From his first key work as a cinematographer and co-director, *Strike City* (1967; co-directed by Tom Griffin)—a moving portrait of a Greenville, Mississippi-based 'tent city' composed of workers who abandoned impoverished near-slavery working conditions at plantations and labored to build their own collective community and housing, eventually marching on Washington to bring national attention to their plight and that of millions of other impoverished Americans—Douglas's films have taken the side of the disenfranchised, particularly those who engage with the struggle against the repressive powers-that-be.

*Strike City*

Among his Newsreel collaborations were *BDRG: Boston Draft Resistance Group* (1968) and *Summer '68* (1968), both chronicling organized student resistance, the latter culminating in some harrowing footage of the Chicago Democratic Convention. This body of work informed Newsreel and Douglas's unique orientation to the Vietnam War presented in *People's War*, which detailed the social structures of North Vietnam society—a culture then at war for a quarter-century—and their ongoing struggle to elevate an underdeveloped nation while maintaining organized resistance to U.S. occupation and aggression. The film was completed despite the seizure of Newsreel's footage upon the filmmakers' return to the U.S.; *People's War* went on to win a Blue Ribbon at the U.S.A. Film Festival in Houston, Texas, and a Golden Bear Award in Moscow, Russia.

With his first solo work, the short *Die-Cast Grills* (1968) meshing news footage and original footage to impressionistically capture (in Douglas's word) "daily life following the King/Kennedy assassinations," Douglas introduced a distinctive vision of meditative montage. Thus, rapid-fire editing and superimposition of seemingly contrasting imagery—the national/international scope of "found" news footage, usually shot from television; the intimacy of filmed reality, regional/domestic in nature—embodies "think globally, act locally" as a cinematic syntax, and even an aesthetic. This vision and approach reverberates throughout Douglas's short films and videos, including his computer-animated creations of the 1990s, right through to *Da Speech*.

Upon his move to Putney, Vermont, Douglas continued chronicling regional eruptions of protest and repression, filming and co-directing *Free Farm* (1970), while adopting a more intimate approach in films like *Cecil* (1970), a portrait of "an old Vermonter who works at the garbage dump, plays Santa Claus for a small rural town, and celebrates Christmas with his wife, eleven children, and forty-one grand-children." [14] Shifting gears, *Kaskawulsh* (1972) offered a powerfully physical, tactile expressionist "diary" of an excursion into the rugged forests, mountains, and glaciers of the Northwest, marvelously photographed and edited. Still, Douglas never abandoned his activist roots, photo-

---

[14] quoted from Douglas's filmography on his website.

graphing and co-directing another dissection of US policies against Vietnam entitled *To Our Common Victory* (1971); Barbara Reilly's dramatization of the Dhoruba Moore trial *The Verdict* (1976); two films detailing the American government's ongoing destabalization efforts in Grenada, *Stand Up Grenada* (1979) and *Grenada: The Future Coming Towards Us* (1983), and photographing another, *Grenada: Nobody's Backyard* (1980); and more.

With *Birds and Buffaloes* (1981), Douglas began to incorporate animation into his work, and he made a crucial transition to video and digital media. Computer animation fused with his political convictions yielded *Love the American People, Not the American Government* (1988) and a video for the Quebec/Vermont artist collaborative, *Acid Rain Project* (1989). This led to a fruitful collaboration with celloist Erich M. Kory on a body of remarkably personal and political animated videos, including *White Noise* (1990), *Thought I Saw* (1991), *The Heart of It* (1992), *Revelation* (1992), *Underneath: A Nostalgia for Paint* (1993), and more. Probably the most widely-viewed of Douglas's computer-animated creations is the haunting *The Whitehouse* (1998/2000), in which skeletal "spirits" engage in a variety of activities, including dancing around a fire, playing the cello, watching television, kissing, conversing via reversed English tracts, and—more ominously—wielding firearms, torturing and tossing a blind-folded prisoner out of a black helicopter, etc., in and around a doorless, windowless "white house" which is slowly engulfed in rising flood waters.

*The Whitehouse*

Simultaneously dreamy and nightmarish, playful and pointed in its subversive attack on the titular seat of U.S. Government, *The Whitehouse* has been screened [15] in a number of work-in-progress variations, though the definitive version to date incorporates footage of the Bush/Gore Presidential debates from the 2000 election, eerie omniscient views of an orbiting government satellite, and concludes with a race between corporate 'copters emblazoned with Coca-Cola and Pepsi logos; a sardonic subtitle referencing the destination "Harvard vs. Yale game," further links the aircraft to 2000 election candidates Gore and Bush, that concludes with explosive results.

*Underneath: A Nostalgia for Paint* explores a sterile art gallery displaying only images—from varying points of view—of the same fenced-in winterscape, sheltering an ominous satellite dish and peppered with cautionary signs; metallic cubes housing TV monitors broadcasting war footage are topped by revolving cubes emblazoned with the stars-and-stripes of the American flag; the military-industrial complex's icy grip on communication is chillingly evoked. A later edition of *White Noise* mounts a scathing attack on the current Bush Administration's diversionary tactics, opening and closing with archival audio and video of Bush's shameless volunteer boosterism while the mournful body of the video—accompanied by more of Erich Kory's cello music—offers impressions of the Iraq wars and air-attacks amid eruptions of static and agitprop text scrolls. The high-contrast, closeup black-and-white video footage, shot from television, of President Bush's features that opens this revised version of *White Noise* were later incorporated into *Da Speech*, along with other iconographic visual elements.

Thus, John Douglas was ready for *Da Speech*, and indeed, the resulting video is absolutely in-synch with the filmmaker's body of work, building upon, while plundering visual elements from, earlier works to mount the most assaultive summary of Douglas's views of the current Administration conceivable—for now, anyway. He began the process by establishing a visual template to match the throbbing rhythm of Stockhausen's composition, working with the key images he'd selected—the black-and-white still closeups of President Bush's face (taken from the revised edition of *White Noise*), and the "Warning: Bad Dog" graphic—to construct a complete video beat track synchronized to *Da Speech*, a process Douglas described during the Q&A session at a showing of *Da Speech* in Norwich, VT, on January 4, 2004. Once established, this video template provided the frame on which the rest of *Da Speech*'s complex tapestry of multi-media images was woven.

Though Stockhausen was clearly working from his own associative elements and influences, his musical composition echoes preceding works, populist and novelty, arguably established with the hit single—which climbed to the #3

---

[15] Including Vermont Public Television screenings.

spot on the charts in the summer of 1956—"The Flying Saucer, Parts 1 & 2" by Bill Buchanan and Dickie Goodman (Luniverse single #107, 1956). Dickie Goodman made a career of such parody "sampler" tunes into the 1970s, e.g. "Mr. Jaws". Similar sampling techniques informed Brian Eno and David Byrne's album *My Life in the Bush of Ghosts* (1981, Sire Records/Warner); "Reagan Speaks for Himself" sound collage by Seattle, WA, artist Doug Kahn (Raw #4, 1982); the works of Skinny Puppy and the sampling techniques which constitute the bedrock of most hip-hop/rap/DJ venues and artists. Similarly, John Douglas' *Da Speech* owes a debt to the unique animation techniques, idiom, and intent pioneered by celebrated American underground filmmaker Stan Vanderbeek, and Vanderbeek's pioneering computer animation works. While animators like Terry Gilliam constructed their own distinctive styles on the bones of Vanderbeek's stop-motion collage animation techniques, few extended the pointed political satire and savagery of collage-animated works like Vanderbeek's *Science Friction* (1959) and, more relevant as an historic precursor to *Da Speech*, *Achooo Mr. Kerrooschev* (1960). Douglas is among the few that has, literally in spades, with the *America's Most Wanted* card set/imagery, which figures prominently in *Da Speech*'s final seconds, and with characteristic clarity and ire.

When I asked Stockhausen about his reaction to John's visualization of his piece, he replied, "His film on *Da Speech* is certainly the most vivid and powerful, everybody here who sees it gets sort of pale and asks for a glass of water."

*"—the Egyptian Islamic Jihad/Osama bin Laden/the giving of blood/the saying of prayers/(known as al-Qaeda)/kill all Americans—"*
*—(cover of Christopher Hitchens' book The Trial of Henry Kissinger) as a black-and-white photo of President George W. Bush (the Department of State insignia) morphs into a portrait of Adolph Hitler—*
*"—Osama bin Laden/(and you know what?)/the giving of blood/the saying of prayers/(known as al-Qaeda)/kill all Americans/(and you know what?)—"*

As *Da Speech* unreels, the ritualistic "mantra" of Bush bytes give way to more snatches of the speech itself, which Douglas undercuts every time with the grim reality of the American and the coalition's occupation and aggression: the President's verbal evocation of Pearl Harbor is matched to television news footage of the initial air strikes on Baghdad—obliquely captioned "Shock and Awe Under Way"—as the military's Saddam Hussein playing card is introduced visually, tipping into the frame as explosions devastate the Iraqi cityscape ("—and you know what?/We will rebuild New York City—").

The dense, audio-visual collage eases to introduce news footage of a later speech by the President which John Douglas seamlessly weaves into Stockhausen's original piece: President George W. Bush's Message to the Iraqi People,

April 10, 2003, in which Bush says, "...whose principals of equality and compassion are essential to Iraq's future. We will help people build a peaceful and representative government, that protects the rights of all people." Stockhausen's composition returns to the fore as the aggressive visual montage reasserts itself, overwhelming the viewer with footage of Iraqi citizen casualties: air strikes, bloodied victims, urban devastation, marines handcuffing civilians, tanks crashing into doors. In a second insertion of new audio-visual material by John Douglas, a blonde female newscaster momentarily proffers: "...the US and the coalition are a compassionate people."

The accelerating images of devastation become more intimate and human:

*Weeping women, babies, families—Bush: "every nation and every region now has a decision to make: either you are with us or you are with the terrorists."—children maimed—"...and those who commit evil in the name of Allah, blaspheme in the name of Allah."—children dismembered/a child's skull on bloodied tarmac, split asunder—"...we are in a fight for our principles, and our first responsibility is to live by them."—the flurry of casualties and atrocities accusatory in contrast with the pious rhetoric of the speech—"... no one should be singled out for unfair treatment or unkind words because of their ethnic background or religious faith."*

For an ominous but wistful moment, the torrent of images yield to the slowly flickering monochromatic image of a solitary bird in flight, soaring against a clouded sky, and the preacher's voice Stockhausen referred to: "...there was a great poet who said, 'harder yet may be the fight and right may often yield to might; wickedness a while may reign, and Satan's cause may seem to gain; Oh, but there is a God who rules above, and he's got a hand of power and a heart of love; and if I'm right, then God will fight my battle—we'll get through it."[16]

But the moment passes: the bird soaring is disrupted by the montage that opens the film:

*b&w high contrast images of President Bush (Warning: Bad Dog/Bush/etc.), vanishing completely as marines hustle a family from their home—Bush's speech returns: "I will not forget this wound to our country..."— the youngest girl's face twisted in terror/wailing faces/flashing images of the Bush Administration's key participants/the family at gunpoint, hands raised—"...freedom and fear, justice and cruelty, have always been at war, and we know that God is not neutral between them."—the opening words of the Kaddish, the Jewish Prayer for the Dead, are repeated—"Yit-ga-dal ve-yit-ka-dash."—US and British flags are torched/angry Iraqi crowds/anti-war*

---

[16] If any reader knows the source of this quote—name, date and location—I would appreciate the information. SRB.

*banners/fists in the air/protesters—"...as long as the United States of America is determined and strong."—the faces of the Bush Administration and inner circle flash by—*

*—and finally, the deck of cards: America's Most Wanted (Jacks, Queens, Kings, deuces: Rumsfeld / Matalin / Lay / Rice / Tenet / Ashcroft / Perle / Poindexter et al.) dealt one by one—'...this will not be an age of terror.'—until the Joker conquers all—...This will be an age of liberty here and across the world."*

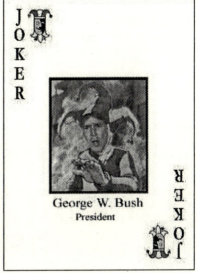

The short history of public exhibition of the *Da Speech* project began with the video installation—featuring multiple monitors screening three 'Waseda Versions'—premiere at the Art and Architecture School of Waseda University, November 3 and 4, 2002. The filmmakers represented at that debut were Satoshi Kubota, Jin Otagiri, and project founder Toshi Fujiwara; the event was produced by Yoichi Sato.

John Douglas's version of *Da Speech* premiered at State University NY at Purchase (SUNY) on May 8, 2003. Later that year, in November, the Vermont Film Commission and the Vermont Arts Council honored John Douglas with the James Goldstone Vermont Filmmakers Award for *Da Speech*, presented at the Vermont Filmmakers Showcase, Vermont International Film Festival, in Burlington, Vermont. It most recently played at the debut presentation of Shelburne Film Series in Shelburne, VT, on January 16, 2004.

The most expansive exhibition of the *Da Speech* project to date remains the international premiere screening of five versions at Emergency Filmmaking Project-RSVP, Singapore, June 10 and 11 2003, presenting *Da Speech* videos by John Douglas, Satoshi Kubota, Jin Otagiri, Toshi Fujiwara.

As a country and a people, we are at a crucial juncture; and it is important to understand the importance of that fateful September 20 Presidential speech, the turning point it represents in our country's history, the United States' relationship to the rest of the world, and the world's perception of our country.

Wielding their usual selective memories and conveniently narrow and revisionist sense of history, pundits and essayists from the Far Right would already have us forget the opening paragraphs of the speech, in which Bush promised, "...on behalf of the American people, I thank the world for its outpouring of support. America will never forget the sounds of our National Anthem playing at Buckingham Palace, on the streets of Paris, and at Berlin's Brandenburg Gate. We will not forget South Korean children gathering to pray outside our embassy in Seoul, or the prayers of sympathy offered at a mosque in Cairo. We will not forget moments of silence and days of mourning in Australia and Africa and Latin America. Nor will we forget the citizens of 80 other nations who died with our own..." Note that Stockhausen included the majority of the latter excerpt in *Da Speech.*

Consider Charles Krauthammer's "To Hell With Sympathy,"  [17] which argues that post-9/11 sympathy/empathy for the U.S. is a myth. Krauthammer states: "It is pure fiction that this pro-American sentiment was either squandered after Sept. 11 or lost under the Bush Administration. It never existed...."

Clearly, Krauthammer had forgotten all President Bush promised we, as a people, would never forget.

Having feigned the September 20 speech is of no consequence, it is thus easy to dismiss the dramatic turnabout the rest of the speech—and subsequent radical, aggressive American policy change and action—embodied, and how clearly it articulated for the planet the realities of the new post-9/11 world, in which brazen American swagger and unilateral action would be taken without regard for anything but the Bush Administration's agendas and perceptions of the world.

If we can forget all Bush promised in the opening text of his September 20 speech we would never forget—label post-9/11 international sympathy/empathy for the U.S. "a myth"—we can also refute responsibility for the extremist new foreign policy ominously outlined in the rest of that speech, though it was decreed by Bush himself. When Krauthammer, in the same essay, singles out "the ur-text for this myth of 9/11 foreign sympathy is the famous *Le Monde* editorial of September 12, 2001, entitled "We Are All Americans." Within months, that same *Le Monde* publisher was back with a small book, *All Americans? The World After September 11, 2001*—note the question mark—filled with the usual belligerence toward and disapproval of America."[18]

Of course, the September 20 speech was delivered after the September 12 editorial, and no doubt prompted the writing and publication of the book. Bush's September 20 speech changed everything: a third of the way into it, the world began to grasp how Bush and his Administration intended to reshape the global arena, and how dire the consequences of those stated intentions and actions would be. The publisher of *Le Monde* understood—just as Stockhausen did as he listened to the speech, which politicized his music for the first time—what so many Americans forget, or still ignore, refute, or simply do not understand.

Krauthammer's venomous essay embodies precisely the perverse xeno-

---

[17] *Time*, November 17, 2003, pg. 156.
[18] Ibid.

phobic rhetoric Randy Newman so causticly personified and satirized in his song "Political Science" back in 1972, whose sly lyric, "Europe's too old," was inadvertantly appropriated by Secretary of Defense Donald Rumsfeld in one of his most hamfisted diplomatic *faux pas*.

The myth of a "Liberal Media" must be laid to rest; the reality is quite the contrary. The extreme Right's domination of American corporate media would have us forget the opening passages of the September 20 speech, and dismiss/forget/ignore the dramatic turning point the body of that historic speech represented in our foreign policy. This was subsequently articulated in a new "Pre-Emptive Strike" doctrine that reversed a century of American foreign policy, and made us aggressors rather than defenders of the principals to which the Bush Administration continues to pay lip service.

The corporate media would have silenced Stockhausen's composition, and did its utmost to do so. You will not hear or see any version of *Da Speech* playing on television, much less American television. If the myth of the Liberal Media were true, Simon Stockhausen's *Da Speech* would have enjoyed airplay above the underground, and John Douglas' *Da Speech* would be unreeling on MTV with regularity.

Thanks to Stockhausen and Toshi Fujiwara and the project, *Da Speech* lives on, reminding us all how historic President Bush's September 20 speech truly was, and what it represented to most of the world.

Toshi Fujiwara's project has grown beyond his and Stockhausen's wildest dreams. Writing for the *Da Speech* website in May, 2003, Fujiwara said, "Thus, *Da Speech* videos became an international collective that respects each individual point of view about the world we are living in right now, and by this very nature of individualistic collaboration assembling perspectives from different political/cultural/social contexts, should be a strong protest against the dangerous path our world seems to be taking now, in this period of so-called 'Globalization,' and simplistic visions propaganded [sic] through the so-called 'international media.' "

By action and example, Stockhausen, Fujiwara, and their collaborators prove the power of art, individual expression, and the truly international media, as opposed to the corporate media. The very forces that tried to silence Stockhausen have only fueled the creative fires that continue to inspire fresh interpretations of *Da Speech*.

Simon Stockhausen expresses his own happiness with the project his composition spawned, pleased that it "...has evolved into a multinational cooperation in which so many aspects and views of the current global situation can be expressed. The vital choice today is: Either you tell the truth or you don't—it's as easy as that!"

For many, it ain't easy. For John Douglas, there's no other choice but to speak the truth, as he has for as long as he's made films.

*Da Speech* tells the truth, circa USA 2003, as John sees it.

*Da Speech: The International Collective*
Music by Simon Stockhausen.
Produced by Toshi Fujiwara.
Films by John Douglas, Satoshi Kubota, Maya Puig, Jin Otagiri, Amir Muhammad, Toshi Fujiwara, Mohamad-Hashim Elkareem, Pascale Feghali, Jean-Baptiste Duez.
Based upon Simon Stockhausen's *Da Speech* featuring George W. Bush (2001, MP3 and CD); note that Stockhausen also composed an instrumental version of *Da Speech* (2003), performed with James Morrison and the Band-Projekt *On The Edge* in the Sydney Opera studio (released as a CD/DVD, 2003).

---

**Sources**:
"*Speech* garners Vermont Film award," *The Burlington Free Press*, Wednesday, Nov. 12, 2003; *Living* section, *Newsmakers*. (Note: This uncredited piece erroneously refers to the award as "the 2003 James Goldstein [sic] award.")
Austin, James and Brown, Hugh, producers: *Brain in a Book: The Science Fiction Collection* (packaged in *Brain in a Box: The Science Fiction Collection*, CD boxed set; Rhino Entertainment Company, 2000); pp. 146-147 (*The Novelty Records*, by Dr. Demento), pg. 174. *The Flying Saucer* (Parts 1 & 2) is included on *Disc 5: Novelty* of *Brain in a Box*.
Kahn, Doug: *Reagan Speaks for Himself*, flexidisc produced and packaged for *Raw* #4, edited by Art Spiegelman and Francois Mouly (Raw Books & Graphics, Inc., New York, 1982), pg. 1 (*For the Record*, by the editors), pg. 19 insert.
Krauthammer, Charles: "*To Hell With Sympathy*," *Time*, November 17, 2003, Vol. 162, No. 20, pg. 156.
Newman, Randy: *Political Science, Sail Away* (Reprise/Warner Records, 1972).

Stern, Chaim, editor: text of *The Kaddish* quoted from *Gates of Prayer: The New Union Prayerbook* (Central Conference of American Rabbis, New York, 1975), pg. 629.
Vanderbeek, Stan: *Stan Vanderbeek: Visibles* (vhs, Johanna Vanderbeek at Re: Voir Video, 2000) - http://www.re-voir.com.

---

President George W. Bush's Address to a Joint Session of Congress and the American People (aka President Declares Freedom at War with Fear; Address to Congress and the Nation on Terrorism), Sept. 20, 2001:
http://www.whitehouse.gov/news/releases/2001/09/20010920-8.html
http://www.johnstonsarchive.net/terrorism/bush911c.html
President George W. Bush's Message to the Iraqi People, April 10, 2003:
http://www.whitehouse.gov/news/releases/2003/04/20030410-2.html

---

John Douglas:
http://www.redrat.net/blackhole/eyes.htm
http://www.redrat.net/years/03/film/index.htm

---

*Da Speech* Project:
http://www.dragons.vg/daSpeech/

---

Simon Stockhausen (including a full listing of his works and discography):
htp://www.simonstockhausen.com
Simon Stockhausen's MP3 site:
http://stage.vitaminic.de/simon_stockhausen

---

Amir Muhammad: The Big Durian website:
http://thebigdurian.tripod.com/

---

Maya Puig: the FilmArch e.V.:
http://www.filmarche.de
NISI MASA (European association of young filmmakers:)
http://www.nisimasa.com

---

Mohamed-Hashim Elkareem:
TAFF, Toronto African Film Festival:
260 Adelaide Street East, Suite 201,
Toronto, Ontario, Canada M5A 1N1
torontoafricanfilmfestival@yahoo.ca

"The Black Hole" - John Douglas' Charlotte, VT studio
(*photo by John Douglas*)

## John Douglas' Filmography

*Skyhook* (cinematography only; training film, USMC Seal Team/Rescue, for the CIA dba: Fulton Co. and OmniVision Inc., 1966).
*Strike City* (30 min. B&W- cinematography, edited, co-directed with Tom Griffin, 1967) (Award: Blue Ribbon, American Film Festival.)
*BDRG: Boston Draft Resistance Group* (20 min.; cinematography, Newsreel Group, 1968).
*Die-Cast Grills* (15 min.; cinematography, edited, directed, 1968).
*Summer '68* (1 hr.; cinematography, edited, co-directed, Newsreel Group, 1968)

*Peoples' War*

*Peoples' War* (50 min; cinematography, edited, with Robert Kramer and Norman Fruchter, Newsreel Group, 1969) (Awards: First Prize, American Film Festival, Golden Bear Award, Moscow International Film Festival.)
*Cecil* (30 min.; cinematography, edited, co-directed, 1970) (John Douglas's first Vermont film.)
*Free Farm* (15 min.; cinematography, edited, co-directed, 1970) (Putney, VT.)
*To Our Common Victory* (30 min.; edited, co-directed, 1971)
*Kaskawulsh* (30 min.; cinematography, edited, directed, 1972) (aka *Glacier Film*.)
*Milestones* (226 min. approx; cinematography, edited, co-directed with Robert Kramer, 1975) (John also acted in this feature; Awards: Critics Choice Award, Cannes Film Festival; New York Film Festival; London Film Festival; First Prize, Internation Film Festival, Portugal.)
*The Verdict* (60 min., video; videography, edited, co-directed, 1976).
*Hunter College Now* (15 min.; cinematography only, 1977).

*Portrait of a Puerto Rican Artist: Jorge Soto* (20 min.; cinematography, research, scripting, 1977).
*Cric, Crac* (cinematography, 1978) (Played international festivals.)
*Barrio Logan Por Vida* (cinematography, 1979).
*Rape of Reality* (60 min., cinematography, 1979) (produced by Cobra Films, Sweden).
*Stand Up Grenada* (60 min., cinematography, edited, co-directed, 1979); (Awards: Latin American International Film Festival, Havana, Cuba.)
*Disarmament: The Question of Conversion* (cinematography, 1980) (produced for the United Nations by Swedish TV.)
*Grenada: Nobody's Backyard* (cinematography, 1980) (Covert Action Bulletin Production.)
*I'm Not Really a Waitress* (15 min., cinematography, edited, 1980) (Played Womens International Film Festival.)
*Birds and Buffaloes* (20 min., cinematography, animated, edited, directed, 1981).
*La Logan* (30 min., cinematography, edited, co-directed, 1981) (Played Latin American International Film Festival, Havana, Cuba.)
*Grenada: The Future Coming Towards Us* (60 min., cinematography, edited, directed, 1983) ( Played at Latin American International Film Festival, Havana, Cuba; Leipzig International Festival Award; The Public Theater, NYC; Nigerian National Television to NHK, Japan; etc.)
*Route One* (editing only, 1988; feature film directed by Robert Kramer, Films D'Ici, Paris.)
*Love the American People, Not the American Government* (computer animation on video, 1988) (Special Jury Award Political Video, National Journalists' Conference Halls/Walls Gallery, Buffalo, NY.)
*Quebec/Vermont Artists: Acid Rain Project* (computer animation on video, 1989) (Work showed in LaMacaza Gallery, Quebec, and Coburn Gallery/Metropolitan Gallery in Burlington, Vermont.)
*White Noise* (4 min., computer animation, 1990) (Music by Erich Kory; Awards: Special Jury Award / Earth Peace Film Festival, Burlington. Also note: a revised edition of *White Noise* was completed in 2000, though John instructed me to not list this as a separate title on this filmography.)
*Thought I Saw* (30 min., computer animation, 1991) (Music by Erich Kory, performed in 'Le Violoncelle a toutes les cordes' Festival, Montreal, Quebec.)
*The Heart of It* (7 min. computer animation, 1992) (Music by Erich Kory; Awards: First Prize, AT&T's 1992 International Graphics/Animation Competition.)
*Revelation* (2 min., computer animation, 1992) (Music by Erich Kory; Produced by P.C.S.I. and Alan Waxenberg, distribution by DIVA Corporation on Interactive-CD Video Disk.)

*The Heart of It*

*Underneath: A Nostalgia for Paint* (5 min., computer animation, 1993) (Music by Erich Kory; shown at the Walker Art Center as part of ISEA'93, ISEA'93 annual show reel.)
*Our Bones* (10 min., computer animation, 1994) (St. Johnsbury screening; part of Vermont Filmmaker Series.)
*Demo Reel* (10 min., computer animation, 1995).

*The Whitehouse*

*The Whitehouse* v.3 (14.4 minutes, computer animation, 1998/2000) (Awards: Bessie Award, 2000, for "Outstanding Creative Vision;" also note variable running times, as there are three versions of *The Whitehouse* extant; two shorter versions were shown in various venues, including Vermont Public Television's "Reel Independents" program.)
*Da Speech* (8 min., computer animation, 2003) (Awards: James Goldstone Vermont Filmmakers Award.)

***Endnotes***:
Re: *Reagan Speaks for Himself* by Doug Kahn. Note that this remarkable satiric collage composition, juxtaposing sound bytes from an interview President Ronald Reagan conducted in 1980, also prompted censure/censorship similar to that suffered by Simon Stockhausen's *Da Speech*. An account of these difficulties accompanying the release of Kahn's composition as a flexi-disc insert—to have been manufactured by Eva-Tone Soundsheets Inc. of Florida—were detailed in a brief editorial in *Raw* #4 (this account was presumably written by the *Raw* editors, Art Spiegelman and Francois Mouly). In short, Eva-Tone refused to manufacture the discs; the manufacturer considered the material "morally objectionable" and a company representative informed the *Raw* editors that the magazine "couldn't use a performer's voice without his written permission." The editorial continues: "We complimented them on their political acuity in perceiving that Reagan is indeed little more than a performer, but that, nonetheless, different rules would seem to apply to a public servant... It soon seemed apparent that if Eva-Tone hadn't used this pretext to squelch our agreement another would have been found. They thought we were being "unfair," since the president was a "swell guy." And, though they admired Doug Kahn's engineering artistry, they were afraid that most of our readers... would believe that our disc was a straightforward transcript!" In the end, a Netherlands-based firm manufactured the flexi-discs.

Re: President George W. Bush's September 20 speech. In my research for this essay, I studied all commercially-available U.S. Government propaganda as well. Though I was primarily seeking a video I could direct the reader to featuring substantial excerpts from President Bush's September 20, 2001 speech, what I found was compelling in and of itself. The only commercially-distributed Bush Administration-sanctioned release featuring a brief clip of the September 20 speech was *Operation Enduring Freedom: America Fights Back* (2002, Artisan Home Entertainment, DVD 12944; running time, 65m, 49s), "produced with the cooperation of the United States Department of Defense" under the supervision of Terry Mitchell, Chief Audiovisual Division, and featuring an introduction by Secretary of Defense Donald H. Rumsfeld, who is also featured prominently throughout. Bush's September 20 speech is only momentarily excerpted (Chapter 7, 18:26-19:46), but the documentary is fascinating for what it does not once mention: the plans to mount the Iraq war, or "need" to remove Saddam Hussein from power. "On September 11, 2001, the United States declared War on Terrorism and the search for Osama bin Laden began," the DVD cover declares, and indeed the sole focus of the film is to trace the 9/11 attack on America to Osama bin Laden, Sheik Omar, the Taliban, and the al-Qaeda, and thus to Afghanistan. "This program is dedicated to the victims of 9/11, the people of Afghanistan, and the men and women of the United States Armed Forces," the final credits begin, after a lengthy appeal, ostensibly presented as being read from a letter from an Afghan woman, pleading for Americans to free Afghanistan from the oppressive rule of the Taliban (Chapter 19, 57:03-1:02:29); this appeal is framed visually with shots of impoverished, badly wounded Afghan women, children, teenagers, and other survivors. Clearly, this appeal—whether real or manufactured—is the film's final pitch to "sell" the war in Afghanistan to the American viewer. In hindsight, the Bush Administration's decision to redirect the "War on Terror" to Iraq, based upon dubious and, in part, manufactured "evidence," mere months after the release of this Pentagon-sanctioned propaganda demonstrates their own cynical indifference to the Afghanistan appeal, the country itself, the pain and suffering of its people—and the reasons given in *Operation Enduring Freedom* for being there. Recommended viewing.

*The Whitehouse*

*Golem, L'Esprit de l'Exil* (1992)
A film by Amos Gitai,
music by Simon Stockhausen

# A talk with Simon Stockhausen
...about *Da Speech* and the Project...
by Stephen R. Bissette

Simon Stockhausen

***Stephen R. Bissette:*** *You state on* Da Speech Project *website that* Da Speech *was your first politically-driven musical composition. Prior to* Da Speech, *had you used sampling of spoken words or speeches in previous compositions?*
**Simon Stockhausen:** Yes, in a composition called *Nights of Fire* for small orchestra and tape (1996) which deals with the bombing of cities in World War II, I included several samples with spoken word from our former German Bundespresident Mr. Herzog (not the Chancellor), so thinking about it, *Nights of Fire* was my first composition with political implications. But it didn't make such a clear political statement as *Da Speech* does, and was much more focused on music. In 1995, during the Yugoslavian war, I started to take samples from the news channels, but I used those samples more as musical textures, not as any sort of statement against or in favor of something. What I meant was that ever since *Da Speech*, I am much more focused on politics in my music and lost my

doubts that we musicians have to engage ourselves and our work in favor of a peaceful and just world, with no bombing maniacs on either side!

*SB:* *Given my American frame of reference to such compositions that use sampled speech from various sources, I am wary of inadvertantly naming possible precursors that might have nothing to do with your work. So, may I ask, what predecessors or existing works would you cite as inspiration for* Da Speech *?*

SS: The speeches of Martin Luther King were a great inspiration to me in the last years. I love the rhythm and the melody in his speeches. When I heard George W. on that day speaking to the congress live on CNN, I was reminded so much of the way Martin Luther used to speak—and that made me sick, because the contents was so terrifying—that I knew: now it's time to stand up. There are no other musical predecessors which inspired me.

*SB:* *I'm curious to know a bit more about the censorship/censure from your site. How soon after you had posted the MP3 did your internet provider take action, and what kind of communication followed?*

SS: On January 13, 2002, Da Speech was taken from my MP3 site [19]. I received a mail saying that I was abusing the copyright of George W. and the American government by using George's voice without asking him. Also, the webmaster said that this was a tasteless piece of music where one could hear things like: "Osama Bin Laden kills all American and Jews"—what a load of crap! The song had been online for about five weeks and luckily several hundred downloads had already been performed. Then they closed down the entire site for about a week, saying they had a technical problem—I guess they checked my other MP3-stuff during that week.

*SB:* *I'd like to ask you about the process of composing* Da Speech*, and what that entailed; the creative decisions, components, etc. First, how did you initially approach deconstructing Bush's speech itself for re-construction into a musical composition?*

SS: The thing that struck me first was the rhythm of "O-sa-ma-bin-la-den—the-e- gyp-tian-is-la-mic-ji-had" both have the same 6/8 groove to them and goes on with "the-gi-ving-of-blood—the-say-ing-of-pray-ers-the-ta-li-ban—" and so on. I also noticed the length of the sentences were structured like bars in a musical piece. The preacher in the end had the same speed and groove like Georgie; I

---

[19] See *Sources*.

didn't have to pitch the sample at all, it just fitted, also the soldiers in the stadium marched at the same speed—just incredible!

*SB: How did the composition process itself then proceed—and at what point were you satisfied it was completed? How long did it take to create, beginning to end?*

SS: I instantly derived that 6/8 groove from Georgie's speech and made the musical structure out of it. First, programming some drum loops creating the "refrain" out of the syllables mentioned above, playing synthbass and keyboard sequencer onto it with a simple four-chord structure and a four-chord bridge in a different key, inserting all the things from the speech valuable to me—of course, very subjective—then, adding my own percussion playing on a big metal flowerpot and asian bells and finally playing my soprano sax on top of everything. Oh man, those were wild days—I was in my studio for 72 hours with only a few sleeping breaks and then it was done.

*SB: Having studied the text of the speech itself, and compared it to* Da Speech, *there seems to be a juggling of rhythmic concerns with content: that is, some rather extensive portions of the 9/20 speech are retained essentially due to content—what is said—while others are included and manipulated for content but primarily for musical/rhythmic reasons. Could you discuss this matter?*

SS: Partially, I've answered this already above; I thought it would take "seriousness" out of the matter by treating the speech as a pool for rhythmical samples, like I would sample a rapper and take some of his very cool words and lines to form something new out of it. I don't usually do that in my music, I did it a few times while working on soundtracks for theatre pieces, without caring about the meaning of it. But of course, I was aware that with this shit I was manipulating facts around, and when I had done the first montage, I liked it.

*SB: Bush's phrase, "the giving of blood," immediately takes on religious, almost mystical, significance in* Da Speech, *wherein the 9/20 speech itself, it is presented rather pragmatically, in context of citizens giving blood for rescue purposes. That subtext grows into an increasingly primal, almost occult beat throughout Da Speech; it becomes a prayer, in and of itself. Why did you seize on to that phrase, or did it assert itself as such during the sampling and composition process?*

SS: Yes, it's totally out of context—but—first: I consider this to be the subtext to Georgie's words, he is giving the blood of Americans everyday for the fight against terrorism, and in this speech he calls for war, war is blood; second: it is one of the grooviest phrases in his speech together with "the saying of prayers."

*SB: There are many Middle Eastern musical, religious, and vocal samples used in* Da Speech; *my wife recognized the Kaddish toward the end. Could you identify for us some of the pieces you used, and why those particular pieces were used?*

SS: All of those sounds were generated during the first big memorial service in the New York Yankee Stadium about two weeks after 9/11. Some of them I used because of their shear beauty, like the Sengalese sikh singing so sadly; others, I reversed and shredded to take some realism out of it. The Kaddish has this great sound, I had to use him. To me, he sounds like Moses himself. As I don't speak any of the languages incorporated in the chanting, apart from the short quote of *The Star-Spangled Banner*, the selection was a mere intuitive and musical one. Actually, I created the bridge of the piece in A-minor because that is the main key everybody was singing in! *The Shofar*, I used for obvious reasons, the rhythm it played wasn't manipulated by me.

***SB:*** *I noticed two points in* Da Speech *where the juxtaposition of text sampled from the 9/20 Bush speech presented wholly new meanings, either from compression of one sample against another, or in the placing of two portions of the 9/20 speech together in a way that suggested hidden subtexts in Bush's rhetoric. One was the statement, "America has no truer friend than Great Britain," in which "the Egyptian Islamic Jihad" almost supplants "Great Britain." The other meaningful and provocative recontextualization I noticed are the couplings of "...and you know what?" with "we will rebuild ." "We will rebuild" is first followed by the repetition of "the Egyptian Islamic Jihad," which seconds later is reiterated as: "...and you know what?" followed by: "we will rebuild New York City." The implications—the Egyptian Islamic Jihad as a "friend," the actions implicit and explicit in the 9/20 speech would only "rebuild the Egyptian Islamic Jihad"—are provocative. Could you speak about these elements of Da Speech and what perceptions of the 9/20 speech and Bush's presidency led to your decision to include them?*

**SS:** Well, you've understood it all Steve. The willingness of people to wrap a belt packed with TNT around their waist and blowing themselves up to do the Jihad-thing in order to kill Americans, Jews, and so on has certainly risen since that speech, and ever more since the occupation of Iraq. So the effect of this intervention is making the Jihad stronger and stronger. Before Osama bin Laden became an alien to us, he was strongly promoted by the Americans, supplied with heaps of weapons and US-dollars, so there is no truer friend than....

***SB:*** *Immediately after the conclusion of the Bush 9/20 line, "No one should be singled out for unfair treatment or unkind words because of ethnic background or religious faith," you transition into the preacher's speech, which as you say on the website makes explicit, in overtly Christian terms, "the purpose of this memorial service was evident—*war and revenge.*" Two questions, then: The first: Do you know who made this speech, and when?*

**SS:** I can't recall the preachers name; I would have to check the original CNN-video with the coverage of that memorial service in the Yankee Stadium, maybe there is a hint about him. "Harder yet may be the fight and yield may often turn to might wickedness or wild may reign and Satan's cause may seem to gain there is a God that rules above..." I have no idea who wrote those lines, they sound old.

**SB:** *And secondly: You specifically cite Dr. Martin Luthor King's speeches as an inspiration to you personally and to* Da Speech. *The preacher's speech in Da Speech evocatively and deliberately emulates the cadence and delivery of Dr. King's speeches; in fact, most Americans I've listened to your piece with, via viewing John Douglas'* Da Speech, *immediately assume the preacher's excerpt is a sample of a Dr. King speech. John tells me one of the videos of* Da Speech *explicitly explores this issue, juxtaposing images of Dr. King with other speakers. This makes the content of that speech, "...and if I'm right, then God will fight my battle -- we'll get through it..." even more chilling, given its bitter context. I'd like you to comment on this matter as you see fit, and will also ask:* Da Speech *makes explicit the implicit religious contexts and connotations of the 9/20 speech, and it is chilling. Would you care to further articulate your feelings about Bush's insistent religious perspective, and that of so many American speakers that followed in the 9/11 mourning. including that which you used in your composition?*

**SS:** This preacher here certainly stands in the tradition of Martin Luther, but what he says has nothing to do with the principles of non-violence. He is abusing people's feelings of grief and sadness, implicating that the Christian God is a God of War, fighting battles against whatever; as subtext, he himself is actually calling for a Jihad against the Muslim world ("God will fight my battle"). So just like George W. himself, he is twisting around Christianity, taking it back many hundred years to a time where it was common to slaughter Muslims and Jews in God's name. George W. to me seems to be some sort of pseudo-religious guy who exchanged his alcoholism against this religous frenzy that helps him to cope with the extreme pressure of his job. The way he speaks of America as God's own country is so anachronistic I can't at all understand why American patriots fall for all that shit. I hope to understand it one day.

***SB:*** *Amen to that. Now, to switch gears: I want to understand the chronology of* Da Speech *in terms of your creative relationship with Toshi Fujiwara, who founded the Project. How did the two of you meet, and what can you tell me about that relationship? Was* Walk *your first collaborative venture with Toshi Fujiwara?*

**SS:** Well, we met in the net. I traced Toshi down because he had been using some of the music I had composed for the Israeli film director Amos Gitai in the early 90's without asking me. So I got angry and managed to contact Toshi via Amos' office in order to say it was *verboten* to use my music without clearing copyrights and stuff. While communicating with him, he was getting sympathetic to me, and so I just sent him a copy of *Da Speech* and other music, not expecting him do start this video-project—but Toshi took action, which made me very happy. Then, as a sort of thank you, I wanted to do a project with him, where the film was there first and the music would enhance the images, and he send me the first cut of *Walk* which I loved. I find Toshi's approach to film and arts very radical and thrilling and I hope to collaborate with him a lot in the future.

***SB:*** *What work did you do with director Amos Gitai? His marvelous films are just beginning to reach us in the US, via video and DVD.*[20]

**SS:** My brother Markus (trumpeter) and I did a series of collaborations with Amos—music for the films *Golem: L'Esprit de l'Exil* (*Golem: Spirit of Exile*, 1991) with Hanna Shygulla, Bernardo Bertolucci, Samuel Fuller, and others; and *The Petrified Garden* (aka *Golem: The Petrified Garden*, 1993).[21] In the theatre: *The War of the Sons of Light Against the Sons of Darkness*, performed in Venice for the opening of the Biennale June 1993, out on CD; and *Metamorfosi di una Melodia*, performed in Gibbelina, Sicily, Italy, in August 1992.

***SB:*** *Thank you. Could you tell me about* Walk? *I've never seen the film...*

**SS:** The film is about walking people in the Tokyo-Metro. You mainly see legs and feet walking in different speeds and the soundtrack plays with different layers of speed, sounds, speech and singing in many languages.[22]

---

[20] See *endnotes*.

[21] See Amos' websites for details, in *endnotes*.

[22] See Toshi's website for details.

*Walk*

**SB:** *What kind of attention did your composition* Da Speech *receive prior to the attempt to suppress it—and what kind of attention, if any, did it receive afterwards, prior to Toshi's attraction to the piece?*
**SS:** Half the people hated it, because they thought I would give George a platform to utter his shit, and they were not willing to accept that George has got the groove of war speech. The other half loved it because they saw the irony in my piece and thought this was the best way to handle Georgie and his falcons. After it had been taken down, people ordered free copies because the piece was getting a sort of *Verboten*-nimbus to it. I never thought that I would enter the subculture this way!
**SB:** *What impact, positive or negative, has* Da Speech *had upon your own life and career, apart from the Project?*
**SS:** It made me aware of my possibilities as a musician to influence people's attitude, politically, philosophically, in certain fields. Also, I learned to let others take control of something that I originated without trying to impose myself on it too much—John was a help with that point!
**SB:** *Were you aware of John Douglas's work before the* Da Speech *Project brought the two of you together creatively?*
**SS:** No, I had never heard of John before the Project.

**SB:** *Given the recent history between Germany and our current President, particularly the tentative but volatile parallels Chancellor Gerhard Schroeder's Justice Minister Herta Daeubler-Gmelin made between Bush and Adolf Hitler during the election season,*[23] *I must ask about your initial reaction upon seeing John's explicit visual juxtaposition of Bush and his circle of associates with Hitler and the Third Reich. This is potent,* loaded *imagery stateside, and it must be even more so in your country! Many Americans bristled when the news was reported here that, in essence, Chancellor Schroeder had compared Bush to Hitler.*

**SS:** Man, our Chancellor never made a comparison like that, that's classical and dangerous misinformation. One of his female ministers made a silly quote in that direction comparing Rumsfeld to Goebbels, she was sacked a few weeks later! Of course, it is a big taboo in Germany to compare somebody with the Third Reich and I got really mad when I first saw the website John had put up for the project, because I felt the comparison was too direct and much too agressive. John later changed the outlook of the site because everybody involved was getting angry. Within John's film, I can now accept this comparison; he has got a point there because George and the hawks started something there that could lead to a disaster much bigger than any Holocaust we've dreamed about and they are using similar means of propaganda and misinformation.

**SB:** *I've only seen John's contribution to* Da Speech *Project thus far, but noted that his version incorporates new audio as well as visual material from two additional, later sources—Bush's Message to the Iraqi People from April 10, 2003 and the female newscaster who briefly appears. Did the two of you discuss this adaptation, and did John's incorporation of this new material work for you?*

**SS:** No, we did not discuss this but it was alright for me, because it brought elements of documentary-film into the project and it included information that I didn't have when writing the piece in September/October of 2001, and so it adds impact on Georgie's words.

**SB:** *What other contributions to the project have impressed you, and could you briefly describe them for us?*

**SS:** They all impressed me a lot. My personal favourites are Toshi's second approach, where he shows tourists at ground zero, John's film, and also Maya's contribution—but I like them all.

---

[23] For more on Germany's former Justice Minister Herta Daeubler-Gmelin's remarks on U.S. policies, see:
http://www.mail-archive.com/antinato@topica.com/msg07039.html
http://seattlepi.nwsource.com/national/87891_germany20.shtml
http://www.mail-archive.com/antinato@topica.com/msg07039.html
http://www.freerepublic.com/focus/news/757325/posts
http://www.ananova.com/news/story/sm_674396.html
.

*SB:* *Are there any plans to showcase* Da Speech *Project in Europe, particularly in your own country?*
**SS:** Not at the moment—people here are momentarily very bothered with themselves and their economic situation. The whole topic—Iraq/the hawks/George—had been on the news for months and most people don't want to be bothered anymore; at least that is my impression. But let's see what happens.
*SB:* *Is the Project continuing to expand? Have there been other filmmakers or video artist gravitating to this collaborative venture?*
**SS:** I've lost track a little bit of how many films have been made and what is going to happen next, maybe Toshi knows more about this. I would love to start the next round with a piece about the current state of the Middle East turmoiled by the hawks. I've already collected heaps of new samples, mainly sounds from anti-war and anti-American rallies throughout the world, and I'm waiting for some time in my life to put them together.
*SB:* *You've made it clear that the 9/20 speech, and the subsequent process of composing* Da Speech *was a political awakening for you as an artist. Where has this led you since, and will this kind of composition—a politicized rap, so to speak—continue to evolve in your work in the foreseeable future?*
**SS:** I make no plans about this and don't try to forsee what will happen next, but the impact of *Da Speech* on my friends, the filmmakers, you and others show me that this art-form is something to pursue. Certainly it has changed my overall attitude towards politics. I don't rely anymore on the information offered to me by all the TV stations and I try to be aware of the things said behind the lines.
*SB:* *What is your current project?*
**SS:** Right now, I am writing a piece for a composition-competition in Dresden sponsored by car maker Volkswagen. I went into the new car factory there some time ago and took samples and now I'm making a piece for 20 musicians out of those sounds. Parallel to that, I am doing the film score for a documentary film and after that I will be working for the theatre. In the spring, I'll go to Australia to play some gigs with James Morrison and our band On The Edge, we will be touring a lot this year.
*SB:* *Thanks for taking the time to talk about your work, Simon, and best of luck!*

*This interview was conducted via email, January 1-9, 2004.*

## Simon Stockhausen
## A Selected Discography

*By request, Simon has prepare a selected discography (with explanatory notes) of his personal favorites among his many CDs—for a complete listing, go to Simon's website.* Simon adds, "Since 2000, nothing of my stuff has been officially published besides the album with James Morrison (2003), where you will also find the instrumental version of *Da Speech*. Nevertheless there have been a lot of works recorded, published, and distributed on a small scale by myself, but here are the most important."

*Works compiled and self-distributed by Simon Stockhausen:*

*Stahlkörper* (*Bodies of Steel*): composition for electronic music and orchestra-studio production (2001).
*Berliner Geschichten* (*Stories from Berlin*): composition for the Ensemble Modern, performed and recorded (2001).
*3-5-8-13*, concert for trumpet, brass ensemble and sampler (2001).
*Da Speech* (2001).
*Jerusalem* 1(performed and recorded live in Paris) (2001).
*Jerusalem* 2 (studio production; including a speech of Dr. Martin Luther King: The six principles of nonviolence) (2002).
*Wintermärchen* (*Wintertale*): electronic music, a requiem for a dead friend (2002).

Simon and Markus Stockhausen

*In collaboration with brother Markus Stockhausen and drummer Jo Thënes:*

*Aparis*: ECM-Records 1404
*Aparis*: "*Despite the fire-fighters efforts...*": ECM-Records 1496
http://www.ecmrecords.com/ecm/artists/139.html
*Clown*: EMI 7243 5 55603 2 2
*Jubilee*, with Markus Stockhausen: EMI 7243 5 56265 2 3
*Possible Worlds,* Markus Stockhausen: CMP CD 68
*The War of the Sons of Light Against the Sons of Darkness* (Biennale Venedig) Agav Films 793 53, collaboration with Amos Gitai, Hannah Shygulla and Markus Stockhausen.

---

*Mir CD* on Academy Label - collaboration with the multiple artist Manos Tsangaris published on Edel Records ACA 0085172 - http://www.tsangaris.de.
James Morrison / *On The Edge* - published by Origin Music collaboration with the australian musician James Morrison and our band.
http://www.originmusic.com and http://www.morrisonrecords.com.au.
*Esperanto*, Lalo Shifrin - Aleph Records.

*Simon Stockhausen (including a full listing of his works and discography):*
http://www.simonstockhausen.com
*MP3 site:*
http://stage.vitaminic.de/simon_stockhausen

*Markus Stockhausen*
http://www.markusstockhausen.com

---

**Sources and endnotes***:*

Amos Gitai:
Facets Video recently released the 5-disc DVD set *Exile*, featuring two of the features (*Golem: Spirit Of Exile*, 1991, and *Golem: The Petrified Garden*, 1993) which Stockhausen scored. Available at the Facets website.
http://www.facets.org/asticat
Amos Gitai's website:
http://www.amosgitai.com

# Haven't Seen *Da Speech*...?
## by Stephen R. Bissette

*"...discourse is itself political activity, not merely its mirror. As industrial production has become increasingly the production of information, political power has lodged more and more in the apparatuses of ideology, and media events have themselves become substantially the activity of the political process."*
- David E. James
*(Allegories of Cinema: American Film in the Sixties)*

*"The first casualty when war comes, is truth."*
- U.S. Senator Hiram Johnson, speaking during WW1

Haven't seen John Douglas' *Da Speech*? Haven't seen any of the international project's videos? Haven't heard Simon Stockhausen's *Da Speech*? What, you never heard of it? Access to *Da Speech* is problematic, at best. As noted in the text and accompanying interview with Simon Stockhausen, swift action was taken to keep the composer from releasing *Da Speech* as an MP3 file, under the most dubious of legal arguments. John Douglas' film, despite winning the prestigious James Goldstone Award, remains difficult to see.

Harder still to see are numerous political short films and documentaries that young filmmakers have produced over the past three years in and about the state. Occasionally, one may merit a brief notice in the regional press—such as Burlington digital filmmaker Art Bell's scathing *Don't Do Bush* spot, completed during a workshop in Rockport, Maine—but these remain by and large invisible, save to the filmmakers' immediate circles.

*Da Speech*—both Stockhausen's composition and Douglas' video—are forceful expressions of their respective creators' outrage. They are arguably creative screeds in the true sense of the term. One can perhaps rationalize, but not excuse, the timidity that has kept *Da Speech* off the airwaves and television screens. But, prior to 2004, other regional attempts to scrutinize, debate, criticize, and/or counter the dominate media push to embrace the Bush Administration's radical post-9/11 policies were similarly discouraged and squashed. Don't forget President Bush's press secretary warning the media and all Americans in the wake of 9/11 to watch what they say, and do. It is discourse and debate itself that is being suppressed in the mainstream arena, as the media falls in lock-step with itself, discouraging anything out of synch with that preordained train of thought.

Despite attempts to arrange public television broadcasts of both versions of Walter Ungerer's post-9/11 documentary—the incomplete edition done in collaboration with Lesley Becker entitled *Ground Zero*, and the complete 80-minute *And All This Madness* (both 2002)—only institutional and regional theatrical showings were ultimately possible. Ungerer's snapshot of regional voices reacting in the immediate wake of 9/11 offers a surprisingly cogent, incisive series of questions and responses, delivered by a diverse group of Vermont citizens; in no way could the film be considered a screed. One could in fact make a strong case that *And All This Madness* is precisely the kind of documentary that public television once would have produced, should be producing, and most certainly broadcasting. Nevertheless, rational contemplation, discussion, and debate were deemed off-limits in the months following September 11, compromising Ungerer's every attempt to mount a broadcast. He was also discouraged from, and/or criticized for, the few public theatrical exhibitions that were scheduled. Simply put, public television venues did not wish to risk broadcasting either version of the film for reasons unexplained.

Make Ice Cream, Not War: Ben Cohen, Jerry Greenfield, image from one of the unaired True Majority commercials (2003).

Similarly, former Vermont ice-cream moguls Ben Cohen and Jerry Greenfield found it difficult to purchase air time for a series of anti-Iraq-War commercials they prepared early in 2003 via their organization True Majority. The group raised approximately $500,000 to produce and arrange the broadcast of a series of anti-war television spots, which featured Ben and Jerry themselves, "a retired admiral, a former U.S. ambassador to Iraq, a Methodist bishop, and entertainers including actress Susan Sarandon and hip-hop artist Mos Def." [24]

The ads were refused by the major TV networks and most local cable venues. Of the major cable venues, one Time-Warner New York-based cable system agreed to run only two of the four spots: "The ads, which show still and moving pictures of soldiers and civilians injured or killed in battle, were deemed too graphic...." Network representatives noted long-standing policies against advocacy advertising; CNN didn't accept the ads, but did invite Ben Cohen to appear on their *TalkBack Live* program; CNN spokesperson Jerry Weiss reportedly said, "while we don't accept their ad or their advertising dollars, we did allow their voice to be heard."

The wider national arena of corporate media successfully kept any critical debate or substantial scrutiny well under wraps for the majority of the current Administration's term. More recently, MoveOn.org's attempts to air their Voter's Fund's *Bush in 30 Seconds* ad on CBS during the 2003 Super Bowl broadcast was refused by the network. In their email campaign to alert the public to the situation (and air their ad online as a result), MoveOn.org wrote, "During this year's Super Bowl, you'll see ads sponsored by beer companies, tobacco companies, and the Bush White House. But you won't see the winning ad in MoveOn.org Voter Fund's *Bush in 30 Seconds* ad contest. CBS refuses to air it." This, just a few months after pressure from the White House and various G.O.P. forces prompted CBS to pull their scheduled broadcast of the made-for-TV biopic *The Reagans* off the air. The MoveOn.org email continued, "Meanwhile, the White House is on the verge of signing into law a deal which Senator John McCain (R-AZ) says is custom-tailored for CBS and Fox, allowing the two networks to grow much bigger. CBS lobbied hard for this rule change; MoveOn.org members across the country lobbied against it; and now our ad has been rejected while the White House ad will be played. It looks an awful lot like CBS is playing politics with the right to free speech. Of course, this is bigger than just the MoveOn.org Voter Fund. People for the Ethical Treatment of Animals (PETA) submitted an ad that was also rejected. But this isn't even a progressive-vs.-conservative issue. The airwaves are publicly owned, so we have a fundamental right to hear viewpoints from across the ideological spectrum. That's why we need to let CBS know that this practice of arbitrarily turning down ads that may be controversial—especially if they're controversial simply because they take on the President—just isn't right."

Of course, a certain "wardrobe malfunction" during the Super Bowl halftime show effectively diverted national attention to more absurd matters, thus

---

[24] Gram, David: "Iraq war foes have trouble getting television to air ads," Associated Press; *The Brattleboro Reformer*, Friday, February 21, 2003, pg. 3.

defusing any scrutiny of the political impact of CBS' policies and practices.

And so it goes.

On True Majority's attempt to find air time for their anti-Iraq War ads, Ben Cohen concluded, "You hear about free speech, and you hear about free press. But if you're not able to get the media to carry your message... it starts sounding like censorship to me."[25]

"Same as it ever was," or: we've been here before—as John Douglas, Roz Payne, and the surviving members of the various Newsreel groups can attest. Long before digital video technology, the internet, online mail-order DVD and video venues, 527-funding, or "rush-releasing" in commercial markets (see below), the Newsreel Groups were creating their own radical media and bringing it to the streets when only three networks controlled national news broadcasting. The opening paragraph of the December, 1967, manifesto of the New York-based Newsreel collective is still timely:

"The Newsreel is a radical news service whose purpose is to provide an alternative to the limited and biased coverage of television news. The news that we feel is significant—any event that suggests the changes and redefinitions taking place in America today, or that underlines the necessity for such changes—has been consistently undermined and suppressed by the media: Therefore we have formed an organization to serve the needs of the people who want to get hold of news that is relevant to their own activity and thought." [26]

While today's funding, methodology, and technology outstrips what was available to grassroots guerrilla 16mm activist filmmaking coalitions like the Newsreel groups, the similarly subversive needs, means, and sense of urgency rings clear. The means of distribution have changed. Newsreel's national cooperative network projected Newsreel films in (and on) any available venue, from university lecture halls to churches, gymnasiums, student unions, and exterior building walls, while the current breed of alternative documentaries can supplement regional theatrical shows with on-line streaming, mail-order, and even commercial video distributors (see below). But this is not the primary difference: working from a vast array of multi-media and broadcast archives and access to relevant speakers and experts, the new breed of political activist documentarians are rarely shooting from the streets. The disenfranchised focus of the current wave of political documentaries are not the minority groups of previous generations—the Latin communities, African-Americans, Native Americans, students, the unemployed, war veterans, women, etc.—who were central to the Newsreel groups (the filmmakers, the films, and their audiences). The post-Millennium alternative media are seeking to address and represent fully half the voting population of the United States, if the corrected 2000 election results and

---

[25] Ibid.
[26] Quoted from Jonas Mekas, *Movie Journal*, pg. 305.

current polls are an acceptable indicator. It is, arguably, a majority being marginalized in our contemporary corporate-dominated, market-driven news culture.

The lie of "Liberal Media Bias" crumbles under even cursory scrutiny. The regional case histories cited above make it clear that public television continues to steer clear of even temperate works like *And All This Madness*. They furthermore demonstrate that network television—which happily joined the Administration in bamboozling the American public in selling the Iraq War as a justifiable military preemptive action though it marked a radical departure from all previous overt American foreign policies—won't even accept advertising dollars for 30 seconds of air time daring to question the powers that be.[27]

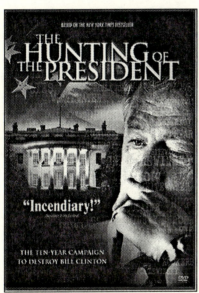 

At the time of this writing, some might argue there has been a climate change. The international and national theatrical release of Michael Moore's *Fahrenheit 9/11* is significant, the current high-water mark—if only in boxoffice terms as top-grossing documentary of all time—dominating an apparent tsunami of documentaries critical of corporate culture, corporate media, the Iraq War, and the Bush Administration. *The Corporation, Unprecedented: The 2000 Presidential Campaign, Outfoxed: Rupert Murdoch's War on Journalism, Control Room, Uncovered: The Whole Truth About the Iraq War, Bush Family Fortunes, The Hunting of the President, Orwell Rolls in His Grave, Horns and Halos, Bush's Brain*, etc. joins and, in some cases, emerges from the ongoing

---

[27] For more sobering national and international case histories, read *Into The Buzzsaw*, edited by Kristina Borjesson; Prometheus Books, NY, 2002.

cottage industry of best-selling books mounting pointed attacks on many alarming public, social, and global case histories involving major corporations, the Iraq War and the Bush Administration.

This vital new wave of grassroots activist documentaries is gaining critical mass while addressing the continuing failure of mainstream media to adequately cover national and international events. These independent documentaries are building on the foundations laid by the Newsreel groups, New Day, and many others, but the spill into mass-market theatrical arenas and video rental venues is unusual. Commenting on this phenomenon, Williams College political science professor Alex Willingham says, "A medium we usually associate with arts and entertainment film operates here to provide coverage—and critical commentary—more like that of traditional print and the mass audio and television outlets." [28] Of these documentaries, only Moore's *Fahrenheit 9/11* has punched a notable hole in the wall of corporate media, a game Moore continues to play brilliantly. But this does not mark a shift in the media: Moore, ever the satirist and cinematic essayist rather than journalist, remains the exception, though he leads by example.

Until the summer of 2004, the internet was the primary vehicle of promotion and distribution for most of these documentaries. In the wake of *Fahrenheit 9/11*'s boxoffice success and video release, more traditional video distribution venues have embraced the opportunity to profit from the controversy: political documentaries critical of the current administration are, for the moment, a bustling niche market, outnumbering pro-Bush offerings like *George W. Bush: Faith in the White House*, *FahrenHype 9/11: Unraveling the Truth about Fahrenheit 9/11 & Michael Moore*, and the Showtime docudrama *DC 9/11: Time of Crisis*. *Outfoxed* is currently available via video distributors like Ingram and Baker & Taylor. *Uncovered*, *Bush's Brain*, *Horns and Halos*, *Bush Family Fortunes* and others will enjoy similar preelection commercial distribution in October. A video industry trade recently reported, "First Run Features is joining the political arena by rush-releasing *Brothers in Arms*, a doc about John Kerry and his unit in Vietnam," [29] offering a narrow window of opportunity for Paul Alexander's film to be widely seen before the election. Many of the titles cited above are also being 'rush-released' into the commercial video market to capitalize on the election, a remarkable ripple-effect from the success of *Fahrenheit 9/11*.

The volatile public visibility and unexpected commerciality of this rush-releasing phenomenon can be further measured by the quick, tactical eleventh-hour addition of David O. Russell's 35-minute documentary *Soldier's Pay* (2004) to the October theatrical and mainstream video market release of Robert

---

[28] Quoted from Janet Curran, *Images Cinema Focus*, September 2004.
[29] *Video Business*, "Vidbits," August 23, 2004, pg. 5.

Greenwald's *Uncovered: The War on Iraq*. Russell [30] had self-produced *Soldier's Pay* for inclusion on Warner Bros. DVD Special Edition of Russell's Gulf War drama *Three Kings* (1999), but "the documentary was deemed too controversial from Warner Bros." [31] and was quickly slated to accompany Greenwald's documentary in its fall theatrical and DVD releases. In fact, "Warners bosses deemed it too much of a political hot potato to release ahead of the November election. The suits were also concerned that the film could end up violating federal election laws.... The $180,000 doc features interviews with Iraqi refugees, human-rights officials and veterans of the Iraq conflict. While it takes an anti-war stance, it avoids taking sides in the presidential race and doesn't mention either candidate." [32] Wary of publicity comparable to Miramax's and Michael Moore's highly-publicized struggle this past spring with parent studio Disney to bring *Fahrenheit 9/11* to market, Warner negotiated terms with Russell allowing him to seek alternative distribution for *Soldier's Pay*. This is highly unusual activity, even more extraordinary for its rapid response to studio-imposed suppression of controversial material, a significant revision of codified studio practices.

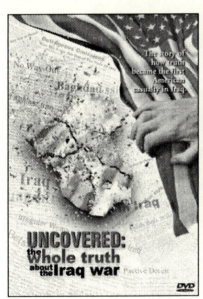

---

[30] Director of *Spanking the Monkey, Flirting With Disaster, I 'Heart'* [Love] *Huckabees*, etc.
[31] Quoting Cinema Libre's September 16th, 2004 email to video retailers.
[32] Josh Greenberg, "Warners *Kings* Controversy," Sept. 2, 2004, http://www.eonline.com/News/Items/0,1,14859,00.html?tnews.

At any previous time in history, either studio move would have almost certainly resulted in the successful entombment of such documentaries into studio vaults, far from the public eye.

Note, however, that the same controversy fueling *Brothers in Arms*' wider video availability has culminated in a legal attack on the means by which many of these films were produced and distributed: the so-called '527' organizations, named after the Internal Revenue Service tax code section covering such groups. By the week of August 23-27, the strident conflict over the Bush reelection campaign's possible ties with the 527 organization Swift Boat Veterans for Truth television spots attacking candidate John Kerry's Vietnam service record resulted only in President Bush calling for legal action against all 527 organizations. Thus, while side-stepping denouncing the Swift Boat ads in particular (as Kerry and his campaign demanded), Bush has established a legal beachhead against activist organizations like MoveOn.org, Disinformation, and others. As Karen Tumulty wrote earlier in the year, concerning the spring attacks on Kerry's Vietnam record, "...the flap is instructive about the kind of traps that the Bush campaign is adept at setting for Kerry..." [33] Another trap was sprung; at the time of this writing, a September ruling by a Federal judge has further complicated the issue. A more devastating trap sprung was the recent CBS News/*60 Minutes* debacle concerning allegedly falsified documentation of President Bush's controversial National Guard record; the damage that *pas de deux* has inflicted on what little remains of active television journalism is impossible to underestimate.

Nevertheless, the alternative documentaries are reaching wider audiences in the final heated 60 days of the campaign season.

Too little, too late?

The November election will tell—but little will change in its wake to allow works like *Da Speech* and *And All This Madness* to reach wider audiences. Whoever wins, the corporate domination of the media, and its ongoing function as a propaganda tool for those in power, will continue.

It's a safe bet that far, far more Vermont teenagers have seen Rusty DeWees's military recruitment video than *Da Speech, And All This Madness*, or a single one of the True Majority spots.

Nevertheless, regional filmmakers—including John Douglas and Walter Ungerer, among others—continue to express their concerns, as artists, citizens, and patriots. They were there early in the process, speaking out, seeking, and, as necessary, creating venues for their own visions to be seen, their voices to be heard.

They aren't alone.

---

[33] *Time*, May 10, 2004, pg. 38.

*See the review of* And All This Madness *on pages 157-165 of this issue. Comprehensive coverage of Walter Ungerer's* And All This Madness *and of the Newsreel Groups, and the films of John Douglas and Roz Payne, will appear in future issues.*

***Sources*:**
Author's interview with Walter Ungerer, June 19, 2003, Montpelier, VT.
Curran, Janet: "The Documentary Through an Unobjective Lense," *Images Cinema Focus*, September 2004, pg. 1.
Gram, David: "Iraq war foes have trouble getting television to air ads," Associated Press; *The Brattleboro Reformer*, Friday, February 21, 2003, pg. 3.
Green, Susan: Art Bell's "Don't Do Bush" spot was covered in Green's column "Flick Chick," *Seven Days*, June 23-30, 2004, pg. 60A.
Greenberg, Josh: "Warners 'Kings' Controversy," *E! Online* "Latest News," Sept. 2, 2004, 3:10 PM PT,
http://www.eonline.com/News/Items/0,1,14859,00.html?tnews
James, David E.: *Allegories of Cinema: American Film in the Sixties* (Princeton University Press, 1989), pg. 166.
Lerman, Laurence: "Vidbits: Kerry Doc in Running," *Video Business*, August 23, 2004, pg. 5
Mekas, Jonas: "January 25, 1968: On Radical Newsreel," *Movie Journal: The Rise of a New American Cinema*, 1959-1971 (The MacMillan Company, 1972), pg. 305.
Netherby, Jennifer and Ault, Susanne: "Doc galore—ditto concerns," *Video Business*, September 6, 2004, pg. 10.
Treston, Arik Ben, VP, Home Entertainment, Cinema Libre Distribution: "Cinema Libre - Breaking News - Date Change," email to video retailers, Thursday, September 16, 2004, 15:40:09. For more, go to
http://www.cinemalibrestudio.com
Tumulty, Karen: "What Kerry Means to Say...," *Time*, May 10, 2004, Vol. 163, No. 19, pg. 38.
*Video Business*, "Vidbits," August 23, 2004, pg. 5
Various emails from Marlene O'Connor (1/22/04) and Barry Snyder (1/23/04) alerted me to the MoveOn.org Super Bowl ad and CBS; the passages quoted herein were from an email MoveOn.org statement credited to "Adam, Carrie, Eli, James, Joan, Laura, Noah, Peter, Wes, and Zack: The MoveOn.org Team, January 22nd, 2004."
For more, go to: http://www.moveon.org
To see the ad in question, go to: http://www.moveon.org/cbs/ad/

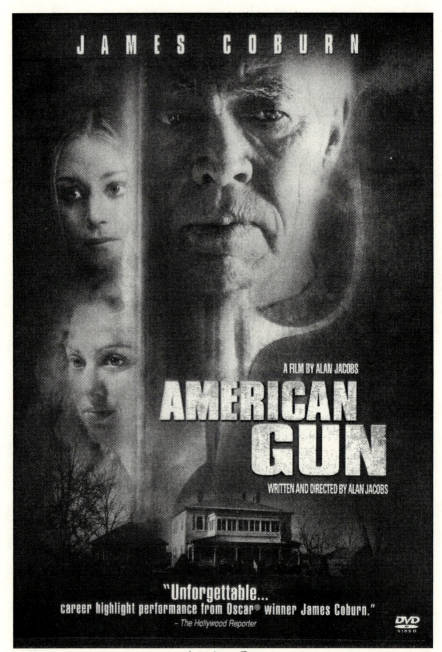

*American Gun*

# Reviews
by Stephen R. Bissette

## *Recently Released to DVD*

*American Gun* (Miramax) - Writer/director Alan Jacobs' long-awaited, sobering follow-the-smoking-gun drama stars James Coburn in one of his last screen roles as a father devastated by the seemingly-random killing of his daughter (Virginia Madsen). Spurred to take some kind of action, if only to put the tragedy behind him, he traces the path of the murder weapon in a harrowing cross-country quest. Coburn's performance lends gravity to the proceedings, embellished on the widescreen (1.85:1) DVD with a sole extra, A&E's *James Coburn: Bang the Gong* biographical documentary.

*Arachnia*

*Arachnia* (MTI) - Tenaciously independent New Hampshire writer/director, fantasist, stop-motion animation & special effects mini-mogul Brett Piper (*They Bite, Dark Fortress* aka *A Nymphoid Barbarian in Dinosaur Hell, Psyclops,* etc.) completed this amusing, entertaining ode to 1950s and '70s giant spider opuses in and around Rutland with the participation of Edgewood Studios. Though it was an unhappy creative marriage, this is big fun for genre fans, recalling films like *The Black Scorpion* (Piper's spiders look like they crawled out of the subterranean fissures of that 1957 gem) and *The Giant Spider Invasion.* MTI used the title as one of their launch points for their genre imprint. Piper has since moved on to work with New Jersey-based EI Independent Cinema studios' Shock-O-Rama imprint, and that seems to be going well. Piper already has two shockers out with stronger sex and gore content, *Screaming Dead* (spring 2004) and *Bite Me!* (October). Also note the recent release of *Raiders of the Living Dead* on DVD (from Image), which includes a bonus second disc offering a murky but watchable transfer of the never-before-released original Piper feature *Dying Day*, from which producer Sam Sherman cut, revamped, reshot, and retrofitted the ramshackle Raiders. MTI offers the usual bonus features on *Arachnia* (audio commentary, behind-the-scenes, and trailers), but there's tons of extras on the EI DVDs.

**Before Stonewall** (First Run Features) - Guilford-based filmmaker John Scagliotti executive-produced this essential documentary tracing the roots and history of the gay community in America pre-1970s; directed by Greta Schiller and Robert Rosenberg. This DVD release sweetens the pot with never-before-seen archival footage of Allen Ginsberg reading two of his poems, and exclusive archival and interview footage. Scagliotti and First Run are already preparing for the DVD release of its follow up, the excellent *After Stonewall*, with more choice extras well worth the cost of acquisition.

**The Big Dis** (Koch International/Go-Kart Films) - John O'Brien, co-pioneer of hip-hop narrative cinema? He da man! Though Koch is promoting the first-time DVD release of *The Big Dis* (1988) with Gordon Eriksen's solo feature *The Love Machine* (1999) as "Two Films by Gordon Erikksen [sic]," the fact is Tunbridge's native son John O'Brien (*Vermont is for Lovers, Man With a Plan, Nosey Parker*) co-directed this innovative urban romantic comedy, marking O'Brien's directorial debut. Though unfairly forgotten today, *The Big Dis* won the Audience Favorite Award at Sundance (the breakthrough festival year of *Sex, Lies and Video Tape*), the Best Film Jury Prize at the Toronto Film Festival and placed on the Village Voice's Ten Best List. Inspired by Spike Lee's *She's Gotta Have It* (1986), O'Brien and Eriksen follow J.D., a young black soldier home on a weekend pass, in his 48-hour quest to "mix bodies with a female" only to be dissed by his dozen select candidates (hence the title) while his mom makes him tend to chores (including buying Grandpa's lottery tickets).

This disarming improvised black-and-white urban comedy still bemuses, anticipating both the style of O'Brien's rural Vermont comedies and the major studio hip-hop comedies of the subsequent decade (*House Party*, *Friday*, *Barbershop*, etc.)—and if that doesn't mark this film for unusual pop culture distinction, I don't know what else could. Still-available on vhs from First Run Features, but this DVD debut offers bonus footage and interviews and streets November 9 (the separate release of Eriksen's mockumentary *The Love Machine* is recommended, tracing an investigative reporter's expose of a fake online sex site; a genuinely funny satire, and it's fascinating to see how the filmmaking paths of urban Eriksen and rural O'Brien have diverged, while both remain active).

***Ghost Story*** (Universal) - Though director John Irvin's adaptation of the Peter Straub best-seller is one of the great missed opportunities of its genre, it boasts a sterling venerable cast (including Melvyn Douglas, John Houseman, Douglas Fairbanks, Jr., and Fred Astaire in his final screen role) and hasn't looked this good since it opened theatrically in 1981. Universal's widescreen transfer (1.85:1) is lovely, showing the Woodstock and Sharon, VT locations at their best (enhanced by Albert Whitlock's matte painting embellishments) and radiant Alice Krige at her most alluring as the angry female spirit seeking retribution. If only the studio had used this release to unveil one of the most startling creations of makeup maestro Dick Smith (*The Godfather*, *The Exorcist*, *Little Big Man*, etc.)—Krige's bathtub manifestation as a faceless, gape-jawed Baconesque being—which was relegated to the cutting room floor. Alas, true to form, Universal elected to place not a single extra on the disc, so we still have to make due with the film's grim procession of soggy specters... another lost opportunity.

*Ghost Story*

**Horatio's Drive: America's First Road Trip** (PBS/Warner Bros.) - Ken Burns' recent Florentine Films documentary streeted in tandem with its PBS debut, tracing the epic 1903 sojourn of Vermont doctor Horatio Nelson Jackson who made history when a fifty-dollar bet sent him motoring across the United States with his dog, on the first cross-country "horseless carriage" journey. Dayton Duncan's script, Ken Burns' patented brand of visualizing the past, and Tom Hanks' steady vocal performance as Horatio himself is graced with a tank full of extras, including a trio of outtakes and *The Making of Horatio's Drive*. Don't go looking for a widescreen edition, as the standard fullscreen version is all there is—don't forget, this was made for television broadcast, hence the original aspect ration is fullscreen. PBS/Warner also just released on DVD the near-complete Ken Burns and Ric Burns collections, meaning the entire Florentine Films catalog is now available on disc.

**Louisiana Story** and **Man of Aran** (Home Vision Entertainment) - Gorgeous new transfers of Robert J. Flaherty's classic documentaries recently came to market, and all are highly recommended. These two titles are of particular interest not only for the films themselves—which have never looked or sounded better—but also for their sterling extras, which offer insights into Robert and Frances Flaherty's remarkable work and lives, including privileged peeks at Robert and Frances' years at the Dummerston, Vermont studio (where work on *Louisiana Story* and *The Land*, which is excerpted on the *Louisiana Story* disc's

extras, was completed) and a taste of the insights that defined the annual Vermont Flaherty Foundation workshops while Frances still lived. Among the abundant treasures here: Both DVDs offer *Flaherty and Film*, a filmed conversation with Frances, and an excerpt from Peter Werner's rarely-screened 1971 documentary on Frances, *Hidden and Seeking*. *Louisiana Story* sports *Study Film*, probing the opening of *Louisiana Story* with audio commentary by cinematographer Richard Leacock and Frances, and *Letters Home*, selections and readings from Leacock's correspondences while filming *Louisiana Story*. *Man of Aran* offers *How the Myth Was Made*, a documentary on the making of the film; and *Looking Back*, Robert Flaherty's own reflections on the film's creation. These are essential viewing!

**Ordinary Sinner** (Wolfe Video) - Recalling elements of Jamie Yerkes' *Spin the Bottle*, John Henry Davis's college coming-of-age (and out-of-the-closet) drama is likewise set and shot in Vermont. Derailed by profound theological doubts, a former divinity student suffers a further crisis of faith when he becomes entangled in an emotional triangle with a former childhood friend and his pal's coed partner... and evidence of a murder. Winner of the Audience Award at the Greenwich Film Festival and Best Director and Best Feature Film at Slamdunk, this accomplished indy melodrama also boasts a DVD commentary track, interview with director Davis and screenwriter William Mahone, outtakes, and preview trailers.

*Peyton Place*

**Peyton Place** (20th Century Fox) - The scandalous novel by New Hampshire's Grace Metalious was one of Fox's premiere hits of 1957, and this lavish Fox Studio Classics DVD restores director Mark Robson's CinemaScope production to its full 2.35:1 widescreen color glory (including the scenic title and transitional shots, some of which were outtakes from *The Trouble With Harry*'s second-unit Vermont landscapes; *Peyton Place* location filming was also shot in Camden, Maine). Along with the ravishing transfer, extras include a commentary track by Terry Moore and Russ Tamblyn, the AMC 'Backstory' documentary on the making of the film, vintage *Movietone News* footage of the film's premiere and the Photoplay Movie Awards. You may pick it up planning on having a laugh, but this epic soap is still remarkably engaging and entertaining stem to stern, with a genuinely affecting performance from Tamblyn and pip of a courtroom finale.

***Phish: It*** (Rhino/WSM/Elektra) - A definitive two-disc presentation of the high-definition video record of Vermont-based band Phish's two-day summer 2003 concert in Limestone, Maine, directed by Mary Wharton (*Legend: Sam Cooke*, etc.) and edited by Emmy-Award winner Thom Zimny (*Bruce Springsteen's Live in New York*). This was Phish's sixth—and penultimate—self-produced "city-size" festivals culminating summer tours built around Phish's music and the active alternative arts and performance community that graced the concert events. Aired on PBS stations throughout August in a condensed 90-minute version, this DVD offers extensive bonus features, clocking in over four hours: over 150 minutes of additional uncut performance footage (bringing the total tunage to 23, plus an extended performance of The Lizards), a trio of bonus interviews, photo gallery (including audio collage by "The Bunny"), and a resonate 5.1 mix by Grammy-Award winner Elliot Scheiner. For more info, go to: http://www.phish.com, and http://www. rhinovideo.com.

***Strangefolk: Garden of Eden*** (Moonshoot Productions) - And if that ain't enough alternative Green Mountain music for ya, Vermont band Strangefolk offer a rich condensation of their August 31st thru September 1st, 2002 concert (staged at Haystack at Mount Snow in Wilmington/Dover, Vermont) on their self-produced and self-distributed (online only) DVD, well worth a watch and listen. Nine tunes in all (including the "Lucy Down" jam), directed and edited by Jaclyn Ranere under Strangefolk's production masthead, and available only via mail order from http://www.strangefolk.com

***Terror Train*** (20th Century Fox) - Jamie Lee Curtis starred in this Canadian/US co-production in the wake of her success as John Carpenter's *Halloween* heroine, primarily filmed in Quebec (November-December 1979) with train sequences reportedly filmed in Bellows Falls, VT. This gender-bender horror-mystery thriller was an early entry in the '80s slasher cycle (released in the US March of 1980) and more generously-budgeted than most (at $3.5 million), but it's Jamie Lee's presence that endeared this to horror film buffs. Though the producers were firmly rooted in exploitation (Montreal-based Astral Films Productions Ltd and Los Angeles-based Sandy Howard Productions), director

Roger Spottiswoode was Sam Peckinpah's key editor and cinematographer John Alcott worked with Stanley Kubrick; co-star Ben Johnson was a vet of John Ford westerns and magician David Copperfield's star was ascending at the time. Long out-of-print on video and rarely screened on television, Fox released this in August on DVD with handsome full-screen and 1.85:1 widescreen transfers, sans extras.

*Terror Train* (courtesy of *Photofest*)

***Valerie/L'Initiation*** (Lions Gate Films/Cine-Maison) – More key Canadian features; these are not Vermont or New England films per se, but they are of interest. *Valerie* (1968) and *L'Initiation* (1969) marked the rise of Quebec's Cinepix "maple syrup porn" cycle, which at the time were considered quite risque adult romances (though they seem quite tame today, easily rated 'R'). Long unavailable in any format and rarely broadcast in Canada, their DVD release (in Canada only) at the end of 2003 is encouraging; could Cinepix's shot-in-St.-Albans hippie-era sex farce *Loving & Laughing* (1971) be far behind? One can hope. The *Valerie/L'Initiation* disc features fine fullscreen transfers of both features (with French and English track options) and a paucity of extras, and is only available north of the border or online from:
 http://www.amazon.ca/exec/obidos/ASIN/B00006BS9K/702-3221303-2450435

***Windy Acres*** (Kingdom County Productions/Rusty D. Inc.) – Rusty DeWees and Sandy Kofoed co-star in this "Farm Fresh Comedy" mini-series which streets day-and-date on October 27th alongside its Vermont Public Television debut (Wednesdays at 9 PM). A real first for regional television in many ways, including this simultaneous DVD and video release! See full write-up in this issue's *In Production/Recently Completed* column.

Danielle Ouimet as *Valérie*

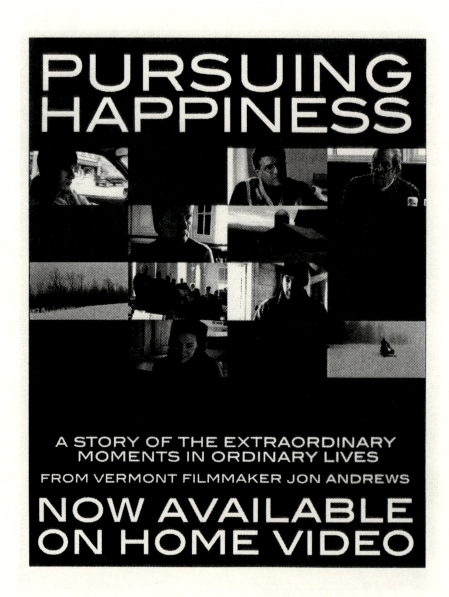

# *Hard Choices:* **Pursuing Happiness**
## by Stephen R. Bissette

*Native son Jon Andrews' drama of three small-town lives shaken by life-altering decision -- and indecision -- offers quiet but compelling viewing...*

"Nanny," an Alzheimer's-afflicted elderly man hesitantly asks his loving wife, "are you having any fun?"

No one is having any fun, really, in *Pursuing Happiness*: a farmer's son facing "what's next" after high school; a young parson facing unrest in his congregation and personal temptation; a housewife in her autumn years dealing with the declining mental health of her beloved husband. Nevertheless, *Pursuing Happiness* seeks and illuminates the ties that bind, steering its put-upon protagonists to the titular promise.Though one might quibble with issues of pacing and rhythm—which are, appropriately enough, leisurely—the film is a gem.

The trinity of narrative threads capture three lives at crucial junctures. Shy, self-effacing teenager Matt (John Stockvis) lives with his single father on their struggling farm, discouraged by a cynical guidance counselor from pursuing his college goals and tentative about his growing attraction for a classmate, Hannah (Suzanne Mozes). Charismatic Pastor Charles (Ted Scheu) seems to be coasting, tending a dwindling church flock and struggling with a marriage that seems somewhat adrift. Both Charlie and his wife Kate (Grace Kiley) are preoccupied with their professions: he forgets their anniversary, transparently consulting self-help books to mend the frayed relations while entertaining—however covertly—his attraction to local teacher Julia (Tara O'Reilly), a new member of his congregation. Most accessible of all is the plight of Nan (Bette Moffett), whose loving care for her utterly dependent husband Harold (Jack Runyon) reaches a crucial crossroads when his forgetfulness causes escalating danger. After a kitchen fire, Nan reluctantly consigns Harold to a nursing home, a decision that does not sit well with her unconditional devotion to Harold and their lifelong relationship.

*Pursuing Happiness* enjoyed its first local showing at Middlebury College in October, 2002, and its "world premiere" at the First Annual Rural Route Film Festival in New York City. Thankfully, the film is reaching a regional audience via a summer showing on Vermont Public Television's *Reel Independents* and Andrews' self-produced video release; like the similarly intimate, moving work of Nora Jacobson, it deserves much wider distribution. This is Jon Andrews' first feature, but not his first film. As a student at Yale University of Art, Andrews received his B.A. with two films to his credit, *The Night Tram* (1995) which was filmed in Prague during a semester abroad studying at the national film academy of the Czech Republic FAMU, and the award-winning *Short Change* (1996).

For *Pursuing Happiness*, Andrews and his wife Lisa returned, after living in New York City for five years, to his hometown of Middlebury, VT, writing the screenplay in the seclusion of his lakeside cottage. Shooting at locations in and about Middlebury, Cornwall, Weybridge, Shoreham, and Irasburg—including familiar Vermont landmarks like Shard Villa—filming began in the winter and spring of 2002. The local community was supportive as Andrews drew his cast from local talent, a precious few of whom had any previous—much less professional—acting experience. The locations, the cast, and Andrews' own life experiences—with area schools, social circles, and growing up the son of the town's Congregationalist Church pastor—lend the film an authenticity, arguably semi-autobiographical in nature, that transcends the easy verisimilitude regional filmmaking habitually taps.

Bette Moffett and John Stockvis inhabit, rather than perform, their roles. Moffett radiates devotion and dignity from her first frame sans pretension or false sentiment—hers is the most affecting story, at least for most adult viewers—while Stockvis communicates every shade of Matt's emotional turbulence despite the tenacious, sullen opacity of his armor. Matt's strength and stoicism is admirable, but we see how it cuts him off from the world and those who genuinely care for him. The toll exacted by the maintenance of his emotional armor against all incursions—acceptance, rejection, disappointment, hope, loss, desire, threat, fear—is depicted with a candor rare to cinematic portraits of teenage life. Painfully vulnerable, Matt keeps his guard up even when confronted with honest expressions of faith in his abilities and love from his father (Steve Small), his uncle Billy (Adam Parke), and Hannah. These, too, are potential threats; in his own eyes, he is unworthy of such attention. Inattentive viewers—like inattentive parents or teachers—might too easily shrug off Matt as incommunicative, but Stockvis' screen presence and Andrews' perceptive framing and direction of the character belies that glib dismissal.

Ted Scheu lends Pastor Charlie the affable, easy warmth that increasingly masks his own cluelessness amid a mounting test of his own faith and monogamy. In telling tableaus, Andrews crafts two sequences demonstrating Charlie's inability to honestly confront his own prejudices and blind-spots: an appeal from a couple seeking marriage in Charlie's—or any—church, and an exchange with a disgruntled congregation member who feels Charlie's stewardship is abandoning what the man considers core values of the church. During the opening credits, we hear portions of Charlie's sermon, including the statement, "Faith is worth nothing unless it is expressed." Charlie, however, seems incapable of honest expression. With succinct economy, Scheu and Andrews convey Charlie's rootless weakness via the pastor's diplomacy which skirts any meaningful discussion or expression of self: affronted by the open, physical expression of affection between the couple and their opportunism in seeking any available venue for their marriage, Charlie lies, claiming the church schedule is full, rather than voice his reservations; tentatively fearful of his confrontational parishioner's criticism of the direction he has taken the church, Charlie accepts the affront without debate, and turns the other cheek by allowing the fellow to run an ad in the church newsletter and later address the congregation directly after a sermon. This carries into his marriage and every glimpse Andrews affords of Charlie and his wife. In their scenes, Nan and Matt are seen to responsibly confront and cope with their respective harsh realities to the best of their abilities; Charlie, a spiritual leader of the community, seems lost in casual self-denial and passive deceit, seemingly ignorant of—but not, I hasten to add, indifferent to—his culpability. Given the destination Charlie literally hurtles toward in the final act, and his implicit acceptance of the consequences as a punitive God's will, Charlie's story may be the most tragic of all.

Equally perceptive and affecting is Jack Runyon's performance as Nan's lost-at-sea husband Harold; his strained expression amid day-to-day events both banal—suddenly forgetting the most familiar of tasks—and, in his world, extraordinary—the diner meal with old friends—asserts a profound gravity. This is buoyed by his obvious enjoyment of ephemeral domesticity and the most modest conquests: sharing Nan's company, brushing their cat with childlike abandon, enjoying his old competency with a household task, asserting his washing of the dinner dishes. The chemistry between Nan and Harold gains crucial momentum, lending tension to their time together: we find ourselves unexpectedly agonizing over the most commonplace tasks, such as the preparations for dinner after Nan returns Harold to their home. We hope nothing will happen to further demonstrate Harold's degenerative condition or inadvertently cause harm, but fear the worst.

Just as vital, and too often overlooked by even the most experienced of directors, every character onscreen is concisely proffered with a clear sense of life lived beyond the narrow parameters of the running time. The hidden depths of many—the forthright Hannah, Matt's father and uncle, Matt's long-haired buddy Pete (played by David Pezzulo), Nan's confidantes, etc.—add resonance to the narrative whole. Clearly, the writer/director knows these characters and has, in his own way, walked in their shoes. That he places us vicariously in their footsteps as well is an act of grace.

*Pursuing Happiness* is an assured directorial debut, extraordinary most of all for the filmmaker's confidence in his material and his characters. With effectively understated patience, writer/director Andrews eschews the high melodrama usually attached to such narratives—any one of which could, and has, been the springboard for countless self-standing features—to explore a quieter, more intimate path. Only Nan seems to really be facing life-and-death decisions which, in the end, impacts on everyone in view, but Andrews doesn't twist his material to favor that conflict over any other. All three narrative threads play out with their own rhythm, occasionally brushing one another—the shared meal of three couples, for instance, is among the film's most deftly conceived, executed, and edited passages—before they believably come together in the final act. That literal collision is one we anticipate—why else would we be watching these seemingly unrelated stories?—and dread as it becomes an inevitability, demonstrating how fully we have emotionally invested ourselves in the lives of these people by the denouement.

To his credit as writer and director, Andrews empathically attunes to the magnitude of each individual's dilemma through their eyes, skirting the falsity of soap opera to evoke life as it is lived by most of us. "I like the idea that this movie takes normal people and makes them stars based on epic moments in their lives," Andrews said in 2002, "I wanted to tell stories about here: this is where the stories are for me, not with people I don't know."[34] True to his intent, Andrews sees no need to artificially inflate the magnitude of the "epic moments," which are momentous enough for these people. For Nan, Matt, and Charlie—and, thus, for the viewer—the problems they face become all-consuming, and cannot be measured by anything but their own experience. Each character struggles with intangible, uncontrollable, and seemingly insurmountable difficulties in their personal arenas, spiraling into increasingly insular circles until their seemingly-unrelated movements bring them together in an accidental crossing-of-paths: an honest culmination, not a disruption, of their stories. Nor does Andrews allow his climax to necessarily thrust his protagonists into revelatory awakenings though the lovely coda—comparable in its gentle power to that which concludes Hilary Birmingham's exquisite *Tully* (2000)—indicates one of them, at least, has finally opened their eyes to new possibilities.

To say any more would be unfair. The film should be experienced on its own terms, just as it invites us to taste the lives of its characters.

The title is apt: pursuit is the coin of the realm, and perhaps all there is. The happiness each pursues is elusive and invariably bound to those they love, and those who love them. The object of pursuit, when it comes, is fleeting at best—a gesture, a glance, a word, a shared meal—and may barely be recognized at all.

The ever-present hope is that, once recognized, the spark can be sheltered long enough to generate—and share—warmth. With his final shot, Andrews suggests this alone is worth the struggle.

Pursuing Happiness *is available in various retail venues around Vermont and online at:* http://www.onticpictures.com/ph/orders/consumer.htm.

---

[34] Quoted from "Local Love Seen Through Silver Screen" by Crystalyn Radcliffe, The Middlebury Campus.com, October 30, 2002.

*Pursuing Happiness* (2002) New Prospect Pictures. Produced, written and directed by Jon Andrews. Starring Grace Kiley, Bette Moffett, Suzanne Mozes, Tara O'Reilly, Jack Runyon, Ted Scheu, John Stokvis, Mark Davenport, Dave Pezzulo, Richard Reed, Shannon Small, Steve Small, Connie Staats.

---

***Sources***:
Mozes, Suzanne: e-mail to the author, September 2004.
Radcliffe, Crystalyn: "Local Love Seen Through Silver Screen," *The Middlebury Campus.com*, October 30, 2002.
http://www.middleburycampus.com/news/2002/10/30/Arts/Local.Love.Seen.Through.The.Silver.Screen-311198.shtml.
Rural Route Film Festival 2003 site.
http://www.ruralroutefilms.com/program.html.
Yale University School of Art: Biographies: "Jonathan Andres [sic], Filmmaker."
http://www.yale.edu/art/biographies.html

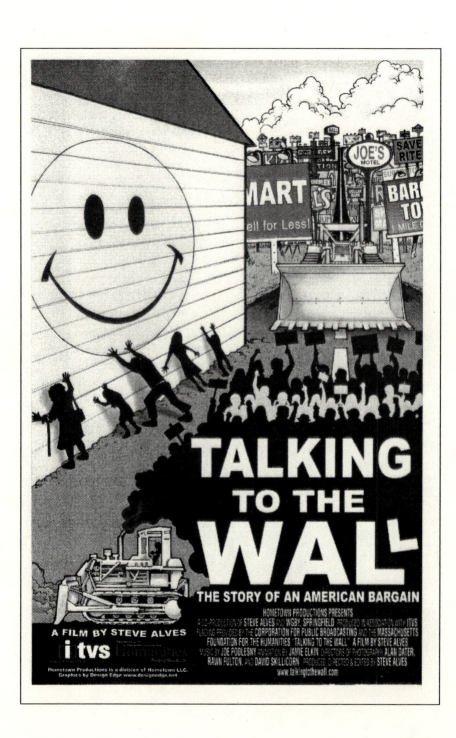

# A Brick in the Wall: *Talking To The Wall*
by Stephen R. Bissette
photos courtesy of Steve Alves

*Steve Alves's testimonial to small-town New England fighting corporate power is a galvanizing testimonial to democracy in action...*

*Talking to the Wall*: Steve Alves, Rawn Fulton

How Long Island native Steve Alves studied at USC, became a Hollywood film editor for a decade, and eventually settled in Greenfield, Massachusetts to become a political activist and member of the Town Council would seem to be peripheral to the substance of his new documentary *Talking to the Wall: The Story of an American Bargain* (2003). It might provide a glib framing device, perhaps, at best. But Alves is adult, savvy, and shameless enough to know we need a hook to draw us into the tale of a small-town New England David struggling to topple as formidable a corporate Goliath as Walmart—and he's as good a hook as any.

His story is our story, he proposes, and he proves such is the case with deft, assured strokes, high spirits, sharp humor, and a keen investigative eye and ear for the nuances of how small-towns and big business communicate—and fail to communicate—and the real stakes of the conflict he probes so lovingly.

In a brilliantly conceived and executed prologue, Alves presents his personal odyssey with enviable economy. Immediately capitalizing on the pop-cultural genre associations with his Long Island hometown of Amityville, NY (renowned as the home of *The Amityville Horror* pseudo-fiction novels and seven-feature-film series), Alves wryly crosscuts between amusingly shrill clips from the films and archival footage of suburban sprawl to evoke "the horror of Long Island—development run amuck." Compressing his personal trek across the country into an intoxicating rush of people, places, and periods, Alves breezes through his Los Angeles years (a city, he tells us, which was "like Long Island on steroids") and skips like a stone to his eventual move to Greenfield, MA. "It reminded me of Amityville before the horror," Alves concludes, establishing both the placing of roots into the kind of small-town community he wished to raise his family within, and his common bond with most Americans, who ache for, or seek to preserve, the same for themselves and their loved ones.

Such community values and bliss may seem illusory to many, but Alves maintains—and, throughout the subsequent feature, demonstrates—that small-town America is still an active—and/or achievable—here and now reality. It is a reality, he argues via the action onscreen rather than with platitudes, we must join and work within if we are to savor and preserve its values; a reality are unwise to so blithely leverage and level in the name of progress, business, or perceived retailer paradises.

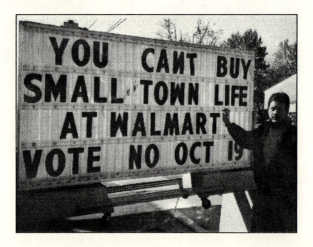

Having found his own place in the sun—and all before the title of the film appears!—Alves just as quickly introduces the central menace of this social/political/economic *kaiju eiga*: Walmart. As surely as Godzilla's roar promises impending destruction, the Fall 1992 announcement that Walmart intended to build a 131,000-square-foot superstore, with additional space predetermined for expansion, two-and-a-half miles outside of Greenfield raised the hackles of adoptive citizens like Alves and a surprising cross-section of its natives. The proposal, which involved rezoning 63 acres of land for commercial use, promised a radical relocation of Greenfield's activities, and—to many—the erection of a tombstone for the town itself.

The repercussions of Walmart's intrusion are carefully traced in all their complexity; this is the narrative thrust of the film, and it is riveting. Given Walmart's stature—still number one in *Fortune* magazine's Fortune 500 corporations, holding the number 12 position among the most profitable and still ranking as the number one employer, with 1,500,000 employees in 2003, presently facing the largest class-action sex-discrimination lawsuit in history—and ongoing expansion into every corner of America, Greenfield's story is arguably Everytown's story. What set the community apart—for a time, at least—was its willingness to take on the corporate monolith.

The unlikely bedfellows in the struggle to oust Walmart—despite the Town Council's initial approval of the development—include elderly die-hard conservative businessman David Bete and hired-gun grass-roots activist Al Norman. Though the generational and political polarities of the participants are self-evident, so is their common ground: Bete pragmatically asserts, "we were looking at the potential collapse of the local downtown business," while Norman echoes, "what this campaign was about was community." Via clips from Greenfield Community Television footage of a debate between local town and business representatives and a Walmart "suit," and the results of an exhaustive 200-page report prepared to propel the debate, the deceits of Walmart's announced employment opportunities for the area—integral to corporate strategy for winning over community support—are exposed with surgical precision: the promised 250 jobs—60 to 70% of which were to be "full benefit jobs"—dwindle to a mere 29 jobs in actuality, with Walmart paying only 20% of the promised health-care benefits of that meager work force. Like the horror films Alves evokes in his prologue, there are even echoes from ancient graves: the construction of the Walmart would necessarily disinter the bones of Native Americans, as the site rests on soil once sacred to indigenous Abenaki tribes.

Despite its rigorous focus, *Talking to the Wall* isn't just about the Greenfield drama. Alves provides sobering glimpses of now-destitute Midwest communities devastated by Walmart's incredibly successful strategies, and cannily charts the dissolution of nearby Orange, MA during the same period in the 1990s. In Alves' original plan for the film, the town of Athol, MA would have also been traced; however, its tragic five-year history paralleled that of Orange precisely, and thus was not included in the final cut. With heartbreaking brevity, we see the complicity of Orange's consumer populace in their own town's destruction—to the strains of the 'superstore's' launch bastardizing "Hello, Dolly" to "Hello, Walmart,"—and all-too-familiar tragedy of the owner of the venerable local hardware store shrugging at his fate, eventually working in the hardware department of the chain that absorbed his once-thriving family establishment. Well-intentioned but misbegotten "town revitalization" projects fail to engage with the core issues, squandering enormous resources and funds to no good end. The community pastor participating in the grand opening ceremonies proclaims "Bless all those who will use this Walmart" with a straight face, but Alves can't resist a pointed bit of mondo-movie shorthand: "Amazing Grace" accompanies footage of the first-day shoppers exploring the aisles of bargains they traded their downtown's vitality for. Another consumerist "church" is filled to the brim with soon-to-be-impoverished parishioners.

This what-if look at what Greenfield could have become is potent, and Alves doesn't orchestrate a glib happy ending. Not content to let the town's apparent victory stand, Alves shows us a still-alive downtown area bristling with Halloween trick-or-treaters, representatives of the Abenaki tribe arranging to buy the intended Walmart site, and a delegations of Japanese merchants visiting to explore the tactics that won the day. But he also makes sure that we know the divisive split in the community caused by the Walmart debacle festers to this day. Already, plans are afoot to invite other retail giants into the area; two community college students seriously assert that the difficulties finding ephemeral Disney Studio merchandise within the town parameters is evidence of the need for change. The viewer's laughter catches in the throat. With the opening of a BJ's in Greenfield only three years later—the largest store in Greenfield's history, but only one-quarter of the size of the planned Walmart facility—we are reminded the war is still brewing.

"I think the future of our country is at stake," Al Norman emphasizes, having gone on to write a book (*Slam-Dunking Walmart*) and working with other towns in over forty states. "To me, this is not the Walmart film," Alves said in a question-and-answer period following the Marlboro College screening I attended, "this is about the failure of government to regulate big business and protect democracy."

*Talking to the Wall* makes a strong case for the truth of both statements.

In an era when our own President suggests the citizenry responds to a crisis like the 9/11 demolition of the World Trade Center towers by shopping, we clearly have passed through the Looking Glass. As Alves provocatively details, the reduction of our status as citizens to a consumer class, and the targeting of communities and surviving downtowns as flocks ripe for the fleecing by omnivorous and outsized corporate consolidation retailers like Walmart, is the result of decades of political lassitude and powerful market forces at work in America. En route through Greenfield's troubled metaphoric sojourn from and back to the Shire, *Talking to the Wall* illuminates a few landmark case histories relevant to the progressive elevation of various supermarket entities at the expense and erosion of suppliers and workers—A&P versus farmers, Sears & Roebuck versus the tool manufacturers. Though fleeting, these reference points provide a necessary context to how American at the Millennial turn arrived at these now-commonplace cannibalizations of communities under the guise of "serving the community." The failures of the Roosevelt era—including the 1936 national "Chain Store Bill," intended to regulate the buying power of powerful retail businesses—demonstratably reverberate to the present, via the saga of the nearby Miller Falls Tools firm, a major multi-generation employer which was sold to a national corporation in 1968, servicing an exclusivity contract to Sears that was eventually canceled to the loss of six hundred local jobs.

The demands of detailing the microcosm under scrutiny in *Talking to the Wall*—the town of Greenfield, and the volatile upheaval provoked by Walmart's proposal—necessarily precludes the intensive analysis required to adequately articulate the national and historical macrocosm involved, but this feature is a lucid and powerful introduction to that long-overdue debate. That the final and decisive vote that arguably saved Greenfield was split by only nine ballots eerily reflects the historic and narrow rift that divided the nation in the 2000 Presidential elections: clearly, active community and individual participation in democracy is more vital today than perhaps ever before in U.S. history.

Thankfully, Alves is already planning a follow up film, chronicling Greenfield's communal saga in the wake of *Talking to the Wall* while more intensively exploring the corporate hegemony on the local, national, and global scale. Alves may succeed in mounting his sequel with the wit, candor, urgency, and clarity of *Talking to the Wall*, but the battle is already shifting in his adopted home town. Greenfield's case history recently culminated in a fourth vote which opened the doors to Walmart and other big-box chain stores entering the community; still, big money has not yet had its way, despite the complicity of the voting community. The activist efforts charted in *Talking to the Wall* have also redirected toward protecting Greenfield's once-thriving downtown from incoming developers, hoping it does not share the dire fate of nearby Orange and Athol. As I said, Greenfield arguably is Everytown, USA... but Everytown rarely boasts as passionate an advocate as Alves.

On another front, however, we must acknowledge a vital new voice in the contemporary international activist documentary movement. This film proves Alves has already raised his voice loud and clear, and his position in the front ranks of the movement is already established. *Talking to the Wall* is one of the key films of the year, regional filmmaking of the highest order, and essential viewing for all.[35]

---

[35] Since the writing of the review, *Talking to the Wall* won the New England Film Festival's Independent Documentary Rosa Luxemberg Award.

*Talking to the Wall: The Story of an American Bargain* (2003) Hometown Productions, a co-production of Steve Alves and WGBY, Springfield, in association with ITVS. Produced, directed, written, and edited by Steve Alves. Associate Producers: Joyce Follet, Anne Letson, Sean Maxwell, Pilar Schiavo. Photography: Alan Dater, Rawn Fulton, David Skillicorn; Aerials: Robert Fulton. Animation: Jamie Elkin. Music: Joe Podlesny.

http://www.talkingtothewall.com

---

***Sources***:
Hjelt, Paolo, "The Fortune Global 500," *Fortune*, July 26, 2004, Vol. 150, No. 2, pp. 163, 182, 184.

# "I don't expect to win, I only expect to fight..."
## Steve Alves carrying on the good fight in and for Greenfield, MA.

*Steve Alves took his activism to the streets and into office as Town Councilor, until voted out of office in June—at which point Steve returned to the streets, active as ever. In three emails over as many months, Steve Alves has kept me posted on the recent developments in Greenfield, MA. Here are vital excerpts, offering more information on the continuing saga of* Talking to the Wall.

*Saturday, July 17th, 2004 11:42:41*
"The Greenfield vote was dramatic and shocking—all moderate growth candidates, including yours truly, were either voted out of office or not elected. Our pro-growth newspaper turned it into a single issue campaign that centered around the re-zoning of 46 acres of land to create a new shopping district... I voted against this measure as did the other councilors who lost. I had a very strong record that I ran on: saving the town millions of dollars and helping many low income residents.... I was tossed out because I wouldn't rezone industrial

land that would allow Walmart or some other big chain to build there. There is already existing commercial land that they could use if they were willing to build a moderately-sized store, an issue that was never brought out in the press. So shopping won out! So much for my one year as an elected official. It has only emboldened me to continuing fighting against the social and economic devastation that results from these unregulated corporate behemoths, and trying to reach bring an utterly bamboozled citizenry who think they are getting a bargain... It's time to start thinking about regulating chain stores like Walmart, as Robert Reich points out—like we did back in the 1930s. I continue shooting footage in preparation for *Talking to the Wall Part 2: Buy Now, Pay Later*. Thank you for your interest."

*Saturday, August 21st, 2004, 19:25:05*
(in response to a rather despondent letter, reflecting my reading of current events in Greenfield):
"Steve: The situation in Greenfield is not as dire as you portray. After getting over the initial shock of the last election, we discovered that there's still plenty of fight left in us. I just spent this weekend working with a Native American group gathering the 600 plus signatures needed to force the recent re-zoning decision to a town-wide binding referendum. The cameras are rolling... Thanks for caring!"

*Tuesday, August 24th, 2004, 14:32:08*
(following my request for a recap of recent events, for publication):
"It's hard for me to sum up what I've been through and what I think is going on in Greenfield. After recovering from the June 8th vote which ended my brief political career and paved the way for Walmart's possible reentry, I believe that things are not much different than they were 11 years ago when the public voted 2-1 in a non-binding vote to welcome Walmart, then three months later the Town Council gave their supermajority rezoning approval. Things only began to change once a group of citizens began to gather the 600 signatures needed to rescind the town council vote. This past week I've been working with a group of Native Americans to organize a citizens' petition to begin that process once again. In a scene reminiscent of my movie it was thundering and pouring rain as people came out in droves to sign the petition. So far we've gathered over 800 names and will probably have 1,000 by the time we submit them to the Town Clerk on Thursday. The battle will once again be on. But this time the debate will focus on the ghoulish events that took place during the summer 1964, when Native American remains were unceremoniously dumped on 10 acres of the land that was recently rezoned for commercial. As the story of what took place 40 years ago becomes known, it has thrown the Town Council and the citizen/consumers into a moral conundrum, and has divided the pro-growth contingent. Taking the 10 acres out of the mix limits the size of any potential devel-

opment. Coupled with environmental problems, it's possible that no large corporate retailer will ever build on this site and Greenfield will once again be saved. Whew! But of course it could go the other way. Whatever the outcome, I presently feel stronger than ever. Having stood up for what I believe in, then suffered the body blow of being de-elected, I am strangely energized. I don't expect to win, I only expect to fight. In my hometown, I take a stand for maintaining the soul of community life. As a filmmaker I fight against the gross distortions of our history and for the birthright of democracy which entitles us to have some control over our lives. Hope this helps. Best regards, Steve Alves."

Jonathan Brandis (1976-2003)
(from *Bop's BB*, December 1995)

# Jonathan Brandis: *The Year That Trembled*
by John Hutchinson

*The young star of* The Year That Trembled *tragically took his own life last year. Television historian and Brandis fan John Hutchinson offers his own perspective on the celebrity, the actor, the man, and Brandis's penultimate role in Jay Craven's latest feature.*

Left to right:
Sean Nelson, Amy Butchko, Marin Hinkle, Charlie Finn and Jonathan Brandis

*The Year That Trembled*, the deservedly award-winning 2002 film which recently came out on DVD and video, tells the story of three teenagers who are afraid of being drafted in 1970-71, at the height of America's involvement in the Vietnam War and the imminent incursion into Cambodia.

It centers on the anti-President Nixon events at the time at Kent State University, and it also gives a well deserved top billing to a very fine young actor who had worked very hard to build up an impressive list of movie and television credits over almost 20 years and who seemed to me at least to have made the transition from "teen idol" to adult actor with a great degree of success.

But the tragic events of November 11 and 12, 2003 would come to mean that—for fans of Jonathan Brandis—a year which had already seen much more than its fair share of death and destruction in other arenas, would become not so much the year that trembled as the year that collapsed completely.

Because November 11, 2003 was the day when, away from the glare of publicity, and in the privacy of his own home, Jonathan Brandis decided to take his own life.

The stories which emerged on the internet and in the press several days later related that Jonathan had been found by a friend just before midnight, at which time he was unconscious but still alive. The friend dialed 911, and Jonathan was rushed to hospital by paramedics, but tragically died from his injuries the following afternoon.

He was just 27 years old. He left no clue behind as to why he had done what he did.

Jonathan Brandis, Kiera Chaplin

I first received this news several days after the event in an e-mail posted on one of my news groups. The details were sketchy and I was tired. But, at the same time, I was so shocked by what I read that I felt almost physically ill, and had to know more.

So, after a long day at work, and at a time when more sensibly I should have been going to bed, I went rampaging round the internet looking for more information.

Eventually I found what I was looking for. Jonathan Brandis was dead and had been so now for something like ten days, and nobody, certainly here in the UK, seemed to have heard anything at all about it until now.

A sleepless night led to an ongoing strong emotional reaction from me to Jonathan's death. This sort of thing has happened to me before. Freddie Prinze, John Lennon, Rick Nelson, River Phoenix, George Harrison... all great favorites of mine who left us before their time and they all took their toll on me.

But somehow this was different. Over several years as a TV fan, I found that Jonathan had enriched my life in many different ways, and I was now looking forward to the time when I could see what he did when he would make good on his ambition to become a writer and director as well as an accomplished actor.

Now, all that was not to be. In common with many of Jonathan's fans, I felt the need to consolidate, and so I set about collecting as many of Jonathan's film and TV appearances on DVD and video as I could.

I also established contact with other fans on the internet, something I certainly could not have done following the deaths of the other celebrities I mentioned. This proved to be a most moving and cathartic experience. We all had one genuine aim in common, and that was to try and do something to ensure that Jonathan was not forgotten—and he won't be.

It was around this time that I first started to hear about a movie entitled *The Year That Trembled*, in which Jonathan had been given the top billing that I always thought he deserved.

Well, I waited with mounting impatience for my DVD of that movie to come through the post and since the day it did (December 19), I have watched it several times. Indeed, as I write this article, it is in the DVD player feeding me with the inspiration and the occasional reminders that I need.

In my view it is a truly excellent film and I am sure that repeated viewings will only enhance this opinion.

To me it is an intimate, high quality film which unfolds at just the right pace, allowing the viewer to get involved with the story and get under the skin of the characters and feel their motivation and their emotions along with them.

I think it is the sort of film which, although it deserves to be seen by the biggest audience possible, really appeals to people like me, who don't always run with the crowd, but do know who they like—Jonathan Brandis, Martin Mull, Meredith Monroe to name but three— what they like—films which deal with recent history and stories they remember from their own childhood even though they were thousands of miles away and still at school themselves at the time— and will count themselves richly rewarded for having been able to see the film.

This is a powerful, honest and emotional film, and the strength of those emotions owes a lot to a superb performance from Jonathan Brandis in the role of Casey Pedersen.

I am very proud to be a fan of Jonathan's and I have to say that after watching this film I feel even more proud of that because in *The Year That Trembled* he is every inch a star of the highest order. In this performance he delivers absolutely everything his fans knew him to be capable of. Passion, humor, and above all an intensity that practically burns through the screen.

Casey is a high school graduate who, along with his friends, is fearfully facing the prospect of being drafted. In my view at the beginning of the story, he is a serious character, working on his school newspaper, standing up for a teacher who teaches boys how to avoid the draft, maybe something of an idealist. But as the story progresses he becomes riven by conflict, both externally and internally. He's thrown into turmoil by what is happening in the world outside, he is thrown into more turmoil when a girlfriend shatters the post-coital bliss by saying that she would not wait for him or remain faithful to him if he were drafted to Vietnam, and thrown through yet another hoop when a set of circumstances over which he does not seem to have too much control lead him into the bed of his best friend's wife—a situation which, with said friend about to be drafted, leads to any amount of inner turmoil. This is only added to when the lady, his former teacher, tells him when he tries to discuss the situation with her that "nothing ever happened."

Charlie Finn and Jonathan Brandis

The suppressed emotions and the turmoil are all brilliantly portrayed by Jonathan whose every emotion can be seen in his face and heard in the deep, powerful voice which on many occasions he raises barely above the level of a whisper, such is the coolness and control of his performance.

Ultimately, Casey's best friend Charlie is drafted and killed in the Vietnam War. It is Casey who is on hand when an Army representative calls to break the news to his widow Helen, who by now is mother to Sarah, a daughter Charlie has never seen. At the end of the film, Helen asks Casey to try and make something of all this, to which he replies he is, he is writing.

That, in the light of events of November 2003, is a quite remarkable instance of art imitating life—because since Jonathan's passing, what is happening is that on paper and on the internet, people are dealing with their feelings about the situation by writing and sharing with others.

Jonathan Brandis in *Stephen King's IT* (1990)

*The Year That Trembled* is a long way removed from the sort of work that Jonathan was doing in the nineties which all heightened his teen idol status and without doubt gave him the experience and confidence he needed to build a successful acting career. Jonathan, who was born in Danbury, Connecticut in April 1976, had actually been acting in commercials since about the age of 5, but as the eighties progressed, an impressive list of guest roles was building up behind him. Shows such as *Murder She Wrote, Full House, Alien Nation, Blossom, The Wonder Years, Gabriel's Fire* and *Saved By The Bell: The College Year* all benefited from an appearance by Jonathan.[36]

---

[36] Jonathan Brandis, quoted in "The Scene: The 10 Sexiest Guys" ("*Seaquest* boy Jonathan Brandis won by a tidal wave") in *Seventeen Magazine* (June, 1994): "If I hadn't gone into acting I'd probably still be in school and working part-time at a hardware store in Connecticut."

However, the role that propelled him to international stardom and for which he is probably best remembered is that of Lucas Wolenczak, the teenage technogenius on board *Seaquest DSV* and later *Seaquest 2032*. This was Jonathan's big break and he gave it all he could, turning in splendid performances throughout the series. Seemingly completely unfazed by acting opposite such greats as Roy Scheider and Stephanie Beacham, Jonathan turned Lucas into one of the most popular characters in the series and indeed it has been documented elsewhere that at least in its later stages, much of *Seaquest*'s success was derived from Jonathan's personal popularity with the younger female audience. [37]

Jonathan's film career had also been flourishing alongside his TV work. The late 80's saw him taking a leading role in *Stepfather 2* and in 1990 he was in the lead for *The Neverending Story 2* and also made a very impressive appearance alongside the likes of Richard Thomas and the late John Ritter in the TV mini series of Stephen King's *IT*. Further movie successes followed with Rodney Dangerfield in *Ladybugs* and Chuck Norris in *Sidekicks*.

Jonathan was also seen during his time on *Seaquest* to great effect in *Born Free: A New Adventure* and *Fall Into Darkness*, a tense thriller in which he gives a completely mesmerizing performance opposite Tatyana M. Ali, with whom he was at one time romantically linked in real life.

With *Seaquest* over, Jonathan further honed his already considerable skills by working with Ang Lee in a supporting role with Tobey Maguire and Skeet Ulrich in the American Civil War film *Ride With The Devil* and with the Farrelly Brothers in their 1999 comedy *Outside Providence* before joining up for *Hart's War* with Bruce Willis and Colin Farrell in 2001.

---

[37] From "Weathering the Storm" by Bill Wilson, *Starlog SF Explorer*, October 1995, pg. 54-55: "Having worked as an actor nearly his entire life, Brandis literally grew up in front of the camera, and his exposure has earned him—or cursed him with—a fanatic following. How difficult is it being a teen heart-throb? 'It gets damn old, to be perfectly frank,' he declared. "I'll do an interview and the publication will refer to me not as *the actor* but as the *teen idol*, and that's very disconcerting. I may have yet to do my best work as an actor, but I feel I've proven myself with *Seaquest* and some other roles in the past. They just don't see that. I got tagged with that label some years ago, and it's difficult to shake. But I get scared when I think that people will read that and think, 'Well, it doesn't mention that he's an actor. Can the kid act?' That really worries me. It's a really tricky time for me as an actor at this stage of my life... Of all the kids I was working with when I was younger, only about an eighth of us are still active in the business. To be honest, I'm surprised I'm still working.' For Jonathan Brandis, the future is still a long way off. 'I really am confident I can make that next step, if I choose my next roles carefully to make that transition. But if it doesn't happen, I'll be happy to move behind the camera, so I figure either way I can't lose.' "

Jonathan Brandis and Kenny Morrison in *The Neverending Story 2* (1991)

Jonathan Brandis in *Falling into Darkness* (1996)

All of these, I feel, can be seen as stepping stones to the starring role in *The Year That Trembled*, which would have been the first of many such performances, I am sure.

I have been asked what I think Jonathan meant to his fans.

In my opinion, he was a great and very underrated actor, always a pleasure to watch, an absolute enhancement to every production in which he appeared, and very high on my list of people I most wanted to meet.

Judging by what I have read lately, I think that he was still held in high regard by many of the young ladies who supported him in the teen idol days.[38] But more than that, I think he also became something of a role model and an inspiration to people in moments of their own crisis. He has inspired people both male and female to follow particular paths in their lives and has made a lot of people feel that they would have loved to have him as a personal friend and wish that they could have helped him when he needed it.

My own view on this is that I believe Jonathan was a thoroughly decent man as well as being a very good actor. He was not dogged by controversy, he did not court publicity, he just got on with what he did so well, and that is what made a lot of people happy.

Of course we must not forget his family in all this. Jonathan's parents must be suffering terribly through everything that has happened and our hearts go out to them. I hope they can find the strength they will need to deal with all

this and that they will draw support from the love and affection that is being demonstrated for Jonathan.

Many people are working hard to ensure that Jonathan is not forgotten. Websites are being set up in honor of him, and the one I have contributed to—www.jonathanbrandis.org—went live on January 1, 2004. Do drop by and give it a look or send a contribution if you can. Other sites are also appearing, and I am sure they will all add to the good work that is being done in Jonathan's memory.

Jonathan Brandis, I feel, was a modest man without any ego but with a huge amount of talent. The fact that he is no longer with us will

---

[38] According to *People's Today Secrets* (March, 1995, pp. 34-37), Brandis was receiving 4,000 fan letters a week in the mid-1990s. The young actor had completed two more leading roles—in the unaired pilot for *111 Gramercy Place*, and playing a CIA hit man alongside Harvey Keitel in the yet-to-be-released *Puerto Vallarta Squeeze*—before taking his own life. SRB.

never ever feel right to me, but at least we can all be grateful for the excellent legacy of work he has left behind him.

God bless you, Jonathan, and thank you.

---

*John Hutchinson is 47 years-old and lives near Leeds in West Yorkshire, UK. He works as a Civil Servant for the British Library and is the Librarian for the Programme Preservation Society, a British based non-profit organisation for those who are interested in the collection of TV programmes past and present. John writes, "in my spare time I enjoy cult tv, sixties music, some classical and country music... helping to run a hospital radio station and writing and contributing to websites." His writings are currently accessible on www.swingin60szone.net, www.cult.tv and elsewhere. John continues, "As far as being a fan of Jonathan is concerned, I think that started probably in the* Seaquest *days or probably a little before... because of my propensity to single out the people I think are really good, I then started looking out for tapes of his other work whilst at the same time making sure I never missed an episode of* Seaquest—*I loved the whole series really, for me it was perfect escapist fantasy adventure TV." Special thanks to Drina Vurbic for her vital role in making this article possible.*

---

**Sources**:
http://www.jonathanbrandis.org
Bio of Jonathan Brandis by John Hutchinson:
http://www.jonathanbrandis.org/bio.html
Programme Preservation Society:
http://www.pps-tv.co.uk

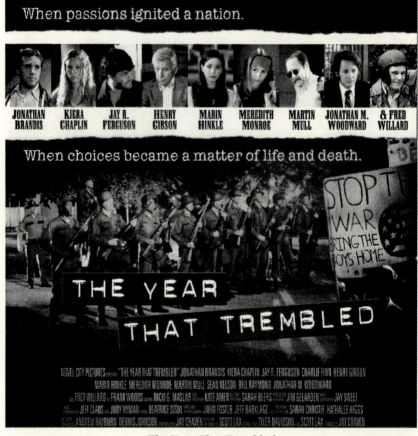

*The Year That Trembled*

# Remembering Jonathan Brandis...
by Jay Craven

*Jay Craven, Director of* The Year That Trembled, *discusses his work and relationship with Jonathan Brandis...*

Director Jay Craven with Jonathan Brandis

Like anyone who appreciated Jonathan Brandis' extraordinary ability as a sensitive and expressive actor, I was shocked and saddened by news of his recent death. I'd seen Jonathan just a month or so earlier, at our Los Angeles opening for my most recent film, *The Year That Trembled*, in which Jonathan starred. He looked great—nicely tanned, slimmed down, buffed up.

Jonathan also seemed a bit distant and unsettled, but I'd come to know this aspect of his personality during the shooting of the film. He made a few sharp and ironic observations during the evening and even pulled a bit of a prank during the Q & A, when a questioner stood in the back and congratulated Jonathan for having been willing to gain weight (which he'd since lost) for the production of *The Year That Trembled*. Jonathan feigned offense with a biting aside, but it was later revealed that he'd planted the guy and the question. Funny.

I first met Jonathan Brandis at a Los Angeles reading for *The Year That Trembled* script, based on Scott Lax's 1970 coming-of-age novel. Jonathan read for the character of Hairball, a quasi-stoner character who serves as a source of humor in the film. Brandis was funny and showed a keen sense of the character's ironic potential. But I instantly saw that he could bring something more and very special to the more complex lead character of Casey.

The casting director pushed another actor for Casey, so it required some maneuvering to get people focused on Brandis. During auditions the next day, we saw more than a hundred actors, including a guy I felt could play Hairball, (Charlie Finn of *Super Troopers* and *The In Crowd* who later got the role). But I didn't see anyone who seemed better than Brandis for Casey. I then learned that he might not be available to play the part. Jonathan had been cast in a role for *Hart's War* and it looked like their schedule would conflict with ours.

I invited Jonathan to join producers Scott Lax and Tyler Davidson, casting director Ricki Mazler, and me for dinner, after the auditions. I urged him to consider the part. From the start, he'd demonstrated that he had the range to play Casey's dark and brooding side as well as his intelligence, ironic wit, indecisiveness, ambivalence, and, finally, his resolve to make sense of all that he experiences during the story's fateful year.

Jonathan Brandis in *Falling into Darkness* (1996)

I knew that we had to look for other actors during the next six months, based on the likelihood that Brandis would not return from *Hart's War* in time. But we didn't find anyone that I felt would be better in the role. We kept the part open until literally the last minute, hoping that Jonathan would return from Eastern Europe in time to play Casey. He returned to LA on literally the day we had to decide. We had another actor ready to go—but Jonathan agreed to essentially get on the next plane for Ohio.

Jonathan Brandis always seemed somehow conflicted and angry about the movie business. I really hadn't known of his teen idol success but I now realize that, during his peak TV success, he was getting 4,000 letters a week from fans and required three body guards to accompany him on the studio lot. In fact, Jonathan had been in front of a camera from the time he was two years old. [39]

As he now embarked on a career as an adult actor, he faced many uncertainties in a business fond of anointing a new flavor of the month and spinning him/her with wall-to-wall media obsession. Jonathan was no longer riding that wave, but he was ready to do more serious work. Would the industry cast him in the roles that would give him the chance to do so? For most actors, this is an unknown. It's truly maddening to have so little control over this looming question — that ultimately decides the size, shape, and trajectory of your life's career.

Jonathan Brandis in Ang Lee's *Race With the Devil* (1999)

The day before we started shooting *The Year That Trembled*, I was having trouble getting through to Jonathan. He seemed troubled, angry, and distracted. I panicked. To be honest, I just didn't know if we could connect for the work needed. I discussed my concerns with the producers and questioned whether this was going to work.

The first day of shooting began to allay my fears. I saw Jonathan working

---

[39] Jonathan Brandis' teen idol days began to slip away in 1995, a process he welcomed. At the time, he said: "I have done teen magazines for a number of years and I think it is time to turn it over to somebody else, like Jonathan Taylor Thomas... I kiss JTT's feet for taking it away from me! I'm not trying to exclude the younger viewers or my younger fans, I just think it's time to move on from certain teen publications." Quoted from "Jonathan Brandis: Is he abandoning his fans?" *Inside Tiger Beat*, February 1996, Vol. 43, No. 1, pg. 28. SRB.

effectively and was able to engage him in discussion about the character of Casey. By the second day, we started to find a rhythm. I quickly came to realize that Jonathan was not "easy"—any respect would have to be earned. I don't know how well I did but I do know that particular moments of opportunity emerged with Jonathan, where he was open and connected. In the private moments that followed, I saw how hard he was working to shape a character that was dynamic, original, and consistent with what I saw and tried to express. He was intensely focused, always prepared, and very aware of energy, movement, and nuanced emotion in each moment. The experiences I had working with him, in those moments, were among the most satisfying I've had with an actor.

Jonathan Brandis in *Hart's War* (2002)

Off the set or in the long interludes between scenes, Jonathan assumed a different face and demeanor. He joked with his buddies and offered his sometimes biting observations about any number of situations and people—on and off the movie. He could seem closed off.

But after each take, Jonathan was unguarded and emotionally spent. We would connect in these moments, sometimes with only a word or a pat on the back. But it was in those largely non-verbal exchanges that we communicated most deeply as he shaped the character. Jonathan worked his ass off for Casey. In my opinion, he expressed a character who is rich and unique to the period, to the complex politics, the shifting relationships, and the impossible choices faced. I could not have been more pleased with the work he did. As the largest role Jonathan had played as an emerging mature actor, I felt that Jonathan's performance signaled great potential, if only it would be noticed, in this most fickle of all businesses.

After Jonathan's death, actor Henry Gibson wrote me a note expressing his sadness and saying how difficult it is to handle early success. He ended with a comment that love is is always more important than acclaim. Jonathan had clearly experienced early acclaim, but I don't know how matters of love affected him—although I do know that he loved Casey and gave all he had to this character. I hope he got something back from it, as well. We'll sorely miss him.

---

*Jay Craven has been an active force in the arts (particularly theater and film) in Vermont since 1975. He established the Catamount Arts in St. Johnsbury, co-founded Circus Smirkus, and started Kingdom County Productions with his wife, Bess O'Brien. Craven also directs Fledgling Films, a filmmaking program for teens, and teaches film studies at Marlboro College, where he has mentored a new generation of very active filmmakers. Though his filmmaking experiences pre-date his move to Vermont, his adopted state remains his key base of operation, where he has made a number of short films (including* Gayleen *and* High Water*) and directed* Where the Rivers Flow North *and* A Stranger in the Kingdom; The Year That Trembled *was filmed in Ohio. He has just completed the six-episode mini-series* Windy Acres, *and is in preproduction on* Disappearances. *Proper career overviews and interviews are already underway for future issues of* Green Mountain Cinema.

Director Jay Craven with Jonathan M. Woodward, Henry Gibson

# The 'Other' *Kent State* Film...
by Stephen R. Bissette

*...was also directed by an 'adoptive' Vermonter, who won an Emmy Award for Best Direction of his* Kent State *docudrama.*

From left to right:
James G. Payne, who played the parts of a Professor and a Guardsman; The National Guard Lieutenant (Larry Jordan) takes a break from shooting a key radical; Robbie Stamps (Peter Moiner) and Sharon (Anne Gillespie).

*Kent State* (originally broadcast in two parts on NBC, Feb. 8-9, 1981) was directed by James Goldstone, after whom the annual Vermont filmmaker James Goldstone Award is named.[40] Scenarists Gerald Green and Richard Kramer (not to be confused with Robert Kramer) crafted their teleplay working from a trio of books: *Kent State: What Happened and Why* (Random House, NY, 1971) by James A. Michener, *The Kent State Cover Up* (HarperCollins, 1980) by Joseph Kelner and James Munves, and the research completed for *Mayday: Kent State* (Kendall/Hunt Publishing Co., 1981) by Dr. J. Gregory Payne; Payne was, in fact, a research consultant on the film.

A diverse cast (including Ellen Barkin, Will Patton, John Getz, and future director Keith Gordon) enlivened this 180-minute fictionalization of the fateful four days culminating in the May 4, 1970 confrontation between anti-war protesters and the Ohio National Guard and the tragic shooting of 13 students. Despite the breadth of material drawn from the three source books, this ambitious drama was still a network undertaking in an era when it required a decade to

---

[40] See our article in this volume on John Douglas's *Da Speech*, this past year's winner.

pass before the volatile Kent State tragedy had cooled enough to become grist for the TV docudrama mill—compared to the mere months needed today: i.e., the TV movies broadcast based upon the respective kidnapping and rescues of Elizabeth Smart and Iraq soldier Jessica Lynch, etc. Arguably, any portrayal of student behavior, anti-war activism, and the actions or inactions of the authorities that led to the shootings and/or involved the subsequent orchestrated cover up, dramatized to pass Network Standards & Practices screening, was by its very nature timid and/or suspect. This film was after all co-produced by Osmond (yup, those Osmonds!) Television Productions.

Weighing considerably in the film's favor was the active involvement of author J. Gregory Payne, who wrote about his experiences with the filmmakers in *Mayday: Kent State*, concluding: "Evaluations of the historical accuracy of Kent State which is contingent upon decisions in the editing room, is, of course, the prerogative of others. The project was punctuated with healthy disagreements as to how much dramatic license had to be employed, and at what points, to keep the audience interested. I am satisfied that every effort was made to expose the producers, director, and writer to the facts about what happened at Kent State in 1970. The real test of the film is the type of reaction *Kent State* generates from its audience." [41] In his book, Payne details his efforts to keep the feature aligned with the facts of the Kent State events, despite network pressure to soften the politics of the script, heavily fictionalize characters, and "develop a romantic theme between some of the principal characters," [42] all while keeping the tightly-scheduled filming, 30 days from first rehearsal to final day of the shoot. There were many setbacks, including malingering and divisive resentments about the Kent State events, the necessity of filming in Alabama's Gadsden State Junior College—Kent State refused to permit filming on their property—resistance from Alabama locals and the National Guard, the Guard's refusal to in any way support the filming requiring the purchase of all uniforms and equipment relevent to the Guard, and a fire destroying a key set before filming was completed.

Concerning his relationship with director James Goldstone, Payne notes, "Jim and Richard [Kramer, co-scriptor and on-set writer] were understandably apprehensive that I would delay the production... Although we were later to haggle over several points, it was apparent from the first conversation that Jim, Richard, and I believed very strongly in the project." [43]

Though most would consider the bulk of director Goldstone's movie and TV work essentially apolitical—with over twenty TV movies to his credit, including the pilots for *The Iron Horse, Star Trek* and *Ironside*—don't forget Goldstone's prior Emmy nomination for the first made-for-TV feature concern-

---

[41] Payne, pg. 158.
[42] Ibid., pg. 130.
[43] Ibid., pg. 143.

ing environmental pollution, *A Clear and Present Danger* (NBC, March 21, 1970); this was the pilot to the series *The Senator*, part of the rotating series *The Bold Ones*, 1970-71, which proved politic enough to be essentially forced off the air. Goldstone also directed *Brother John* (1971) from fellow 'adoptive Vermonter' and vet radio, TV, and movie writer Ernest Kinoy's screenplay. Goldstone was born in Los Angeles, CA (June 8, 1931); he was a Dartmouth graduate and earned his master of arts in drama from Bennington College before working in the movie and television industry. He later settled in Shaftsbury, VT and was head of the Vermont Film Commission; he succumbed to cancer in Shaftsbury on Nov. 5, 1999.

Catherine Burns, director James Goldstone and Richard Thomas: stars and director of *Red Sky at Morning* (1971)

*Kent State* co-scriptor Gerald Green entered television adapting his 1959 novel *The Last Angry Man*—previously filmed in 1959 by Daniel Mann, starring Paul Muni—into a teleplay (ABC, April 16, 1974).[44] Green won an Emmy for scripting *Holocaust* (NBC, April 16-19, 1978), scripted *Wallenberg: A Hero's*

---

[44] Note that Goldstone produced and directed the strikingly similar contemporary telefeature *Dr. Max*, which was telecast on CBS two weeks earlier (April 4, 1974)!

*Story* (NBC, April 8-9, 1985) and *Fatal Judgement* (Oct. 18, 1988), and co-produced Oliver Stone's *Salvador* (1986), among others.

Co-scripter Richard Kramer had cut his teeth scripting the TV series *The Paper Chase* (1978); he later wrote the TV movie *Amos* (CBS, Sept. 29, 1985) and episodes of *Thirtysomething* (1987), *Tales of the City* (1993), *My So-Called Life* (1994), *Queer as Folk* (2000) and more.

They all came together on *Kent State*, which deserves fresh attention and re-viewing in light of *The Year That Trembled*. Alas, the film has only surfaced once on video, in a severely-truncated version—shorn of a full hour—and is long out-of-print.[45]

---

*Kent State* (Made-for-TV, NBC, 2/8-9/81; InterPlanetary Productions/Osmond Television Productions) *Dir*: James Goldstone. *Scr*: Gerald Green, Richard Kramer. *Pro*: Lin Ephraim. *Expro*: Philip Barry, Micheline Keller, Max A. Keller. *Pho*: Steven Larner. *Mus*: Ken Lauber. *Edi*: Edward A. Biery, John Ward Nielson. *Prod Des*: Tracy Bousman.
*Cast*: Jane Fleiss, Ellen Barkin, Charley Lang, Talia Balsam, Keith Gordon, Jeff McCracken, Peter Miner, Michael Higgins, John Getz, Michael Horton, Ann Gillespie, Sheppard Strudwick, Roxanne Hart, Steve Beauchamp, David VandeBrake, David Marshall Grant, Gretchen West, Margaret Dirolf, Frederick Allen, Bill Moses, Jerome Dempsey, George Coe, Barry Snider, Ron Frazier, John Kellogg, Betsy Banks Harper, Daniel Aguar, Mark Chamberlin, Rikke Borge, Will Patton, Christopher Murney, Lenny Von Dohlen, Arthur Weaver, Josh Clark, Richard Kusyk.

---

***Sources***:
Duffy, John J.; Hand, Samuel B.; Orth, Ralph H. (editors), *The Vermont Encyclopedia* (University Press of New England/Hanover & London, NH, 2003), pg. 139
Marill, Alvin H., *Movies Made For Television: The Telefeature and The Mini-Series*, 1964-1986 (New York Zeotrope/Baseline, NY, 1987), pp. 22, 76-77, 115, 187, 206, 220-221, 235, 363, 440.
Payne, Dr. J. Gregory, Mayday: *Kent State* (Kendall/Hunt Publishing Co., Dubuque, Iowa/Toronto, Ontario, 1981), pp. 125-162.
http://www.abebooks.com
http://www.imdb.com/name/nm0326360/

---

[45] If anyone has a recording of the full, uncut original broadcast version they'd be willing to share, please contact me! To be reviewed in a future issue. SRB.

# A Look Back...

## Walter Ungerer's *And All This Madness*
by Stephen R. Bissette
photos courtesy of Walter Ungerer

*Amid the recent 9/11 eulogies, this film was sadly absent, though it remains the sole chronicle of Vermonters responding to the tragedy in its immediate wake. Having driven out of New York City mere hours before the 9/11 attacks, veteran Vermont filmmaker Walter Ungerer was driven to respond as only a filmmaker can.*

Walter Ungerer is among New England's most valuable artistic treasures. Ungerer is a warm, soft-spoken man, but he's an eloquent advocate of the arts and his own work. His unyielding devotion to his art, path, and vision is nothing less than inspiring. He is also one of the pioneers of regional filmmaking, having stayed stubbornly in tune with his private muse for four decades in the face of changing times and venues in a marketplace that remains hostile to the idiosyncratic features, short films, and videos Ungerer has devoted his life to.

A quick crash-course on Ungerer is in order. His earliest short efforts of the 1960s were overtly surreal works, culminated in the quintet of *Oobieland* films (1969-74). The first two *Oobieland* films were completed while Ungerer still lived in New York, growing into a four-film "universe." The first two entries layered imagery and sound impressionistically before transmuting, with Ungerer's move to Vermont, into the more narrative, dreamlike live-action shorts that concluded the foursome. The domestic tensions of the Vietnam War era informed Ungerer's first feature, *Keeping Things Whole* (1972), opening the door to a fresh expansion, in intensity and scope, of Ungerer's cinematic canvas, and a body of more ambitious work. With *The Animal* (1976) and *The House Without Steps* (1978), Ungerer refined his cinematic vision using the Vermont landscape as his stage. [46] *The House Without Steps* is Ungerer's most satisfying traditional narrative work, a somewhat caustic drama in which a single woman new to a small Northern Vermont village is gradually forced out of the community by the petty frustrations and desires of those around her. It offered ample proof of Ungerer's matured vision, which he further refined with the more introspective and challenging tenor, tone, and content of his semi-autobiographical *The Winter There Was Very Little Snow* (1982) and *Leaving the Harbor* (1992), his final 16mm feature which took a full decade to complete.

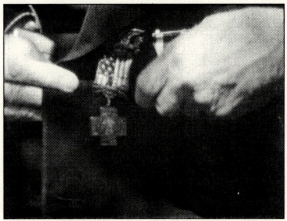

*Keeping Things Whole* (1972)

---

[46] *The Animal* is my personal favorite of Ungerer's features, set in a blinding winterscape in which the emotional distance between a strained husband-and-wife relationship blurs into a waking nightmare in which the wife mysteriously disappears... or does she? SRB.

Much of the difficulties Ungerer struggled through to complete *Leaving the Harbor* were due to financial constraints: federal and state government funding of the arts was drying up, and Ungerer was forced to seek completion funds elsewhere. In due time, the reality of the situation forced Ungerer to redirect his creative energies completely, abandoning expensive features and film itself to embrace the increasingly accessible, and much more affordable, video and computer technologies. In the early 1990s, Ungerer creatively entered the videosphere, and embraced this ideal just as a new era of digital tools and technologies made access to the media more feasible than ever before.[47]

Walter Ungerer

---

[47] Interesting to note, too, that veteren Charlotte, VT filmmaker John Douglas made a similar primary shift in his own creative life during this same period; for more on Douglas's work, see the article on John Douglas and *Da Speech* elsewhere in this issue. SRB.

While working and teaching as a visiting artist at Syracuse University, Ungerer created a six-screen video installation entitled *The Syracuse Tapes* (1991) and the more expansive installation shot with advanced production students at the University of Vermont, *6X6* (1993). During this period, he taught himself the necessary skills to create, animate, and manipulate imagery via computer graphics. This necessary reorientation of Ungerer's efforts eventually opened imaginative new vistas to the artist. The earliest of these new works were elegant, essentially playful animated shorts, including *Birds - 2/93* (1993), *A Warm Day Comes After a Cold Winter* (1994) and a collaborative effort with his daughter featuring a very odd menagerie of creatures shambling across the screen.

Upon this unassuming bedrock, Ungerer built a denser, more meditative series of short films. These comprise the core of an entirely new eddy in Ungerer's pool of work. *Relatives in X, Y, and Z* (1996) is an eerie, evocative, oddly moving tableau of imagery melding old family photographs and live-action to potent effect; in its own way, the film echoes and extrapolates upon the faded old photos glimpsed on the walls of the possibly haunted house of *The Animal* 20 years earlier. *Kingsbury Beach* (1999) carries the allure of mediated, manipulated photographic imagery further, while the most recent of Ungerer's short works breaks fresh ground. Ultimately screened in three variations, *Untitled*, *Untitled 2* and *Untitled 2.1* (all 2001), the video defies description altogether: it is, in its way, a primal mediation on the act of seeing itself. Again, its imagery reflects Ungerer's earlier work: a passage composed of streaking car headlights shimmering in the night recalls the mesmerizing opening of *The Winter There Was Very Little Snow*, as headlights from a distant icy road illuminate the brittle frost patterns laced upon a window pane.

The characteristically introspective nature of these short digital works were disrupted by the nationally/internationally traumatic events of September 11, 2001. Indeed, it was as if Ungerer had been shaken out of a trance: due to his own accidental proximity to the World Trade Center the day before its collapse, 9/11 had a devastating personalized impact on Ungerer's life.

In short order, Ungerer began to chronicle the wake of 9/11, working with musician and teacher Lesley Becker, who had studied film in Ungerer's Goddard College class thirty years before. Ungerer and Becker had driven home from New York City mere hours before the planes crashed into the Twin Towers on September 11. "We got back home at 3 or 4 AM," Ungerer told Susan Green in June of 2002, "I had a class at Goddard that same morning at 9. That's when I discovered what was taking place." [48] Ungerer and Becker returned to the World Trade Center site on September 23 to film the physical devastation and the transformed cityscape from the streets. In the weeks and months following, Ungerer and Becker traced the shock waves through their community—Mont-

---

[48] Quoted from Susan Green, "Flick Chick," *Seven Days*, June 5, 2002, pg. 38a.

pelier and nearby towns—interviewing as many willing citizens as possible.

There are a few familiar faces among those that made the cut: Anthony Pollina,[49] American Friends Service Committee Field Secretary Joseph Gainza, Eleanor Ott of the Women's International League for Peace and Freedom, etc. Equally expressive and eloquent are the interview subjects who live and work outside public and political arenas. Their faces and names may not be familiar, but all are recognizable as neighbors and Vermonters: these are the people many of us live among, exceptional only in that they chose to air their opinions on camera.

By the spring of 2002, Ungerer and Becker were ready to tour with their current edit of *Ground Zero: Perspectives from Vermont*, presenting the feature to audiences and inviting discussions afterward throughout that summer and fall. Community reactions, before and after the showings, proved at times volatile: *Ground Zero* was a tangible ripple in the increasingly divisive 9/11 shockwave moving through the state. The roadshow and audience reactions further shaped Ungerer's perspective on the film, which he considered very much a work-in-progress. Becker did not share this view. By 2003, the collaborative effort phased into a negotiated legal separation, leaving Ungerer free to complete work on his expansive revision of the material.

The full story behind the making—and unmaking—of *Ground Zero*, and the eventual completion of Ungerer's own revised, expanded edit *And All This Madness* will be covered in a future issue (via an exhaustive, definitive interview with Walter covering his entire career, conducted between August 2001 and June 2003). Just as *Keeping Things Whole* represented a dramatic departure from Ungerer's enigmatic, experimental *Oobieland* quintet to address broad cultural, political, and personal issues relevent to the Vietnam War era, *And All This Madness* is a major shift from the meditative video shorts Ungerer created during the prior decade. It also marks Ungerer's return to the feature-film format, which continues as he labors over *Down the Road*, a new autobiographical work.

Suffice here to say that in the wake of a personal ground zero, Walter emerged from the emotional and legal rubble with *And All This Madness*, a timely, concise, intensive analysis of the context of 9/11 events and subsequent War on Terror declared by the Bush Administration, and a testimonial to the immediate wake of 9/11 as it was experienced and expressed by many Vermonters, including, via the film itself, by Ungerer. Interweaving historical and cultural contexts for these on-camera reactions and conversations, Ungerer successfully transcended the regional focus of the interviews themselves to connect its participants to the world at large, bridging the reactions of his immediate geographic neighbors with the global impact of the event. By doing so, Ungerer in-

---

[49] Director of the Vermont Democracy Fund, at the time of filming the Progressive candidate for Lieutenant-Governor.

deed captured the immediate regional impact of 9/11 with sometimes startling intimacy, clarity, and gravity. *And All This Madness* is a more aggressive and carefully-mounted polemic than *Ground Zero*, juxtaposing the onscreen testimonials of Vermonters with a comprehensive chronology and canvas of the 9/11 event itself and its echoes.

The film opens with a condensation of news reports, from the first hijacked passenger jet's collision with the north tower of the World Trade Center at 8:45 AM to the second airliner's plunge into the south tower, the third plane's crash into the Pentagon, the collapse of the Trade Center's south tower, the crash in Pennsylvania of the fourth hijacked plane, and finally the collapse of the Trade Center's north tower at 10:28 AM. This segues into Ungerer's own September 23rd footage at the demolished WTC site; thus, the rest of the film moves out from Ungerer's own experience of 9/11, to the first testimonials from Vermonters. Prominent among these is the first from John Sinzer, an options trader at the American Stock Exchange who lives in Marshfield, VT, who describes a final phone call from a colleague's son ringing from under a desk on the Trade Center's 90th floor. Ungerer establishes the touchstone testimonial interviews he will return to throughout the film: Eleanor Ott, Joseph Gainza, PBS Frontline producer Martin Smith, Paij Wadley-Bailey (of Montpelier, VT), Denise Youngblood (Professor of History, UVM), and Darini Nicholas (of Berlin, VT, faculty member at the Institute of Social Ecology), who candidly admits, "I wasn't surprised by it," noting she was visiting Sri Lanka at at the time. As we shall see, Gainza, Ott, and Nicholas prove to be the most lucid and outspoken voices.

162

Among the significant revisions made to the film's earlier incarnation is material providing a historical context for 9/11, specifically the post-World War I carving up of the Middle East via secret treaties between the victorious Allies dividing the spoils. Relevant archival film and television footage graces excerpts from "Islam, the Middle East, and the West," a lecture delivered by Frank Nicosia (Professor of History at St. Michael's College in Colchester, VT), concluding with scrolled text of the November 1917 Balfour Declaration, Britain's promise to Israel of a national homeland in Palestine. Ungerer interjects the timely Bertrand Russell quote that contextualizes the film's title: "And all this madness, all this rage, all this flaming death of our civilization and our hopes, has been brought about because a set of official gentlemen, living luxurious lives, mostly stupid, and all without imagination or heart, have chosen that it should occur rather than that any one of them should suffer some infinitesimal rebuff of his country's pride." Ungerer returns to Nicosia's lecture: the Balfour Declaration left nothing for the Arabs. Nicosia details how US support for the State of Israel foments ongoing conflict with Islamic culture, and how the humiliating 1967 defeat of the Arabs at the hands of the Israelis in the Six-Day War marked the crucial turning point: "It's here where Islamic fundamentalism begins to take hold."

Given this context, Ungerer returns to the interviews: Gerard Renfro and Chris Stellar seated at a picnic table, discussing the patriotic flaunting of the American flag as an immediate response to 9/11. Gainza and Pollina elaborate on this widespread nationalistic reaction before Darini Nicholas's statement that the World Trade Center was a correct target as a symbol of Western capitalist power is punctuated by footage of a woman and her family breaking down in tears at Ground Zero. Thus, Ungerer reinforces the reality of grevious personal loss in the debris of a Western power symbol: this is how ideology ravages individual lives. It is a point Gainza returns to later in the film, saying, "Those planes went into two symbols of American power in the world: corporate capitalism and the military. Those planes are as much a symbolic act—as horrible as they were—as anything else, and we need to wake up to that reality."

Gainza provides the segue into discussion of the corporate domination of American media, citing how that consolidation of power is narrowing, not broadening, debate and discussion of 9/11 ("an absolutely impoverished discourse"), and the "media warmongering" that followed. Further insights emerge through excerpts from a Champlain College Diversity Forum, "Hunting Bin Laden," in which Dr. Mohammed Turki, Martin Smith, Abbas Alnasrawi (UVM Professor of Economics), Francis Gregory Gause (UVM Professor of Political Science), and others further articulate these issues. This material essentially stood on its own merits in the film's earlier edit; here, Ungerer provides further context and emphasis of key points via intertitles, including web links to the Media Reform Information Center and The Center for Democratic Communications of the National Lawyers Guild, [50] a graphic emphasizing the consolidation of media giants—from fifty in 1993 to only six by 2000—and clips of actual media and news coverage leading to the war in Afghanistan. With the surgical integration of such imagery and excerpts, Ungerer reinforces the powerful arguments the testimonials present.

The disconnect between the American public's perception of events leading up to and following 9/11 and the world's perception of America is given intense scrutiny; ignorance of our government's destruction foreign policies, rabid consumerism, empire-building, and national culpability emerge as a key points, articulated by average Vermonters along with the more expert voices. Bennett Shapiro says, "I really think we need to look at our own behavior;" Chris Steller, sitting at the picnic table with Renfro, puts it bluntly, "to me, September 11th was about a group of individuals... saying to a bully, 'you might be big and powerful, but we can get you.' " Most affecting are the comments of VT Air National Guard soldier and F16 Aircraft Mechanic Dana LaBounty, who served in Saudi Arabia and stands alongside his wife Diane in a field in Moretown. "American as a country is overly ambitious," Dana asserts, "all we're geared toward is success and excess... we need to learn modesty."

*And All This Madness* builds a powerful, multi-layered series of arguments concerning aggressive U.S. policies that precipitated the 9/11 attacks, and have only further antagonized the world since. A broad spectrum of policies, including political assassination of elected foreign leaders, overt military intervention, and genocide, unknown to or ignored by most US citizens is evoked, and not only by activists like Gainza and Nicholas. Standing in that Moretown field, Dana LaBounty reminds us of how blissfully unaware most Americans are of our own government's domestic policies; "life is convenient," he shrugs, summarizing the narcotic cocoon we live within until a cataclysmic event like 9/11 forces some awakening. Footage of Norwich University's October 23, 2001 forum on "Counter terrorism: Military and Intelligence Aspects" excerpts talks given by Norwich Professor of Linguistics and Anthropology George Shelley and Former Chief of CIA Counter terrorism Staff Haviland Smith on destructive US policies abroad. As Gainza touches upon US military plans for "Full Spectrum Dominance," in which our government finds it "necessary to the United States to dominate space militarily in order to provide stability," the scope of Ungerer's film becomes truly devastating. Where can this lead but disasters like 9/11? The cumulative impact is impossible to shake, and the conclusions are sobering: "Every empire has overstretched itself and has come to fall apart as other nations group themselves against it," Gainza explains; Ungerer caps this with a closeup of Paij Wadley-Bailey's interview comment, "all empires fall, don't they. Do they not?"

En route, without losing the film's relentless cumulative focus, Ungerer

---

[50] http://www.corporations.org/media/ and http://www.nigcdc.org.

manages to address a multitude of other post-9/11 issues: the media smokescreen ("It evades the reality that there's actual war going on"), the repression of free speech and constriction of civil liberties, racism and xenophobia, the patriarchal overtly-male rhetoric of power, the power-brokers backlash against female perspectives, and spiritual consequences of "all this madness" via Eleanor Ott's discussion of soul loss, speaking from the haven of her Maple Corner, VT abode. Still, we are attuned throughout to Vermont's community-level alternatives to the crushing forces at work: Ungerer reminds us via glimpses of, for instance, the Montpelier Farmer's Market, a poster proclaiming "Vermont Says NO to War," and the constant presence of the Vermont faces and voices that constitute the film itself.

In the end, Ungerer returns us to Ground Zero, the smoking rubble of the World Trade Center itself only two weeks after 9/11. In the end, the perverse point is made that it has taken 9/11 to force us to finally join the world community. "It is estimated during the last century over 188 million people were killed in wars, genocide, and oppressions," an intertitle explains amid a montage of frightening historic images of Dresden, Hiroshima, Nagasaki, explosions, wars, fires, and expanses of the dead. "As a culture, we haven't had a war on our shores since the Civil War," Joseph Gainza concludes, "we haven't learned as a culture how to hold the tension and the fear that so many other people have had to learn."

Clearly, we have much to learn: ever the trickster—this is, after all, the creator of *Oobieland* behind the camera—Ungerer concludes the film on a sardonic note. The camera tips up from the rubble of Ground Zero to the sky amid audio and interview bytes concerning the peace movement, and the final credits unreel. On the soundtrack, a National Public Radio clip from November 20, 2002 cites a post-9/11 National Geographic Roper study of 18-to-20 year old Americans' geographic ignorance—83% of those polled were unable to locate Afghanistan on a map.

That *And All This Madness* remains so neglected and rarely-screened through the annual din of broadcast 9/11 threnodies is tragic in and of itself. Amid all this madness, the faces and voices of all those Ungerer and Becker interviewed still ring loud and clear—once they are seen and heard. *And All This Madness* remains a vital, even primary, document of its time, place, and people, and as such is absolutely essential viewing.

---

*Ground Zero: Perspectives from Vermont* (2002) Produced and directed by Walter Ungerer, Lesley Becker.
*And All This Madness* (2003) Produced and directed by Walter Ungerer.

Sue Ball in *My Mother's Early Lovers*

# Nora Jacobson's *My Mother's Early Lovers*
by Stephen R. Bissette
photos courtesy of Nora Jacobson

*With Nora Jacobson's* Nothing Like Dreaming *opening throughout Vermont this fall and winter, now is the time to re-assess Nora's first narrative masterwork,* My Mother's Early Lovers...

Nora Jacobson and her mother, Geraldine Jacobson (Mrs. Fricket) on the set of *My Mother's Early Lovers.*

With one documentary feature under her belt, Nora Jacobson produced, directed, edited, and co-scripted the remarkable *My Mother's Early Lovers* (1999), an introspective drama that established a new high-water mark for regional filmmaking when it surfaced on the festival and regional circuit five years ago.

Nora's potent feature eschewed nostalgia and romanticism to weave its tangled, troubled generational web with moving clarity and sometimes startling emotional impact. Though its premise—a daughter's revelatory discovery of her mother's secret diary and letters, and the impact these have upon the family—echoes that of Robert James Waller's maudlin 1990s best-seller *The Bridges of Madison County*, *My Mother's Early Lovers* is drawn from Townsend, Vermont native Sybil Smith's unpublished autobiographical memoir, originally entitled *A Strange Kind of Music*, inspired by actual events—including the discovery of her mother's diaries—which anchor Nora's film adaptation.

Upon reading, Nora was immediately drawn to Sybil's manuscript. "It really struck me," Nora recalls; she was initially drawn to Sybil's parents' participation in a 1930s socialist commune near Jamaica, Vermont that remains central to the film. "That kind of utopianism interested me," she explains; "My own father had moved to Vermont in 1936 from New York City to be a farmer, and so I related to that kind of history." The emotional meat of the story—the wellspring of the family, the responsibilities of parenting, and its generational toll—only intensified Nora's attraction to Sybil's memoir, and they began to work together on the screenplay. In the process, Nora and Sybil thoroughly restructured the story, changing what were three distinct and separate passages in the book into carefully interwoven narrative threads. "When you're trying to adapt something—a novel—into screenplay, there's so much condensation that has to go on," Nora explains, "so we found ourselves having to bring together elements that were scattered throughout the whole book."

Sue Ball and Rusty DeWees

After three years of ongoing work, the script was ready, and with the help of Norwich natives Bill and Jane Stetson (credited as executive producers) Nora raised $200,000 in seed money to launch filming in June, 1996. Working with a tight six-week shooting schedule (the film was shot and edited on Super-16mm, later blown up to 35mm), the timely arrival of non-profit grants, and a full year of editing, Nora completed her first dramatic feature on a modest $250-300,000 budget—a remarkable achievement in this day and age. Belying its modest means, *My Mother's Early Lovers* boasted a rich luster, narrative density, and unexpected emotional intensity.

George Woodard and Sue Ball

The film's central character is Maple (played by Sue Ball), whose discovery of her mother's diary and letters sets *My Mother's Early Lovers* in motion. Maple is a psychiatric nurse and a poet (as is co-author Sybil Smith), and it's her voice that serves as our guide into this treacherous family turf, vicariously talking "to" her mother Louise (Molly Hickok) and, via sepia-toned flashbacks, opening the film's window to the past. Thus, the film develops two parallel narrative threads: the contemporary here-and-now in which Maple and her siblings deal with the changes initiated by their father's sale of their home, and the historical chronology of their mother Louise's adult years culminating in her marriage to Wendell (played as an elder by Gilman Rood, and in the flashbacks by Gilman's real-life son Dudley Rood).

Wendell is the family's aging widower patriarch, whose need for assistance leads Maple to find Louise's papers. This discovery, and the revelations hidden therein, eventually sends shock waves through the lives of Maple's sisters Anne (Kathryn Blume) and Delsey (Kim Meredith) and their wayward brother Calvin (George Woodard). Obsessed by the diary and letters, Maple initially keeps her mother's secrets while doing her level best to help Calvin weather eternally-stormy relations with his estranged partner Sandra (Darri Johnson), their son Adam (Jacob Crumbine), and Wendell. But the diary's revelations of Wendell's strange and violent "courtship" of their mother cuts to the heart of the family's rifts, and Maple is unable to keep its secrets for long. The inevitable emotional eruptions and confrontations drive *My Mother's Early Lovers* to its poignant final act, in which Maple comes to terms with the ghosts that haunt her.

Nora Jacobson's deft shaping of this volatile material into a cohesive and profoundly touching whole cannot be fully appreciated in a single viewing, though I hasten to add the film works beautifully first time around. Her orchestration of so many excellent collaborative artists—from the fine ensemble playing and Roger Grange's cinematography to the earthly, uncanny resonance between David Ferm and Jeremiah McLane's lovely musical score and George Woodard's onscreen guitar pieces—without compromising her own vision demonstrates considerable artistry. The multi-layered tapestry of the film builds with deceptive simplicity to its final act, when things seen, heard, and those barely seen or heard—and all that remains unspoken—assume a devastating cumulative power.

Rusty DeWees and Molly Hickok

"I don't know if it's a weakness or a strength," Nora says, "but I do tend to layer things a lot; I'm interested in complexity, and I'm not sure movies are the best medium for an artist who is interested in complexity."

Ah, but Nora's grasp of cinema is sure, and her eye and ear is true. The seductive interplay between Maple's vision of her mother's past and the family's present almost convinces the viewer of its objective "truth" until one reflects upon its details, and how Maple's subjectivity literally colors what are, after all, her—not Louise's—reveries. The fact that some actors play dual roles is key to Nora's vision of the story, rather than being a budgetary constraint. For instance, the "strange and beautiful soldier" Louise makes out with on the bus in the opening "memory" is played by Rusty DeWees, who co-stars as Calvin's friend and co-worker Tom, a Gulf War veteran ("I get back here and it's a video game") whom Maple is drawn to later in the story; in retrospect, Maple's "casting" Tom as her mother's passionate bus companion foreshadows and anticipates the relationship Maple kindles with Tom. Similarly, Louise's passive suitor Andy is played by Michael Keene, who also appears as Maple's partner Nate; Louise's rejection of Andy in the past anticipates the direction Nate and Maple's relationship takes in the future. This dreamlike attention to Maple's association of her own life with that of her mother achieves an almost sublime Bunuelian power when a prisoner (Carlos Spaulding) who makes obscene facial expressions at Maple when she visits Calvin in jail appears as a lecherous garden visitor in Louise's "memories," or Calvin himself pops up as a guitar-picking farmer in the same garden.

This delicate interplay of reality and dream culminates in Maple's ultimate confrontation—and interplay—with her ghosts in a stirring moment that recalls the touching coda of Robert Benton's fine *Places in the Heart* (1984). More to the point, the moment is in tune with the "magic reality" of writers like Borges and Gabriel Garcia Marquez (*One Hundred Years of Solitude*), suggesting a direction implicit in Nora's commitment to an as-yet uncompleted film project with the working title *Sol Y Luna*, which conjures its own spell in its tale of a Mexican theatrical troupe performing a play drawn from their cultural myths chronicling the birth of the sun and the moon. [51]

This distinctive approach to narrative is further refined in Nora's latest feature, *Nothing Like Dreaming* (2004), wherein "magic thinking" is central to how one lead character (the homeless artist Sonny, beautifully played by George Woodard) perceives the world. In *Nothing Like Dreaming*, George's unsettled

---

[51] Working with artists, puppeteers, and performers from the Dragon Dance Theater in northern Vermont, Nora completed a half-hour springboard for this project under the working title of *Sun and Moon Were Children and Lived on the Earth* (2000).

and unsettling character plays a vital shamanistic role—a stark contrast in many ways to the same actor's role in *My Mother's Early Lovers*, charting Calvin's wayward self-destructive spiral. Whereas Sonny struggles with loneliness and mental illness seeking clarity, autonomy, resolution, and self-expression, Calvin drowns his sorrows with alcohol, numbing a deeply-rooted pain he cannot define and threatening what bonds remain with his immediate family, his ex-wife, and his young son—note, too, that now-teenage Jacob Crumbine reappears in *Nothing Like Dreaming* in a pivotal role. Fine as Sue Ball and the rest of the cast were, George's performance as the troubled Calvin remains in many ways the soul of the film, a breakthrough performance from a beloved Waterbury Center native who somehow tends his family dairy farm, plays music, and helms his own theatrical company while appearing in a succession of films.

Gilman Rood in *My Mother's Early Lovers*

*My Mother's Early Lovers* played theatrically throughout Vermont and New England and the independent film circuit in 1999-2000, earning Nora's modest masterwork the kudos of critics and fellow filmmakers like John Sayles. Nora's debut dramatic feature also earned a bevy of indy awards, including a trio of 'Bessies,' the 'Best Independent Film Award' in Mexico's Ajijic International Film Festival, the Audience Award at the Maine International Film Festival, and the Jury Award at New Haven's Film Fest. Nora self-distributed the feature on video in 2000, and it is still available on vhs.

Her prior feature, the documentary *Delivered Vacant* (1993), debuted at the 1992 New York Film Festival and was selected for competition in the 1993 Sundance Film Festival, going on to win critical praise and the coveted Golden Gate Award at the San Francisco Film Festival. *Delivered Vacant* detailed the devastating impact a spate of profit-driven urban renewal projects had upon a number of Hoboken, New Jersey communities (where Nora lived through the 1980s), chronicling the behind-the-scenes business, political, and personal upheavals involved. Nora spent a full eight years (!) on the project, and her intensive dissection of the process—including the efforts tenant activist groups to protect their homes and neighborhoods—is surprisingly engaging and moving. *Delivered Vacant* is also available on vhs, and is highly recommended.

*My Mother's Early Lovers* remains an unrecognized jewel, one of the key independent films of the 1990s. A revival of the film (and long-overdue publication of Sybil Smith's moving source novel) would be timely in the wake of the release of Nora's newest feature, and might at last bring *My Mother's Early Lovers* to a wider and more receptive audience.

---

*My Mother's Early Lovers* (1999) Off the Grid Productions. Produced, written, and directed by Nora Jacobson, based on the novel "A Strange Kind of Music" by Sybil Smith. Executive Producers: E.W. Stetson, Jane Watson Stetson. Starring Sue Ball, George Woodard, Rusty DeWees, Molly Hickok, and Gilman Rood.
*Delivered Vacant* (1993) Produced and directed by Nora Jacobson.

On the set of Jay Craven's *Windy Acres*:
Jay directing Felicia Hammer, who plays the character Annika Burns.
(*photo: Kingdom County Productions*)

# In Production/Recently Completed
by Stephen R. Bissette

*Plagues and Prophets, DJs and Activists, Princes and Prisoners, Troubled Teens and Tightrope-Walkers, Hitchhikers and Baby Bears: Here's some of what's happening in and about the state:*

* *7 To 10 Days*: Geoff Eads and Carrie Sterr's harrowing chronicle of a young couple whose summer camping trip proves disastrous when they are exposed to an unknown contagion or toxin completed filming early in 2003, and in its final edit and post-production stages as the New Year turned. Though the premise invites thriller expectations, it isn't a genre piece—this intimate, understated drama is based upon a real-life encounter which, happily, did not spin as tragically out-of-control as the reel-life extrapolation. The story was conceived in August of 2002, scripted by Eads and Sterr, both of whom have worked on numerous features in various capacities, including *The Year That Trembled*, *Senses of Place* and *The Undeserved*. Sterr was also one of the creators of the moving documentary *Losing Sleep* (1999). Scripting and pre-production continued from November of that year through April of 2003, and the shoot was completed in June 2003. Post-production was completed in mid-November 2003, and in mid-December Geoff reported, "now we are in sound and color correction and preparing the web site... the 'decorating the cake' part." One of Vermont's few naturopathic physicians, Jody Noe, plays herself in the film; Noe had practiced in Brattleboro for seven years, and left the area in January to relocate to Tulsa, OK, where she has joined the staff of the Cancer Treatment Centers of America, "overseeing the centers' resident program and opening "a naturopathic medicine clinic for hospital staff," according to an article by Joseph G. Cote. [52]

* *American Wake*: Talented 23-year old Brattleboro musician Sam Amidon makes his film acting debut in a lead role in Cambridge, MA filmmaker Maureen Foley's feature *American Wake*, a Hazelwoods Films/small angst films production which debuted on July 28th at Loews Boston Common Theatre as part of the Democratic National Convention. Foley co-scripted with Billy Smith, a NYC stage actor and writer who also served in the Gulf War, in the UN peacekeeping forces in East Timor, as an English teacher in Thailand, and in the Boston Police Department; Smith co-stars as a firefighter named Jack whose life is changed when his best friend dies in a blaze. Jack's story is paralleled with

---

[52] Quoted in *The Brattleboro Reformer* (January 15, 2004, pg. 9).

that of Niall (Sam Amidon, *left*), an Irish fiddler torn between his relationships with his party-hearty artist girlfriend (Anastasia Barnes) and his father (Brian Delate), who wishes Niall will return with him to their homeland. Foley cast Amidon after seeing him perform in Massachusetts with Assembly, a Celtic-influenced band Amidon formed with his younger brother Stefan and bandmates Keith Murphy and Thomas Bartlett, who also appear in the film—along with their music, complementing the original score by Seamus Egan. Sam and Stefan Amidon grew up playing music with their family—their parents are very well-known and beloved throughout the Northeast—and with their Assembly bandmates, they have deservedly earned strong reputations for their inventive fusions of folk, jazz, Celtic, and other forms. The band was formed in 1994 under the moniker Popcorn Behavior by Sam (fiddle), Stefan (percussion), and Thomas (piano), then aged 13, 10, and 12, respectively. They were later joined by guitarist and vocalist Keith Murphy. They have released five albums to date, and just played their 10th anniversary concert on August 31 at The Iron Horse in Northampton, MA. Sam's own CD Solo Fiddle (2001) is still available and highly recommended. The film's title is from Greg Delanty's book of poems, and refers to an Irish tradition, an all-night party celebrating an emigre's last night in Ireland before sailing for America; Delanty's poems punctuate the film, and mark another Vermont connection (born in Cork, Ireland, Delanty now lives in VT and teaches at St. Michael's College). This is the second feature from Foley, whose grandparents hailed from the Aran Islands of Galway Bay; her first was *Home Before Dark* (1997). *American Wake* was filmed in and around Boston: Cambridge, Quincy, Brookline, and on the Charles River and Atlantic Ocean. One to watch for, indeed; for more information, go to:
http://www.americanwakefilm.com

\* ***America's Heart And Soul***: After refusing to distribute Michael Moore's *Fahrenheit 9/11*, Disney Studios courted further unexpected controversy releasing the feel-good *America's Heart and Soul*. Vermont celebrities George Woodard (actor, farmer, musician) and former Ben and Jerry's CEO Ben Cohen appear in this new feature from Disney, offering a little Green Mountain spice to the tapestry of American heroes, homebodies, and eccentrics featured throughout. After over a decade of film work (including roles in caustic dramas like *Ethan Frome* and *The Mudge Boy*). George is particularly pleased with his role in this production, playing—well, himself! In a completely uncharacteristic bit of ballyhoo, George wrote, "They filmed me and my son Henry here on the farm a while ago and put it in this film along with the stories of other people from all over the US of A. I saw a preview of the film a few weeks ago and it is really something... I'm awful proud to have been a part of it, so much so that I'm actually stickin' my neck out and letting you all know about it... It's not one of those high profile films with big stars and a lot of hype... it is just a great film about America and I hope you can find some time to go see it when it comes out." (quoted from a June 17th email). Director Louis Schwartzberg's patriotic ode to one-of-a-kind American citizens opened from Buena Vista (Disney) on July 2nd to dismal grosses ($300,000+ to date) and decidedly mixed reviews. While some critics championed the film's intent, content, and tenor during a turbulent post-9/11 election season summer, others damned it. Here's a fair sampler: Family First's website touts it as "...a celebration of people, a journey that travels through each region of the country offering touching vignettes and heart pounding cinematography... This is first class entertainment that will inspire you and make you proud to be part of this great country." [53] Roger Ebert wrote that the film "may be the first feature-length documentary filmed entirely in the style of a television commercial... Even though the method of the filmmaker, Louis Schwartzberg, is slick, superficial and relentlessly upbeat, the people he finds are genuine treasures. I wanted to see a whole film about most of them, which means this film is a series of frustrations.... I give four stars to the subjects of this movie, and two stars to the way they have been boiled down into cute pictures and sound bites." [54] AlterNet Movie Mix critic Max Blumenthal blasted it as "...a right-wing anti-government commercial insidiously cloaked in a *Morning in America* aesthetic that is calculated to deceive..." [55] reading ominous overtones even in George's wise-cracks. George came across as to Blumenthal as "a quirky Vermont dairy farmer who milks cows day and night with his son by his side. In a non-sequitur remark, Woodard says that the best thing about working with your son is that 'you don't need any daycare'..." Blumenthal also bristles at its caricature of Ben Cohen, sans any apparent political convictions, as "a zany businessman out to whip up a good batch of ice cream and make a whole lot of money." Blumenthal adds, "never mind that he's chairman of the Progressive Business Alliance, a liberal lobbying group working to oust

---

[53] http://www.familyfirst.com/archives/006407.html—but be careful, their site popped all kinds of stuff into my computer!
[54] http://www.suntimes.com/output/ebert1/wkp-news-america02f.html.
[55] http://www.alternet.org/movies/19184/%20-%2023k%20-%20Aug%2015,%202004.

Bush"—and True Majority. [56] Judging from all I've read or heard, I reckon your own response will depend on whether you see the film as a welcome tonic or unwelcome corporate narcotic. Your move—I look forward to seeing it if only to spend some screentime with George and Henry, who are two of the finest folks I've ever had the pleasure to know on God's green Earth.

* ***Birth Of Innocence***: Two Marlboro filmmakers, documentarian (*Blanche, A Love of the Land, Bridge of Fire, Home to Tibet*, etc.) Alan Dater and vet Andy Reichsman (*Signs of Life*, etc.), have been hard at work on this feature film for almost two years now, and shooting continues all over the Green Mountain State. Producer Mac Parker (famed Northern Vermont storyteller) prefers to keep this under wraps, for now; hope to offer more info in the future. For more on Alan Dater and Lisa Merton's own Marlboro Productions projects, see *Sanctuary*, below.

* ***Coincidence Turbulence***: This new documentary short by Tom Brennan of Westminster West, VT and Oakland, CA recently screened at the Third Annual Oakland International Film Festival (September 15-19, 2004), selected from over three hundred entries. The film, and Brennan's production company Orthopedic Dance Media, grew from a 1995 vehicular accident the filmmaker survived which resulted in the below-the-knee amputation of his right leg. See "Westminster filmmaker chosen for Oakland fest," The Brattleboro Reformer, September 9, 2004, pg. 23; for more info and to view Coincidental Turbulence, go to: http://www.twwusa.net.

* ***Dangerous Living***: Since late fall of 2003, celebrated Guilford, VT documentary filmmaker John Scagliotti (*Before Stonewall, After Stonewall, Oliver Button is a Star* and the PBS series *In the Life*) has been busily touring major US cities, festivals, and the world with his latest feature *Dangerous Living: Coming Out in the Developing World* (2003). Via unflinching testimonials and survivors' accounts of brutal imprisonment and torture inflicted on those who dare to stray outside the strict parameters of heterosexuality in global southern nations, Scagliotti—aided by producers Janet Baus and Dan Hunt, editor and fellow Guilford-based filmmaker Michael Hanish—composes a heartbreaking and inspiring portrait of intolerance, persecution, and an ever-growing international movement to free gays, lesbians, bisexuals, and transgenders from the torments of repressive government and fundamentalist religious regimes. Among those who share their frightening personal accounts of prosecution and escape is Egyptian Ashraf Zanati, one of fifty-two men arrested in May of 2001 to be jailed for thirteen months and tortured simply for gathering at a disco in Cairo; Ashraf has since fled to Vancouver, Canada, but his is one of the more inspiring tales. Many are

---

[56] See *Haven't Seen Da Speech...?* pgs. 101-108 in this issue.

executed for such "crimes of debauchery." Janeane Garafalo narrates, and has been shown locally a number of times—I caught it at the School of International Training in Brattleboro. If we can corral globe-trotting John long enough for an interview, we'll be dedicating an issue to the film and John's remarkable body of work. Go to http://www.afterstonewall.com for more information, and if *Dangerous Living* pops up in a festival or screening venue near you, seize the opportunity! First Look Features released a DVD edition of *Before Stonewall* (executive produced by Scagliotti; directed by Greta Schiller and Robert Rosenberg) this May; well worth picking up, especially for its remarkable bonus footage of Allen Ginsberg.

*Dangerous Living*

* **Devotion**: Dan Seitz's third feature film completed its final stages of post-production as of this writing; an early cut of the feature opened the Vermont International Film Festival in October, 2003. Building upon writer/director Seitz's experience making the time-travel fantasy-drama *Shift* (1999) and the horror film *Lost Lives* (2000), *Devotion* offers a fresh spin on the stalker archetype, and was filmed in and around Burlington and the UVM campus. Dan told me that he enjoyed working with a strong cast—which includes Nathaniel Wayne, Alex Bone, Nicole Staudinger, and Kristy Wagner, whose key role required extensive rewrites during the shoot—and that he "finally locked print" at the end of February. "*Devotion* is being considered for the Fall Mountain Film Festival, the Ottawa Student Film Festival, and the Digital Independent Film Festival," Dan added. "The producer plans to submit it to at least six other festivals in the coming months." Dan graduated from the University of Vermont this June, and will be back behind the camera soon. I'm eager to see what he cooks up next...

* ***Disappearances***: The elusive, long-awaited feature-film adaptation of Howard Frank Mosher's debut 1977 novel by Barnet-based Kingdom County Productions' Jay Craven recently suffered another delay, as the planned fall 2004 shoot fell through when star Kris Kristofferson had to postpone due to another feature-film commitment (in the DreamWorks production *Dreamers*, with Kurt Russell, Kelly Preston, and Luiz Guzman—who, BTW, lives in Vermont). Jay tells me filming is now scheduled for the spring of 2005. *Disappearances* was the first of celebrated Vermont author Mosher's novels to see print (from Viking Press); set in 1932 prior to the end of Prohibition, the novel vividly follows the adventures of a desperate whiskey-smuggling Northeast Kingdom family as they brave the wintery Kingdom cedar swamps, Quebec wilderness, and border patrols for a sorely-needed score, plagued by the relentless hijacker Carcajou. It was *Disappearances* that initially prompted Craven to adapt Mosher's novels to film, beginning with Craven's adaptation of Mosher's short story *High Water* (1991), continuing with feature-length adaptations of Mosher's *Where the Rivers Flow North* (1993) and *Stranger in the Kingdom* (1998). Sad to hear of this fresh setback, though Jay says the extra time will only help with the necessary pre-production on this sprawling tale; fortunately, Jay and Kingdom County have the TV mini-series *Windy Acres* in the can (see below), and Jay will be returning to Marlboro College to teach the fall semester.

* ***Down the Road***: Walter Ungerer's latest autobiographical feature—a return to form after the September 11, 2001-inspired documentary *And All This Madness*— continues to evolve. During a visit to Walter's Montpelier, VT studio in early summer of 2003, he shared about a half-hour of the film (then titled *Dukkha*), and what I saw was an engaging and profoundly intimate, moving experience: in part an introspective road movie, in part a probe of family ties, bonds, and boundaries. Walter subsequently mailed me a copy of a later edit, which was excellent, and as of mid-August writes: "At the end of every day of editing, I think I'm closer to finishing it. That's still my impression, but it's still not finished. It has become much more a personal narrative and much less a documentary than when you saw it." I don't want to say more, since what I've seen is very much a work-in-progress, still taking shape; hopefully, we'll all have an opportunity to savor the completed work later this year. Work on the film continues, even as Walter has moved his base of operations and home from Montpelier to Maine. A complete and long-overdue overview by yours truly of Ungerer's innovative work is currently underway, with an exhaustive interview already completed.

* ***Falls***: The latest evocative short film by Michael Fisher (*Noir, Love of My Life, Burgundy*, etc.) was completed in the fall of 2003, and made the rounds this festival season. Inspired by Michael's own experiences with the first training camp session of the now-celebrated Circus Smirkus, *Falls* tells the tale of a

farmer's daughter who becomes obsessed with her dream of joining the circus to be a tightrope walker; despite the hardships her obsession causes, her father is afraid that his interference—or her failure—may drive her to, as Michael puts it, "follow in her mother's footsteps to the falls." Michael describes *Falls* as a film "about the passionate single-mindedness that is necessary to pursue an out of the norm life path, such as a career in the arts. To make that choice, you have to be dedicated to your craft body and soul. If you fail after giving yourself over so fully, what other life choice remains? You may decide that you want that goal that so deeply captured your heart and imagination or nothing at all. I feel the image of a person struggling to walk a tightrope is an apt metaphor for such an obsessive and potentially damaging situation. You are either on the rope, single-minded, utterly focused, or you have fallen...to what?" Starring in *Falls* is Ariel Kiley, who has appeared in numerous shorts, independent films (*Billy528*, 2001; *The Deep and Dreamless Sleep*, 2004), and TV series (including *Law & Order* and—most memorably—on *The Sopranos* 2001 season as the doomed Tracee), including Jay Craven's soon-to-debut *Windy Acres* with her actress mother Grace Kiley (see below). Also starring is George Woodard, vet Vermont actor, farmer, and filmmaker whose work you'll have a nodding acquaintance with if you haven't already by the time you finish this zine (see *Nothing Like Dreaming* and *Whatever Happened to Baby... Bear?*, below); review in our spring issue. Boston-based cinematographer/videographer Tom Robotham shot *Falls* on Super 16; Michael met Tom through local AC Rich Fredette, who also worked on the production. *Falls* screened as a work-in-progress at the October 2003 Vermont International Film Festival; its final edit debuted as part of the January 16 opening night of the Shelburne Film Series, played at the Slamdance Film Festival on January 18 and 19, and was broadcast on Vermont Public Television's *Reel Independents*—accompanied by an interview with Michael—in February.

\* **The Flatlanders**: Writer/director/actor Jeff Miller was seen in downtown Brattleboro on July 5th filming scenes for Los Angeles-based Sherpa Films Inc.'s feature-in-progress *The Flatlanders*—what the hell, I stopped on my way to work to watch. Cinematographer Eric Tremi was behind the camera, shooting a bicycle-fall stunt performed by vet stuntman Ian Quinn. Miller's recent purchase of Jacksonville property and Miller and co-director Kim Gillingham's reported plans to periodically return to the area to continue filming during each season implies a long shoot, working from Miller's script about a same-sex couple who move from New York City to Vermont to raise their child. When a tragic turn of events leaves the surviving father alone to parent their 12-year-old son (played by Philadelphia first-time actor Jarrod Gandy, now 14), the community provides unexpected support. Miller co-stars with Michael Chaban. For more information, see "Lights! Camera! Action! Region will be backdrop for L.A. film company" by Justin Mason, *The Brattleboro Reformer*, July 6, 2004, pp. 1, 6.

*Free RFB*: An FCC agent speaks to Larry Bloch during the June 2003 bust. (*from footage shot by Ian Kiehle*)

* *Free RFB*: Tim Wessel of Vermont Digital Productions (see *Ladies Against Women*, below) in Putney, VT is currently at work on this feature-length documentary portrait of Radio Free Brattleboro aka rfb,[57] an independent community radio station in Brattleboro, VT which has stirred much local controversy of late. In June of 2003, rfb was ordered shut down by the FCC for broadcasting without a license; in the wake of that event, the station rallied local support and fought for the freedom to broadcast and serve the community, despite ongoing FCC opposition and the current climate of increasing corporate control of the airwaves. Given the heated controversy over attempts to further deregulate corporate consolidation and ownership of multiple media outlets, the potent stance and legal plight of rfb is particularly vital. Tim writes, "the documentary follows the all-volunteer DJ/members as they struggle to continue with their five-year-old station, and looks into the implications of restrictive FCC regulations which make legal community broadcasting nearly impossible." At the time of this writing, over a year after the initial government raid, they're still broadcasting and have mustered considerable support from the community and its officials despite ongoing threats from the FCC to silence the station, though their ultimate fate has yet to be decided by the courts ("Rfb Awaits Decision" by Daniel Barlow, *Brattleboro Reformer*, June 9, 2004, pgs. 1, 6) and the station remains a viable and very active presence in the community. Shot and edited by Tim Wessel, with additional footage provided by Ian Kiehle and others; Tim continues to seek funding. He presented an exhibition of the film as a work in progress as part of the Westminster West Festival, and a more recent edit on July 13 at an fundraising event at the Hooker-Dunham Theater in Brattleboro. For more information, or to aid with funding this important project, contact Tim at: Vermont

---

[57] Lower case letters used here per the station's own publicity.

Digital Productions, P.O. Box 326, Putney, VT 05346; call (802)387-2600.

Adam Soto in *Freebox*

* ***Freebox***: Co-winner of the top prize for "best regional film" at the 2003 Northampton (MA) Film Festival, Shandor Garrison's latest (as writer/director/co-producer) will be making the rounds this year at a variety of festival venues, and is well worth seeking out. This 22-minute drama tells the tale of an HIV-positive teenager (played by Adam Soto) and his unusual mentor (Stephen Girouard); Garrison's original screenplay was inspired by his own volunteer work at a residential facility for troubled boys. The cast also includes Theo Stockman, Doug Marsden, Spencer Smith, Nick Santos, and others, and the high-definition film was shot (by NYC-based Melissa Donovan) in February, 2003 in Massachusetts, in and around Truro, Wellfleet, and Falmouth. Shandor heralds from Putney, VT, trained at the Center for Digital Art in Brattleboro, VT and at the Williams College Video Art Department, and was one of the co-founders of Zwack Collaborative, a digital video collective started in southern Vermont with the brothers Jake (*Judgement*, 2001) and Alex (*Painful Grace*, 2001) Stradling, which is now based in Cambridge, MA. Shandor was recently named "Most Promising New England Director" at the 2002 Boston Underground Film Festival. Shandor's first narrative film, *No One's a Mystery* (9 minutes, 2001), was adapted from the short story by Elizabeth Tallent; in a succinct exchange of dialogue between a cheating husband (Doug Smith) and his young teenage lover (Maiana Borsody, now Maiana Vazy, a Smith College theater major also featured in Alex Stradling's *Painful Grace*, 2001), the film

weaves richer, more resonant characterizations than most feature films manage in ten times the running time—for my money, this poignant gem remains one of the best short films I've ever seen. *No One's a Mystery* was screened at numerous festivals, scoring for Best Cinematography at the 2001 Woods Hole Film Festival, and Maiana deservedly won the 2002 New England Film and Video Award for Best Performance. For *Freebox*, Shandor reunited with actress Maiana Vazy and Executive Producer David Lubin (again serving that function on *Freebox*); Lubin previously founded two companies, served on the faculties at Harvard and Tufts University, and holds patents for his original work in multi-media. Fellow *Freebox* Executive producers John McNeil and Mark Donadio have won numerous awards as Boston-based film and video producers for almost twenty years (previous credits include *The Good Son, Gettysburg, Outside Providence, Session 9, Southie*, and others, including David Mamet's *The Spanish Prisoner* and set-in-but-not-shot-in-Vermont *State and Main*). Producer Mike Bowes is co-founder/director of the Cambridge, MA-based non-profit firm Central Productions (http://www.centralproductions.org). Shandor was also aided by the Moving Image Fund, a special initiative of The LEF Foundation's New England office dedicated to supporting New England film and video artists (http://www.lef-foundation.org); the LEF introduced Shandor to producer MacNeil and provided grants for pre-production and production. *Freebox* also boasts editing by Cherry Enoki, production design by Wayne Kimball—who has worked with Roger Corman, James Toback, and Ellie Lee, among others—and an extraordinary musical score by The Alloy Orchestra. The Orchestra made their mark creating soundtracks for classic silent films, including a recent Bellow Falls showing of Buster Keaton's classic *The General*, while scoring contemporary films by directors Errol Morris and Jane Gillooly, and commercial videos for IBM, UPS, the MFA in Boston, the National Park Service, etc. [58] *Freebox* has already played in May at the Independent Film Fest Boston at the Somerville Theater, and the Institute for Contemporary Art; keep your eyes peeled for showings near you.

* **Homeland Security**: Activist artist/photographer/filmmaker/animator John Douglas (see our article on *Da Speech* in this issue) is at it again! Isolationism, vulnerability, cold steel, human flesh, and latent violence seethe in *Homeland Security*—no, it isn't a film or video, it's the latest provocative series of photographs from the veteran Charlotte multi-media creator. Sporting an M16 and nothing else, Douglas appears in this series of images as a literal "one-man army"—duplicated photographically and armed to the teeth in a procession of tableaus that confront the power and impotence of firepower. Sans any associa-

---

[58] see my interview with Alloy Orchestra's Ken Winokur in *Video Watchdog* #75, Sept. 2001, pp. 29-33; visit Alloy's website at: http://www.alloyorchestra.com

tive figures but male replicas of himself, supplanting the male organ in almost every pose with M16s (or flags), *Homeland Security* offers a sardonic dissection of America's current pre-emptive 'go it alone' military foreign policies and a delirious portrait of primal 'citizen soldiers' in native habitats (trailors, tracks, flag-draped coffins, and—most chilling of all—seated stoically around a TV set in the darkness, lit only by its cyclopean light). It's brilliant, funny, unnerving, confrontational, disturbing stuff; you haven't lived 'til you've seen a small platoon of nude, armed, and dangerous Douglas clones poised for action. *Seven Days* offered a generous spread on *Homeland Security* in its June 30-July issue (pp. 24A-26A), and Douglas enjoyed a gallery exhibition of over 35 prints from the series at the University of Vermont's Living & Learning Gallery in October (thanks to Joanne Watson and Chad Harter); the reception was held on Monday, October 4, with Erich Kory and Chuck Eller providing live music. You should visit John's website at http://www.redrat.net/work/photographic/homeland_security/collection.htm to view the gallery in your own home.

*Homeland Security*:
John Douglas, John Douglas, John Douglas, John Douglas

* **IT: A Phish Concert Special** and **Undermind**: Before the Vermont-based band Phish spawned the Green Mountain State's largest population center for one weekend this August, they did the same for Limestone, Maine in 2003. That concert lured 60,000 fans and was dubbed "IT," and thereafter documented (in high-definition video) in *IT: A Phish Concert Special*, which debuted on PBS on August 2 (see this issue's "New to DVD" listing). Along with the 2003 concert footage, *IT* chronicles the band's formation and evolution. Their final thirteen-date summer tour (promoting their tenth studio album Undermind, 2004) was launched on June 17 in New York City, a concert that was simulcast nationwide

in forty-seven theaters. The tour ended with the Coventry, VT August 14-15 blow-out concert celebrating the band's final performance after 21 years together, which will undoubtably yield another feature-length production. Phish bassist Mike Gordon is a filmmaker in his own right; his first full-length feature was the delirious experimental oddity *Outside Out* (2000), followed by the fine music documentary *Rising Low* (2002); according to *Rolling Stone*, the decision to dissolve the band was reached on May 21 in Gordon's Vermont home. [59] Also note that original limited edition of the CD *Undermind* was packaged with a bonus DVD sporting Danny Clinch's short film *Specimens of Beauty* (2004). Proper coverage of Gordon's films and Phish-on-philm in a future issue!

* **Jean Stark**: Writer/director Michael Fisher took a break from editing *Falls* (see above) in the spring of 2003 to shoot *Jean Stark* in mid-May. The titular character (played by 13-year-old Sarah Wolfe of Strafford, VT) lives with her caretaker (Rusty DeWees) in a vast mansion overlooking a small farming community; daughter of a rich and unloved family, Jean struggles to redeem her lineage in the eyes of the village. Ed Tyler of Lyme, NH is also in a key role, and Michael reports, "we did some scenes in Shard Villa, which was exciting for me." Shard Villa is an uncanny historic mansion in Salisbury, VT with an adjoining mausoleum; its construction began in 1872, and it is a strikingly odd three-story, thirty-room structure with an equally odd reputation. [60] In the healthier climate of Waterbury Center, Michael worked on editing *Jean Stark* at George Woodard's farm during the fall; "George picked up a Final Cut Pro editing system, which is pretty hilarious to come across in his old farmhouse." Michael also shot *Mind's Eye*, written and directed by Burlington College student filmmaker Matthew Walters, before the snow fell. "We shot with the new Panasonic 24p DVX100 camera," Michael explains, adding that the film "is an urban story about two brothers, one of them a little 'slow,' who have a rough childhood and get involved in crime... they finally come to terms with their relationship when a robbery goes awry." More on both films in our spring issue, and a full overview of Michael's work to date is planned for a future issue.

* **Ladies Against Women**: More from the Putney-based Vermont Digital Productions: VDP completed this lively 8-minute documentary in December, 2003. Director/editor Tim Wessel calls it "a fun look at a group of ladies who believe we should return to the days of old, when women knew their place." Sophie Bady-Kaye, Ellen Kaye, Bari Shamas, Peggy O'Toole and Betsy Williams are the "Ladies," who marched this past year in the Westminster West parade, "to cheering crowds and appreciative husbands," Tim tells us. Don't get your dan-

---

[59] Will Dana, "Phish Split," *Rolling Stone* #951, June 24, 2004, pg. 37.
[60] See Joe Citro's *Green Mountain Ghosts, Ghouls & Unsolved Mysteries*, 1994, pp.46-49

der up just yet: note the placards the Ladies wielded at the parade ("Ban the Environment: It's too Big and Difficult to Keep Clean," "Preserve Marriage and Pickles")—this is grass-roots gender-centric satire of high order. They declare, "Keep our nation right on track—One step forward and three steps back!" The Ladies Against Women brought their boisterous brand of performance-art-parody to the aisles of the Brattleboro, VT Home Depot this past spring. The film also features Bob Bady, Evan Griffith, Barry Shaw and Isaac Porter.

*Ladies Against Women*

*Landslide*

\* ***Landslide***: Director Neil Kinsella's latest actioner for Rutland-based Edgewood Studios is wrapping up. Alas, mishaps involving a Federal Express package of completed effects material and an X-ray prompted legal action and forced extensive reshoots of the lost material, which should be completed by now. Vincent Spano, Alexandra Paul, Jay Pickett (of *Port Charles* fame), Jaime Gomez, and Luke Eberl star; this is Kinsella's latest project for Edgewood, extending their successful run of made-for-TV disaster thrillers for Porchlight, to be broadcast on the PAX family network. These include last year's *Killer Flood: The Day the Dam Broke*. Kinsella previously directed *Frozen Impact*, and was first assistant director on *Lightning: Fire From the Sky* and *Trapped: Buried Alive*, among other Edgewood productions, and an extensive career dating back to TV series like *Land of the Lost* and *Pee-Wee's Playhouse*. David Giancola (co-producing with long-time partner and Edgewood co-founder Peter Beckwith, who scripted this feature) handled the second unit filming; Jeffrey Seckendorf was director of photography. Pre-production began in October of 2003, with the bulk of the shoot completed in November. In the meantime, work continues on Boston-based director Jeff Rechert's documentary on (and produced by) Edgewood, which is being shot on digital video; Edgewood also partnered with director Shawn Sweeney for post-production on *Most People Our Age Are Already Dead*, which concerns the plight of the elderly in America and their right to die with dignity. Visit Edgewood's website: http://www.edgewoodstudios.com/

\* ***Love's Labor***: Author, poet, and Marlboro College professor of philosophy Neal Weiner brought a fresh approach to his filmmaking endeavors with a September 28th exhibition at the Marlboro College Whittemore Theatre of the current edit (23 minutes) of his new work *Love's Labor*—and filmed the events following the showing. The exchange between audience members and those on stage after the screening—Weiner and a number of the Windham County individuals who appeared in the version shown onscreen—will now become an integral part of *Love's Labor*'s final edit, currently in progress. In the version of the film exhibited, intimate interview footage of eight locals (Rupa Cousins, Jerry Levy, Tom Mansfield, Beverly Miller, Emily Pillinger, Skarrn Ryvnine, John van Ness, Carrie Weikel) was distilled into an evocative dialogue on their personal philosophies of love: spiritual love, love and sexuality, expressions of love reflected in acts of generosity, sacrifice, and selfishness, etc. The intent of the film itself is to "start a real dialogue with the viewer," Weiner explains. The filming of live interaction between Weiner and those appearing in the film (discussing Weiner's assemblage and distillation of their interviews, each of which were originally an hour in duration), and subsequent dialogue between Weiner, the interviewees, and the audience, will actively extend that dialogue, to be incorporated into *Love's Labor*'s definitive version. "The film is not supposed to be passive entertainment," Weiner says, "I don't think real art is ever that." [61] This is Weiner's third film; his interest in exploring the media began as Weiner began posting his photographs alongside his poetry on his website, which cul-

---

[61] Quoted from "Weiner to screen *Love's Labor*—and the audience plays a role," *The Brattleboro Reformer*, September 16, 2004, pg. 23.

minated in his first fusion of text and imagery into digital video. The result was *Genesis* (2002, 45 minutes), "a cosmological poem and film," which wove interpretive visuals around Weiner's titular poem (read and presented as intertitles) on the creation of the universe. The latter debuted at the college, subsequently playing to capacity crowds in Brattleboro's Hooker-Dunham Theater in February and March of 2003, and most recently at this summer's Hollywood Spiritual Film Festival. *Genesis* and Weiner's meditative film *Snow* (2004) will be shown on Vermont Public Television's *Reel Independents* this year.

* ***Naked Hitchhiker***: Animator Eleanor "Bobbie" Lanahan's ambitious, introspective (literally!) animated feature is in production. After four years of work and a screening on Vermont Public Television's *Reel Independents* of a short sequence from the work-in-progress, Bobbie presented an eye-popping 27-minute condensation of *Naked Hitchhiker* in its current form to an enchanted audience at Nora Jacobson's January 3, 2004, gathering of friends in Norwich, Vermont. The fusion of Lanahan's own distinctive cartooning, exquisite environments composed of customized photographs, 19th-Century pulp illustration collages, and various computer-synthesized and/or created graphics was often dazzling, and surprisingly cohesive (primarily thanks to the film's consistent emotional and narrative voice), given the diversity of visual styles at work. The most beguiling sequence depicted the titular hitchhiker's internal thought processes upon being complimented, subjecting the object—both desired and dreaded—to elaborate scrutiny and rigorous tests in an before responding. Edited in collaboration with vet filmmaker/cinematographer/editor/animator John Douglas, who also provided some of the vocal characterizations, *Naked Hitchhiker* is an inventive delight; more on the film, and its creator, soon!

* ***Newsreel***: Newsreel Group vet and archivist Roz Payne taught a workshop dedicated to the Newsreel Group's history, legacy, and body of work at Burlington College this fall, October 8-10. As part of the class, Payne organized a free public showing on October 9th of Newsreel's activist films and films distributed by Newsreel. The weekend workshop and the five-hour evening program unreeled in Burlington College's Community room, and featured and featured *No Game* (1967), *Yippie* (1968), *People's Park* (1969), *Summer '68* (1968), *Amerika* (1969), *Only the Beginning* (1971), *Free Farm* (1970), the Black Panther film *Off the Pig* (1968), *El Pueblo se Levanta* (1971) and others. Roz was joined by Newsreel members Jane Kramer and John Douglas. The October 9 presentation. This October 9 presentation was free and open to the public. For a description of the films and more information, go to http://www.newsreel.us and go to Newsreel Films.

* ***Nothing Like Dreaming***: Nora Jacobson's eagerly-anticipated second narrative feature, following the excellent *My Mother's Early Lovers*, has enjoyed a

number of private screenings of the work-in-progress over the winter, including a recent one for the youthful cast, was featured in the 2003 IFP Film Market in NYC, and has thus far screened as a work-in-progress at the Green Mountain Film Festival, The Women's Film Festival, and the Lake Placid Film Festival. Having seen three versions of the film over the past year, I'm happy to report *Nothing Like Dreaming* is well worth the wait; simply put, it's a masterpiece. Filmed in Montpelier—including key locations in the Capital and State House—Barre, Norwich, and some Enfield, New Hampshire locations from November 2002 through January of 2003, *Nothing Like Dreaming* is a powerful coming-of-age drama in which an enigmatic, disturbed homeless artist (George Woodard, delivering another superb performance; see *Whatever Happened to Baby... Bear?* below) becomes an unlikely lifeline for a teenage girl (Morgan Bicknell, a revelation as an actress) traumatized by the untimely death of her best friend. Their relationship, her path of healing, and the construction of an incredible "fire organ"—a very real outsized sculptural musical instrument, designed and built for the production by Michel Moglia—provide the heart of this exquisite film, which also boasts top-drawer performances and technical credits all the way around, including exceptional photography by Lasse Toft, who has racked up a remarkable number of credits in the past year, including *7 to 10 Days* and *The Undeserved*. First-time screen actress Morgan Bicknell and vet Vermont actor and farmer George Woodard carry the film with their uncanny performances, and Jacobson has once again forged a potent feature which builds to a stirring final act punctuated by the intoxicating unveiling and music of the fire organ, which is key to the emotional climax. *Nothing Like Dreaming* already ranks among the best films of the year for me. Not to be missed.

*Nothing Like Dreaming*: Morgan Bicknell and George Woodard
(*photo: Thomas Ames, Jr.*)

* ***Orwell Rolls In His Grave*** and ***Outfoxed: Rupert Murdoch's War On Journalism***: Congressman Bernard Sanders (Independent, Vermont) appears in two recent independent documentaries scrutinizing corporate control of the media, a topic near and dear to Sanders throughout his career. In tandem with its New York City opening at the Angelika Film Center, Robert Kane Pappas' *Orwell Rolls in His Grave* opened July 26 at Merrill's Roxy Cinema in Burlington with director Pappas and Congressman Sanders fielding audience questions—an extension of the popular town meetings Sanders has hosted all over the state on the subject for over a decade. Pappas' documentary offers a chilling, insightful chronology of American government and corporate media's effective practices of Orwellian information control, doublespeak and domination of the populace, while spotlighting those dedicated to countering this ominous threat to a practicing democracy and true freedom. Sanders also appears in Robert Greenwald's *Outfoxed*, which narrows its focus from corporate control of news media to the Fox Network in particular, and its overt tabloid distortions, GOP affiliations, and flagrant right-wing orientation. In his onscreen interview, Sanders blasts Murdoch's news empire and its brand of yellow journalism. Greenwald also directed *Uncovered: The Whole Truth About the Iraq War* (2003), and *Outfoxed* is an engaging and invaluable successor. *Outfoxed* and *Orwell Rolls in His Grave* are still showing theatrically throughout the election season, and are available for purchase online.[62] *Outfoxed* will also be available through commercial video distribution and retail venues in October. Also note the appearance of Vermont native and Nobel Peace Prize Laureate Jody Williams in Jeremy Earp and Sut Jhally's *Hijacking Catastrophe: 9/11, Fear and the Selling of an American Empire* (2004), concerning the Bush Administration's use of the 9/11 attack to sell radical pre-existing foreign policies.

* ***The Perfect Goodnight Kiss***: Writer/director Bill Simmon (who recently made in appearance, in cartoon-form, in Burlington cartoonist James Kochalka's online sketchbook diary) shot his segment of this semi-autobiographical romantic short throughout November and December 2003, which is actually just part of a three-way filmmaking venture, a portmanteau featurette. As Bill himself describes it, "The film is being made three different times by three different filmmakers. I myself (a straight man) directed the lesbian version of the film; San Francisco-based filmmaker Alex Woolfson (a gay man) directed the straight version; and Burlington filmmaker Alexis Holloway (a straight woman) directed the gay-male version. Same script—three different perspectives." A romantic

---

[62] For *Outfoxed* on vhs or DVD, go to: http://www.outfoxed.org. For *Orwell Rolls in His Grave* on DVD, go to: http://www.buzzflash.com/premiums/04/05/pre04014.html or send a minimum donation of $30 to Support BuzzFlash.com, P.O. Box 618354, Chicago, Illinois 60661-8354; also see: www.orwellrollsinhisgrave.com.

*Rashomon*? Can't wait to see it! Bill writes, "It will be submitted to film festivals throughout 2004 with an eye on the bigger festivals in the fall: Sundance, etc. Executives at Miramax Films and the Independent Feature Project have already expressed interest in seeing the film." Bill's portion of the film was shot in November 2003 in an empty flat in the Woolen Mill in Winooski with two performers, Alex Sevakian and Katrin Redfern, with Mark Sasahara photographing (using a Panasonic DVX100) and the participation of Jeff Haig (Production Manager/AD), Jeff Lawson (Sound Recordist), Matt McDermott (AC/swing), Seth Mobley (Grip), Emily Stoneking (Art Director/Set Dresser), Shayne Lynn (Stills Photographer), Nick Haggerty (Set PA) and Weston Nicoll (Runner/PA). Alexis Holloway directed her segment in an office in Colchester late in November. Bill writes that Alexis shot her portion of the film "in one long continuous take... and despite my initial skepticism, after looking at the results, I have to say it was a complete success." Director Alex Woolfson's sequence was scheduled to be shot in San Francisco, but ended up being shot in Vermont with Woolfson and his two actors, Kari Wishingrad and John Pennington, arriving in Burlington to complete their efforts before Christmas. The musical score is composed by Vermont/NYC musician Neil Cleary (visit Neil's website at: http://www.stratfordprojects.com/neilcleary/). *The Perfect Goodnight Kiss* premiered at Estrogen Fest in Burlington on February 20; check out the interview with Alexis in our spring issue! For more information, visit Bill's *Perfect Goodnight Kiss* website at: http://www.candleboy.com, or go to: http://www.candleboy.com/candleboy%20TPGNK.htm.

*The Perfect Good Night Kiss*

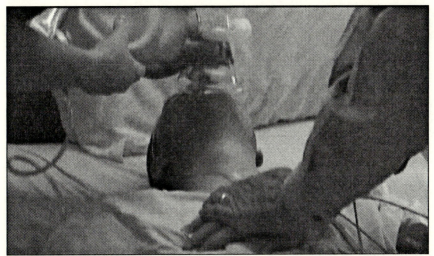

*Prophet*

* ***Prophet***: This is a new film by Jesse Kreitzer of Marlboro, VT, graduate of Brattleboro Union High School and Michel and Linda Moyse's Center for Digital Art program; it won first prize at the 2004 Castleton Videofest and debuted on the big screen at Brattleboro's Kipling Cinemas on Saturday, January 10th. *Prophet* tells the tale of a young man named Daniel (played by Roger Gorton III) who suffers an unexpected collapse which prompts him to question every aspect of his life. Recovering but struggling with the drastic changes in lifestyles his medical condition requires, frustrated with the lack of empathy from those closest to him, including his girlfriend (played by Tessa Deyo), and feeling trapped by his situation, Daniel begins to place an inordinate amount of faith in the prophetic powers of the local newspaper horoscope column. Inevitably gravitating to the writer of the column, Daniel becomes obsessed with the writer, intent on uncovering whatever insights, truths, or secrets the astrological "prophet" may hide. Jesse Kreitzer scripted, directed, filmed, recorded, and completed a rough edit of Prophet on Final Cut Pro during his senior year at BUHS as part of his scheduled CDA digital editing and filmmaking studies. Scenes were filmed in and around Brattleboro, including Brattleboro Memorial Hospital, Bruegger's Bakery, China Buffet, Fitness Barn, the Kipling Cinemas, and the Brattleboro Reformer's printing facilities. Also featured in the film are local talents Burt Tepfer, Katherine Clarke, Crystal Parent, Avi Ovadia, Austin Gorton, Roy Krause, Tyler Saunders, Corey Leary, Tosh Leary, and Dalin Lin. The film earned applause and high praise at the public showing of CDA class video projects in June, 2003. After graduation, Kreitzer continued work on *Prophet* with the blessings and cooperation of the Moyses, completing his final version before the end of 2003. The definitive revised 30-minute version is con-

siderably refined from the earlier version screened in the spring. This is Kreitzer's second narrative film; his first, *Cycle* (2002, also completed at CDA), portrayed a loner (played by Jesse's brother and musician, Zeke Kreitzer, who also has a key role in and scored *Prophet*) drifting through life, in but not of the day-to-day grind, shunning all others who intrude or invite contact. Both *Cycle* and *Prophet* show remarkable maturity of intent and content, orchestrating their respective performances, photography, pacing, and musical scores with imagination and considerable impact. *Prophet* represents a clear evolution in Kreitzer's filmmaking skills. He is currently working on a music video with his brother Zeke to accompany the release of Zeke's upcoming album *Subtex-Vital Nerve*, which features portions of *Prophet*'s original soundtrack. Kreitzer also taught a six-week video production class as part of Marlboro Elementary School's Afternoon Enrichment Program. This yielded two shorts which were exhibited with *Prophet* at the Latchis Theater on Saturday, August 21: *The Reason* (2004), by Jesson Simon (grade 7, with whom Krietzer also worked one-on-one over the summer), and *Remote Control* (2004) by Charlie Greene-Kramer (grade 5), Zoe Reichsman (grade 6), and Jesse Simon. According to Kreitzer, *The Reason* is "the tale of a man struggling to find a balance between his self-contentment and personal obligations," while the playful *Remote Control* "is a light-hearted fable about a magical remote control and the responsibilities that come along with it." Kreitzer just began his freshman year at Emerson College in Boston, where he is working toward a degree in film.

*Redbelly*

\* **Redbelly**: Ever since I first saw a clip from this work-in-progress a little over two years ago, I haven't been able to shake its spell. John DiGeorge and his creative collaborators have just completed the final year of the planned five-year shoot (!) for their stunning modern fairytale, filmed in and around Dummerston, VT. John DiGeorge heralds from Atlanta, GA; drawing and painting since childhood, John studied filmmaking at Harvard University under Hungarian director Miklos Jancso, and spent several years in NYC working in the visual arts before making the big move to Dummerston. Co-writer and lead actor Justin Allen conceived the original story concept in 1999, and remains DiGeorge's key creative partner; I must say, though, as co-scripter, Justin sure has put his character—and thus himself—through some gruelling paces.

The story: An evil king (Michael Nethercott) banishes his young son and daughter to selfishly preserve his reign. She (Erica De Milio) is imprisoned in a remote tower where her mind crumbles and by night she soars in her bed to dream netherworlds; the mute boy is plunged into a swamp with the strange glass vessel—his externalized stomach (!)—where an opportunistic moonshiner (J.R. Whitcomb) enslaves the boy and uses his belly in his distillery. The teenage Prince (played by Justin Allen) finally escapes, only to be devoured by a monstrous bear, within which perpetual winter howls and the boy wanders the freezing wasteland in search of an exit. The cast also includes Debbie Therrien as the Queen and David Rogers as the Hermit. DiGeorge and his collaborators constructed a number of elaborate full-size sets—including a stone tower, the spectacular and atmospheric outdoor moonshine-distillery, and a cannibalistic ogre's charnelhouse shack with breakaway walls to allow filming from any angle—and assembled a marvelous cast. Having completed filming on the film's key sequences, John and associates are hard at work on the last phase of production with a full year of editing and soundwork ahead of them.

"We plan to have a cut of the film to submit to festivals by September 2005," John recently informed me, "which would mean a total of six years in production from conception to finish." A true labor of love... Soren Oberg is producing, Veda Crewe Joseph created the costumes, and John's brother Brian DiGeorge supervised the construction of the amazing sets and myriad props. Everything I've seen to date associated with *Redbelly* has been simply stunning, unlike anything ever produced in New England—or much of anywhere, really. *Redbelly* promises a bizarre fusion of the Brothers Grimm, Jean Cocteau, David Lynch, and Guy Maddin, but I hasten to emphasize John and Justin's vision is utterly unique. I've already said too much.

A full story dedicated to John's uncanny, dreamlike production is in the works; explore the mesmerizing website at: http://www.redbelly.net.

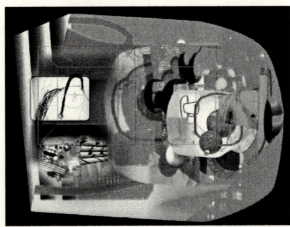

*The Round Schoolhouse: Meditation & Metaphor*

\* ***The Round Schoolhouse: Meditation & Metaphor***: Painter, filmmaker, teacher, and video artist extraordinaire Michel Moyse showcased his stunning video installation *The Round Schoolhouse: Meditation & Metaphor* (2004) at the Brattleboro Museum & Art Center this spring-summer (May 15 through July 5). Moyse's evocative installation opened the museum's summer exhibit "Artists Define Place," curated by Linda Rubenstein (followed by an exhibition of works by woodturner and carver Michelle Holzapfel, July 9-August 29), and was sponsored by the Chittenden Bank. Michel Moyse was born in Geneva, Switzerland, and emigrated to America in 1950. A graduate of Brattleboro Union High School and Marlboro College, Michel earned his Masters Degree in Art Education from New York University before moving into feature film post-production in 1963. He worked as sound editor for directors like Otto Preminger (*Such Good Friends*, 1971), Brian DePalma (*Dressed to Kill*, 1980; *Blow Out*, 1981), George Roy Hill (*The World According to Garp*, 1982), Jonathan Demme (*Something Wild*, 1986), Woody Allen (*Radio Days*, 1987), and others. His television sound editing credits include TV series such as *The Defenders, The Nurses, N.Y.P.D., Coronet Blue*, and television features including *Skokie, Martin Luther King* and *Charlie Chaplin*. Michel had moved back to the Brattleboro area in the early 1970s, shifting from the demands of Hollywood productions to more intimate efforts—including a period away from filmmaking altogether in order to focus on painting. Michel co-founded Domilin Films, Inc., an acquisition and development company, for which he co-produced the television feature

*Why Me?* (1984). Michel subsequently founded MLM Studios, a video production company, in 1986, and completed a number of documentaries, including a portrait of his father Marcel Moyse, *Grand Old Man of the Flute* (1986), followed by *The Brattleboro Music Center* (1987) and *Heartwork: Art Emerging from Silence* (1993). With his wife Linda, he also co-founded the Center for Digital Art in 1996, an independent organization dedicated to the international video arts which also provides educational resources, job training, and teaches digital editing to Brattleboro area high school students. Amid this whirlwind of activity, Michel completed two arresting multi-screen experimental video features that stretched the emotional power of the medium. *The Runner* (1994) was a nine-screen (!) "moving painting" adapted from the 1982 O'Henry Literary Award-winning short story by Vermont author James Tabor; the second multi-screen feature *Cowards* (2001) consumed over five years of his creative life. Like *The Runner*, *Cowards* was filmed in and around Brattleboro (photographed by Michel's brother Claude Moyse) in 1995, with post production and editing completed in Michel's home studio and the Center for Digital Art. *The Runner* was selected for inclusion in the competition of the 8th Biennial of Moving Images at the Center for Contemporary Images in Geneva, Switzerland in 1999; *Cowards* won first prize in the 2002 Experimental Category from the New England Film and Video Festival in Boston. *The Round Schoolhouse* builds upon those efforts, though the complex interaction of video and painted images within the "Artists Define Place" gallery space was an entirely environment/experience/emotion-fueled installation, eschewing the narrative threads central to the prior two multi-screen features. Moyse's distinctive video abstracts punctuated both *The Runner* and *Cowards*, but *The Round Schoolhouse* is primarily composed of such imagery: "I call them 'motion paintings,' to reflect the fact that they exist in duration as well," Moyse noted in the Museum's flyer "Exploring Place." "This gives me the opportunity of working with motion and audio, two realms hitherto absent for traditional painting." The image reproduced here as an illustration (see p. 196) affords some information on the nature of the installation: "It belongs to the large projection screen when it's correctly set up," Michel explained. "This work consisted of two digital videos—one large, the other small—plus a window resting against the wall—projection images reflected on and thru it—and a white plastic chair perched on top of a white pole resting on the tv monitor. Hanging from the chair were two sheets of paper with text, pedagogical in nature." Thus, the multiple and multi-layered, ever-shifting images and audio tracks were integrated into, and constantly altered, the created environment. The title *The Round Schoolhouse* evokes the legendary but very real round "Lookout Schoolhouse" in Brookline, VT, built in 1822 by teacher and physician Dr. John Wilson; after Wilson's death in 1847, it was discovered that he was in fact the infamous British highwayman John Doherty, aka

"Captain Thunderbolt," who had plundered Ireland and the Britain/Scotland border for over a decade with his accomplice "Mr. Lightfoot." [63] Some of Doherty/Wilson's possessions, including his cane sword and false heel, replacing his which had been shot away, still reside in the collection of the Brooks Memorial Library in Brattleboro. "The piece was based, as you correctly infer, on the legend of Thunderbolt and Lightfoot," Michel acknowledged. "In fact, the middle section of the work combines graphics with sepia exteriors of the round schoolhouse in Brookline. I originally started with the idea of documenting, to some extent, the lives of this duo, but as time went on and I worked on it I selected the fact that Doherty/Thunderbolt assumed an identity as a teacher, commissioned the round schoolhouse, and taught for several years. My piece refers to teaching principles, methodology, bureaucracy, and learning—all, admittedly, in pretty sketchy and obscure ways. I was primarily interested in exploring relationships between moving images, sound, and text based loosely on the legend." In conjunction with the installation, Michel also presented "Art and Meaning in Our Contemporary Environment" on the evening of June 17, discussing his own work in the broader context of the value of art within our culture and its importance in the new digital era. At present, Moyse has no plans to publicly exhibit the installation in the immediate future.[64]

* *Sanctuary* and ***Wangari Maathai and The Green Belt Movement***: Alan Dater and Lisa Merton of Marlboro Productions (in Marlboro, VT, natch) are hard at work "on two documentaries that we are producing," Alan writes. *Sanctuary* involves the tragic December 2, 2001 shooting and death of Robert Woodward at the All Souls Unitarian Universalist Church in West Brattleboro, VT. Woodward, of Bellows Falls, VT, appeared before the congregation that morning in a highly agitated state—which has been the cause of much speculation and debate— seeking sanctuary while wielding a pocket knife, with which he threatened to injure or kill himself, and making statements about the environment and the government; the two local police officers who arrived on the scene ultimately shot Woodward seven times—witnessed by the congregation—and Woodward subsequently died. A controversial Vermont attorney general's office investigation cleared the officers of all wrongdoing, but the tragedy continues to send shockwaves through the church, the community, and the state, and became an issue of contention in the Howard Dean presidential campaign. In December, "Justice for Woody" organized their second annual march and vigil

---

[63] For more on this legend and Lookout Schoolhouse, see *Curious New England* by Joseph A. Citro and Diane E. Foulds, University Press of New England, 2003, pp. 264-265.
[64] For more info, see "Michel Moyse discusses *Round Schoolhouse* at BMAC," *The Brattleboro Reformer*, Thursday, June 10, 2004, pg. 29.

in downtown Brattleboro, commemorating Robert Woodward's death while still demanding answers, investigations, and a fair resolution.[65]

Moving from the local to the global, Alan describes *Wangari Maathai and the Green Belt Movement* as "a film about an amazing woman who works with poor rural Kenyan women. Over the last 25 years these women have planted over 20 million trees and have become a force to be reckoned with. Wangari Maathai, who was awarded the 2004 Nobel Peace Prize, is a passionate advocate for women's rights, Democracy and Kenya's environment. This film will primarily be shot in Kenya over the next year." Meanwhile, the celebrated Marlboro Productions library of Alan and Lisa's previous films remain as vital as ever: "Our productions *The World in Claire's Classroom* and *Home to Tibet* continue to attract audiences and are both available from us directly or from New Day Films, a cooperative distribution company, of which we are members." For the record, Alan has photographed a number of other recent films: "This past year several films that I was the DP on were released: Steve Alves's *Talking to the Wall* (see pgs. 126-134), and Julie Akeret's *Someone Sang for Me*, a beautiful film about the singer/teacher Jane Sapp, who works with kids in schools in Springfield, Mass. Currently Julie Akeret is finishing a documentary I shot with her about Tom Boys. It is due to be completed in the next couple of months." He also continues to work on *Birth of Innocence*. More on Alan, Lisa, Marlboro Productions, and their extraordinary films in future issues; for information or to arrange access to or exhibition of their works, visit their web site: http://www.marlboroproductions.com.

\* ***Senses of Place***: Filmmakers Patrick McMahill and Matthew Temple teamed up to make this timely drama about a political candidate's struggle to maintain his footing—and family relations—in the wake of his wife's accidental death. Returning to his family roots and struggling with his responsibilities to his stepdaughter, he inevitably is forced to question his own ambitions. "Ambition is a theme I've been interested in for a while," Temple commented, "I see ambition as creating almost a series of obstacles in terms of personal and spiritual growth." [66] Temple, McMahill, and cast and crew struggled with numerous obstacles while filming in and around Brattleboro and Marlboro, VT in the fall of 2002; weather complicated the shoot considerably, as Vermont autumns histori-

---

[65] Note that the Brattleboro-based Center for Digital Art has yielded one timely student documentary on the subject, Jim Millett and Roy Anderson's *Tragedy: The Death of Robert Woodward*, 2002, which deservedly won the first-ever "Enterprise Award" at the Castleton State College 2002 Castleton Videofest, designating documentary work of true social significance; more on this film in a future issue.

[66] quoted from the Associated Press story "Marlboro grads to screen film at Lake Placid fest," *The Burlington Free Press*, Saturday, May 22, 2004, pg. 1D.

cally do. The film was completed early in 2003. Henry David Clarke delivers a sympathetic performance in the lead role, supported by David Storrs, Eric Bass, Rusty DeWees, Morgan Eckert, Kate Fellows, Bev Miller, Brooks Brown, and others, including a cameo appearance by Fred Tuttle—reportedly his last, along with his appearance in John O'Brien's *Nosey Parker*. The original script—conceived as a period piece before budgetary and other concerns thrust the setting to contemporary times—was crafted by producer Matthew Temple (who also edited, scored, etc.), working on the revisions along with Mike Harrington, Carrie Sterr, Jay Craven (who also functioned as faculty advisor and executive producer), and director McMahill; the feature also boasts more sterling cinematography from Lasse Toft. *Senses of Place* won a Silver Remi from Houston's Worldfest, and enjoyed its "world premiere" at the Lake Placid Film Festival on June 2nd. Full review next issue; in the meantime, check out http://www.sensesofplace.com.

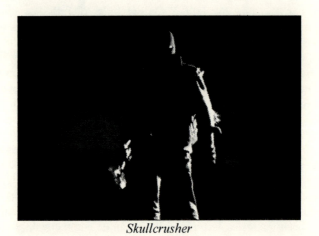

*Skullcrusher*

* ***Skullcrusher***: Over the past two years, Ben Coello has worked on numerous Vermont features in a number of technical and production capacities; now he's working on his own narrative feature. Ben and Nathan Caswell's original screenplay about a backwoods quarry-town haunted by a vengeful loner nurturing a preternatural bond with his sledgehammer and a taste for taking out misogynists is gearing up for filming in 2005. "I like to think of it as a fractured fairy tale," Ben explains, "that uses the genre conventions of a horror film to tell the story of mentally disturbed vigilante hero and the relationship he forms with a young woman. They're both outsiders... and they both need saving in their own way. It's in one another that they find what they're looking for. It's going to be dark, violent and probably a bit disturbing, but I'm hoping people will be

able to see through all that to the heart that lies at it's center." The 35mm promotional trailer I viewed last spring was quite impressive, and Ben and Nathan have been hard at work on rewrites, polishing this horror thriller (boasting a strong heroine lead, the beauty complimenting the titular beast) for his directorial debut. Working with Carrie Sterr and others late in the summer/early fall of 2003, Ben also shot and edited a trailer for another planned thriller, as yet untitled.

\* *The Undeserved*: New York City-based independent director Bradley Coley's coming-of-age drama was shot in and around Rockingham, Westminster, and Bellows Falls for an extended six weeks (July-August, 2003), with an additional week of shooting in the late fall. The $300,000 feature is Coley's directorial debut. Using Westminster's Compass School as their base of operations during the summer, Coley coordinated the efforts of Lasse Toft (cinematographer), Carrie Sterr (script supervisor), Geoff Eads, Ben Coello, and other already-veteren young filmmakers working on the production, which was reportedly filmed in improvisational sessions, John Cassevetes-style. Thus, the narrative the film began with as its bedrock transmuted as the production was underway. The cast includes Paul Sado (**right**) and James Martinez, who moved from New York City to Bellows Falls for the summer and fall to inhabit their roles as seniors in a small alternative school; Sado told *Brattleboro Reformer* reporter Howard Weiss-Tisman, "Brad's process is unique and different," and Martinez added, "It is the kind of process where you have to be committed 100 percent." [67] Reportedly filming continued into well into the fall, and the film is still in postproduction. Ben Coello told me, "We shot it Super 16 on an ARRI SR3 camera, using Fuji film stock. We didn't use any prime lenses but instead one zoom lens (10-100mm, I think)... It made for quicker set ups. We used daylight-balanced 500 speed film for many of the night exteriors, which was an interesting artistic choice made by Lasse. Then I think we had 250 speed in tungsten for interiors and daylight for exteriors.... We spent a lot of the beginning of the movie shooting on sticks, then went on the dolly as much as possible in the middle, and in the end we were going handheld almost all the time."

---

[67] "Compass School hosts film crew," *The Brattleboro Reformer*, Friday, July 18, 2003, pg. 1.

* ***The Voices Project***: Currently in development from director/ producer Bess O'Brien (***left***) (*Where's Stephanie?*, *Here Today*, etc.) of Kingdom County Productions is this two-year theater and music initiative for Vermont teenagers, "gathering teen stories to be adapted into an original theatre production with original music based on teen voices," Bess explains. The state tour begins spring of 2005, and the video production will be distributed through Vermont after the live tour. More info as the project evolves.

* ***Whatever Happened To Baby... Bear?***: Vermont treasure George Woodard made his mark as an actor in *Ethan Frome*, *Mud Season*, *My Mother's Early Lovers*, *The Mudge Boy* and many more (also see *America's Heart and Soul* and *Nothing Like Dreaming*, above) put the final touches to this lively short film this past winter, his first as a filmmaker, and was touring with it in February and March (Vergennes, Barre, and Waterbury) as part of his and his son Henry's "Off the Top of My Head: Old Music, Old Stories, and Old Cuss, and a Dirty Boy" stage show. Shot on 16mm in the fall of 1997 as part of his Burlington College film studies with Joe Bookchin (who has already mentored a generation of filmmakers), George says *Whatever Happened to Baby... Bear?* grew out of a series of assignments. "Joe would give us a reel of film, and say one week, 'Go shoot a place'," George recalls. "Then the next week, it was, 'Go shoot a continuity,' then 'Go shoot a chase scene'—well, I needed five rolls of film for my chase scene!—then 'Go shoot a dream sequence.' This all grew out of that." A little boy (played by George's son Henry, then five years of age) leaves his favorite stuffed baby bear on the running board of a truck, losing it when the truck drives away. It is found by three boys, who tangle with a farmer (Kevin Draper), leading to a merry chase and a heartbreaking finale. This was a real family affair—Henry Woodard, Suzanne Woodard, Matthew Woodard, and Willy Woodard co-star—and may pop up again as part of the various live-performance shows

George—who founded and continues to perform the Groundhog Opry annually—produces and stars in. The proceeds of these events will go toward George's planned directorial debut feature (!), to be shot late summer of 2004. More on George's feature film in future issues...

*Whatever Happened To Baby... Bear?*

* ***Windy Acres***: Kingdom County Productions announces the completion of filming on Jay Craven's independently-produced six-part television series *Windy Acres*, scheduled for broadcast on Vermont Public Television this fall (Wednesday evenings at 9 PM starting October 27) and on Mountain Lake Public Broadcasting for upstate New York audiences. The first episode will run an hour, with the remaining five shows clocking in at a half-hour each. Filming on the modestly-budgeted $300,000 series was completed over a six-week stretch in and about West Barnet, Peacham, and St. Johnsbury this June and July; Charles and Iris Morrison's West Barnet farm on Old West Road was the primary exterior location, leading the Morrison's to dub their village "Hollywood East." At the time of this writing, post-production is underway, though the October 27th debut will likely come and go before you read this. Kingdom County claims *Windy Acres* is "the first regional TV program of its kind in the United States." Though such programming has been the norm in TV for Canada and the UK for decades, don't forget the mini-series format wasn't embraced in the U.S. until the mid-1970s—with *Rich Man, Poor Man* and *Roots* among the landmarks—and has remained the pricey province of major networks, cable, and studios ever since. If *Windy Acres* is a success, Craven would love to expand it to an annual event, continuing the first season's narrative or pursuing other series concepts. "What's important here is the notion of series television," Craven told Associated Press reporter Tim McCahill. "Television that originates in Vermont, that is rooted in

Vermont story-wise but has the potential to reach out to other parts of the country." [68] Rusty DeWees stars as "love-starved" Kingdom farmer Lucien LaFlamme, who tangles with NYC marketing maven transplant Stephanie Burns (Stephanie Kofoed, replacing Jery Lynn Cohen, who had to be replaced mid-shoot due to illness) and her two daughters after their move to the fictional Blodgett, VT, attracted by a website promoting "agricultural tourism" and the rustic allure of Lucien's farm. Lucien and Stephanie inevitably butt heads, further complicated by the schemes of Lucien's Uncle Garald, aka UG (Bill Raymond), and romantic entanglements involving Stephanie's teenage daughter Titiana (Ariel Kiley) and local outlaw Turkey Tatro (Stivi Paskoski).

This comedy mini-series marks the first expansive creative collaboration between Craven and DeWees, though their relationship goes way back (to Craven's casting assistance on the Hollywood feature *Ethan Frome*, landing Rusty his first onscreen role). Rusty has appeared in all of Craven's Vermont-lensed features to date, including the Fledgling teen-collaborative feature *In Jest* (1999); other Kingdom County vets co-starring include the marvelous Tantoo Cardinal (also of *Dances With Wolves, Legends of the Fall, Silent Tongue, Black Robe, Smoke Signals, The Education of Little Tree* and more) and Bill Raymond (also of *Dogville, Summer of Sam*, HBO's *The Wire* and others). Joining them in the cast are Seana Kofoed, Charlie McDermott (who made his film debut this summer in M. Night Shyamalan's *The Village*), members of NYC's Upright Citizens Brigade, and Vermonters Grace Kiley (recently featured in Jon Andrews' fine *Pursuing Happiness*), Abby Paige, Sarah Yorra, John Griesemer, and 10-year-old Felicia Hammer, making her debut (who, according to Jay, "charmed all of us at a Burlington audition"). Jay co-scripted, basing the series on an original story by Randi Hacker; Hathalee Higgs and Lauren Moye produced with VPT's Enzo DeMaio and Dan Harvey. A dozen Marlboro College students and alumni participated, including Carrie Sterr (Script Supervisor and head of the editing team; see *7 to 10 Days*, above), Geoff Eads (rental equipment; also see *7 to 10 Days*, above), Brad Heck (chief camera operator), Andrew Hayes (2nd camera), Andrew Hood (key grip), T.J. Hellmuth (gaffer), Jesse Hannah (grip/electric), Mike Jensen (2nd assist camera), Sonia Darrow (PA), Ivy Robert (art department and 2nd 2nd AD), Chris Lewis (boom operator), and Pat McMahill (see *Senses of Place*, above). Jay's son Sascha Stanton-Craven worked in the art department and is one of three editors currently working with Carrie Sterr; Sascha graduated in May from Wesleyan University's film program (with high honors), and his senior thesis film *Blood Jaaker: The Movie* won the Frank Capra Award for Best Student Film.

---

[68] "Filmmaker Craven works on TV project," *The Brattleboro Reformer*, Thursday, June 10, 2004, pg. 3.

Jay Craven's *Windy Acres* (left to right):
Ariel Kiley, Seana Kofoed, Felicia Hammer, Tantoo Cardinal, Rusty DeWees,
Bill Raymond and Charlie McDermott
(*courtesy Kingdom County Productions*)

Rusty will be releasing the complete three-hour mini-series on DVD in late October via his independent multi-media venue rusty d. inc, and it will also be available through Kingdom County Productions for $24.95 suggested retail; the DVD will also feature and exclusive behind-the-scenes documentary and deleted scenes. To order *Windy Acres* or for more information, contact Kingdom County Productions at 949 Somers Road, Barnet, VT 05821, FAX 802-592-3193, call 802-592-3190, or log on to http://www.kingdomcounty.com or e-mail to kcp@pshift.com. Note that KCP also sells DVD and vhs of Craven's films *Where the Rivers Flow North*, *A Stranger in the Kingdom*, *The Year That Trembled*, *In Jest* and *High Water*, along with Bess O'Brien's documentaries *Here Today* and *Where Is Stephanie*. Or write Rusty at rusty d. inc., RR #2, Box 1770, Stowe, VT 05672, or FAX your order info to 802-888-1686; don't forget Rusty still offers both installments of *The Logger* on vhs and DVD and the shot-in-VT feature *Mud Season*, along with "Best in Show" (the 2005 Logger calender), Logger audio cassettes, and more.

*You Can't Be Neutral...*
Howard Zinn, WWII bombardier
(*Personal collection; compliments of Deb Ellis*)

* ***You Can't Be Neutral On A Moving Train***: This feature-length documentary chronicling the life and times of renowned historian, educator, playwright, author, and activist Howard Zinn—now in his 80s, and best-known for his bestselling *A People's History of the United States*, 1980—has played festivals, been picked up by First Run Features, and will enjoy a theatrical release in 2004. Zinn's untiring activist activities have made him a champion to a new generation, as his views, rooted in his firm knowledge and profound perceptions of American history, became increasingly relevent in the contemporary post-9/11 policies of our current government. As the filmmakers note on their website, world events over the five years of the documentary's production pushed it into unforeseen directions; indeed, the film "has evolved into a statement about the nature of war and a call for social activism expressed through the life of Howard Zinn." Co-produced by multi-award-winning Vermont filmmaker Deb Ellis (*Skin Deep, Unbidden Voices, Doris Eddy, Before She Knew*, etc.) and Chicago-based Dennis Mueller (*I Would Never Do That Again, Citizen Soldier: The Story of Vietnam Veterans Against the War, The Twentieth Century*, etc.), work on the project began in 1997. Ellis and Mueller previously collaborated on *The FBI's War on Black America* (1990), when Ellis lived in Chicago; she completed her graduate film studies at Northwestern University. Her initial involvement with the Zinn project as editor soon blossomed into another truly collaborative venture with Mueller. Matt Damon spices the soundtrack with readings from Zinn's works, and Noam Chomsky, Alice Walker, Marion Wright Edelman, Tom Hayden and Daniel Elsberg are among those who appear discussing the man, his activism, and his writings.

*You Can't Be Neutral...*
Howard Zinn, his wife Roz, and co-producer Deb Ellis
(*Personal collection; compliments of Deb Ellis*)

A version of the film was completed in the fall of 2003. The final, revised edit was completed by Ellis and Mueller in January 2004, and the success of two pre-release screenings of that cut—one in Chicago, the other at the October 2003 Vermont International Film Festival, where Burlington Mayor Peter Clavelle reportedly introduced Howard Zinn to audience of "The Peoples' Republic of Burlington"—boosted the filmmakers' efforts to secure distribution, culminating in their contract with New York City-based First Run Features. Prior to First Run Features' involvement, various fundraising events around the country—including Vermont—supported the venture, thanks to the efforts of New-York-City-based Seven Stories Press and Boston's The Joiner Center for the Study of War and Social Consequences; funding was also provided by the Illinois Humanities Council, Illinois Arts Council, Puffin Foundation, Anne Slade Frey Trust, Vermont Council on the Arts, Lucius and Eva Eastman Fund, Green Valley Media, Jo McInitire Peace and Education Fund, Hugh M. Hefner Foundation, A.J. Muste Foundation, and individual donors, with additional fiscal sponsorship from The Chicago Filmmakers.[69] For updates and more information, go to: http://www.agitfilm.com.

---

[69] http://www.chicago filmmakers.org.

*And that's just what I know about at the moment—I've no doubt neglected something important. Apologies to any filmmakers or video events I've missed; it's up to you to fill me in! The editor invites and welcomes any and all news, information, updates, clippings, notices, corrections, discoveries, graphics, or videos: msbissette@yahoo.com; PO Box 47, Marlboro, VT 05344. Thanks!*

Jay Craven on the set of *The Year That Trembled*

# End Papers

## *Screening Vermont Films*
## by Kenneth Peck

*Kenneth Peck, Ph.D.—Filmmaker, Professor, Art Administrator, and Writer—on the new Shelburne Film Series, The Vermont Filmmakers Forum and Vermont Public Television's* Reel Independents: Vermont's Film Showcase.

On the set of Jay Craven's *Windy Acres*: Rusty DeWees, Tantoo Cardinal
(*photo: Kingdom County Productions*)

If a film is made but never shown, does it exist? Unlike a painting or a sculpture, film exists only when it reaches a screen. Few Vermont films find venues for their projection. Far more are seen annually on TV screens from VHS and DVD copies than ever reach a large screen.

And if a film surmounts those odds and finds a projector and a screen but nobody is watching, does it exist then? These postexistential questions are not as ridiculous as they sound. But where does a local filmmaker find an audience?

In Shelburne Village, two rivers first came together in January 2004 in the old Town Hall. The Montpelier-based Vermont Film Commission is supporting a statewide venture to develop greater local film culture throughout Vermont by working with town and county arts groups to promote regional film screenings including presentations of their work by Vermont filmmakers. The Shelburne Craft School developed a film series to show all manner of cinema to small local groups in an attempt to bring a stronger film culture to their community.

The January event was the kick off of both ventures. Five films were shown (*Ice* by Art Bell of Burlington, *Perfect* by Robert Wurzburg of St. Johnsbury, *Falls* by Michael Fisher of Burlington, *Da Speech* by John Douglas of Charlotte, and *Arms for the Poor* by Anne Macksoud of Woodstock) with three filmmakers present. Ninety people came on a cold wintry night.

In June, Jay Craven did a special screening at Shelburne Orchards of two early films, the narrative *High Water* and the documentary *Gayleen*. Nora Jacobson will be bringing her *Nothing Like Dreaming* to the same audience this Fall, as part of a statewide tour of the feature. The relationship developing between local filmmakers and community is at the heart of the success of the Shelburne Film Series.

The Vermont Filmmakers Forum, a 501(c)(3) organization under the aegis of the Film Commission, coordinates Vermont Filmmaker shows throughout the state as part of its mission. Towns that have demonstrated significant interest in the public screening of films (not necessarily just Vermont works) are being approached to present local filmmaker evenings, similar to the Shelburne shows.

In late March, there was a panel on contemporary independent film distribution held in Montpelier as part of the Green Mountain Film Festival. Panelists included John Pierson, Larry Meistrich, David Klieler, Lisa Merton, and John O'Brien. The discussion covered narrative and documentary film, and looked at the course of independent film distribution over the past decades.

Vermont Public Television broadcasts *Reel Independents: Vermont's Film Showcase* most every Friday night at 10:00 p.m. The length of the weekly show varies in accordance with the length of the film, video or animation being shown. The average program is one hour in length and consists of a pre-screening interview with the filmmaker, the work being shown, and a post-screening interview. When more than one work is broadcast, we often have brief interviews between the different works.

Last season brought the Vermont public films by Anne Macksoud and John Ankele (*William Sloan Coffin: A Lover's Quarrel With America*), David Millstone and James Valastro (*What's Not to Like?: A Community Contradance*), Tim and Ben Kahn (*The Last Link*), Jay Craven (*A Stranger in the Kingdom*), Art Bell (*Only a Farmer* and *Ice*), Michael Fisher (*Falls*), Joe DeFelice (*Down the Yellowstone*), Nat Winthrop and Gary Miller (*Rookies at the Road*) and others.

The VPT website [70] provides information regarding submissions for future broadcasts. A programming committee watches everything submitted regardless

---

[70] http://www.vpt.org/programs/reel.html.

of content, style, and production values.

The 2004-2005 season is currently being programmed. I have the pleasure of being host to the show.

Morgan Bicknell, Alex Sevakian, Ruby Ferm, Siri Baruc
in Nora Jacobson's *Nothing Like Dreaming* (*photo Thomas Ames, Jr.*)

As mentioned above, Nora Jacobson is taking *Nothing Like Dreaming* on the road this Fall to over a dozen Vermont communities, plus screenings in New Hampshire towns along the Connecticut River and the Northhampton (Massachusetts) Film Festival in late October. There will be shows at theaters and old opera houses, conventional cinemas and town halls. Her Montpelier-filmed feature is being scheduled for a week-long run at the Savoy Theater before the holidays.

Self-distribution (and at some venues, even the projection) of one's film is a means of ensuring one's work is seen and provides a direct relationship between the viewer and the filmmaker. The experience can be enriching for both, but the task of coordinating a statewide tour is enormous and can be exhausting, if its expenses remain minimal. In our contemporary media culture, DVD sales of a feature often prove more lucrative than box office receipts. John O'Brien has successfully placed *Nosey Parker* in retail stores all over the Green Mountain state.

Two prominent local directors have chosen to pursue very different projects this year fully outside of the film market. Jay Craven created *Windy Acres*, starring Rusty DeWees, directly for television. The six-part situation comedy will begin broadcasting on VPT in late October. John Douglas designed his digital photographic series, *Homeland Security*, for website [71] and for art gallery (at UVM's Living & Learning Gallery throughout October). Both products bypass the question of how a filmmaker gets his work seen in contemporary media manners. Craven will return to feature film production in 2005 with *Disappearances*, starring Kris Kristofferson and Geraldine Chaplin, his third narrative feature based on the work of Howard Frank Mosher.

The two most interesting local works that I saw in 2004 were by Bill Simmon (*The Perfect Goodnight Kiss*) and Rob Koier (*Love/Hate*). Both are short narratives exploring the intricacies of interpersonal dynamics; both are original works that are far above average in their writing, acting, cinematography, and editing. Will you get a chance to see these works on a screen? I don't know, but I can assure you that they do exist.

*Kenneth Peck (photo by John Douglas) is the coordinator for the Vermont Filmmakers Forum for the Vermont Film Commission, host of Vermont Public Television's* Reel Independents: Vermont's Film Showcase, *and of the Key Sunday Cinema Club at Burlington's Roxy Theater. Over the past year, he wrote and directed a pair of documentaries for Burlington's Intervale Foundation,* The Old Intervale *and* The New Intervale. *Formerly the Chair of Burlington College's film program (1995-2000), which he founded in 1995, and the Executive Director of the Vermont International Film Foundation (1996-1999), he lives in Charlotte with his wife, ten year old son, two cats and a dog. He will begin teaching at Marlboro College in January 2005. He also co-authored the entries on "Films of Vermont" and "Films and Filmmakers" for* The Vermont Encyclopedia *(2003, University Press of New England).*

---

[71] http://www.redrat.net/work/photographic/homeland_security/collection.htm.

## *Bob Keeshan: A Final Tip of the Cap to the Captain.*
## by Stephen R. Bissette
## with Mark Evanier

As this year began, we received news of the passing of another beloved performer who was a neighbor to us all throughout much of our lives.

Bob Keeshan had lived in Hartford, VT since 1990. After struggling with a long illness, Keeshan died at age 76 on early the morning of January 23rd, 2004, at the Mount Ascutney Hospital and Health Center in Windsor.

I was seven months old when *Captain Kangaroo* debuted on CBS; living in northern Vermont, that meant I visited the Captain's *Treasure House* via WCAX-TV, Burlington. My generation literally grew up with the Captain. He was more often than not the first thing we watched each and every weekday morning as pre-schoolers, kindergarteners, and grade schoolers. And just when we thought we'd completely outgrown the Captain, we occasionally found ourselves watching it with preschool relatives.

Outside of our parents and siblings, Bob Keeshan was the first person we spent time with in the mornings, and that time was precious. We didn't know that, but Keeshan did, and for over a quarter-century, he made extraordinary use of that privileged doorway into every weekday of our young lives.

Born in Lynbrook, NY, Keeshan entered television working as a page for NBC while still in high school, seeking, according to *TV Guide*'s obit, "a quiet study place to become a lawyer," leaving for a stint in the Marine Corps in 1945, before returning to NBC and working his way up to become an assistant to "Buffalo" Bob Smith on *The Howdy Doody Show* (1947-60). Keeshan created Clarabelle the Clown for the program; his five-year tenure as the silent Clarabelle the Clown ended just prior to Christmas of 1952. This devastating turn of events opened the door for a period of experimentation for Keeshan, culminating in the debut of *Captain Kangaroo*—when Keeshan was in his twenties—in the fall of 1955.

The rest is television history.

In stark contrast to the ear-splitting bombast of most 1950s children's programming, Keeshan's heavyset Captain was a calm, friendly, impeccably mannered, and seemingly unflappable—but gullible—gentleman. The live program seemed almost surreally shapeless, drifting amicably through skits, music, dance, book readings, and bemusing antics by a variety of performers (led by Hugh "Lumpy" Brannum's forever likable Mr. Green Jeans), puppets (Dancing Bear, carrot-greedy Bunny Rabbit and practical joker Mr. Moose were predominate, as were ping-pong balls) and a steady stream of *Treasure House* guests human (including the delirious Banana Man), animal (often cuddled in Mr. Green Jeans' arms), and animated *(Tom Terrific* and Manfred, his mighty wonder dog). But Keeshan's Captain, with his cap, uniform, walrus moustache, impressive chops and trademark sugar-bowl haircut, was the anchor, tying all the *Treasure House* activities together with avuncular conversation. While most TV kid's show hosts shouted and carried-on with false bravado, Keeshan steadily talked to us in a quiet, straightforward manner few adults in real-life managed. He talked to us as individuals, it seemed, and that was something precious few adults seemed to do, least of all those on television. Though fantasy was the meat of the program, it was a gentle, inviting, caring, engaging, and, unbenownst to us, educational breed, forever fun, an imaginative tapestry threaded by the Captain's chatty manner.

Keeshan and his program won our eyes and hearts as it won kudos, citations, and awards from parents, parents groups, teachers, educators, and broadcasters, including six Emmy Awards, three Peabody Awards, and three Gabriels. By 1959, Keeshan's popularity as the Captain was such that he expanded his agenda to elevate children's pop culture by mounting a series of children's classical concerts in major cities, conducting the symphony orchestras himself. He remained an articulate advocate for progressive, substantial children's media to the end of this life.

By the late 1970s, the slow-and-steady pace of the Captain's visits began to seem sluggish in the increasingly competitive, hyper-frenetic context of children's media. In the fall of 1981, alas, CBS cut the Captain's one-hour visits to half that length; by 1982, the program was bumped from its classical 8 AM timeslot to 6:30 AM to make more room for the network's program for adults

*Morning*. Already invisible to the generation he had helped raise, an anachronism to the next generation who were more enamored of Big Bird and Oscar the Grouch, and now rendered barely-visible to a new generation, the Captain closed the CBS-based *Treasure House* once and for all in 1984, still the longest-running children's program in television history—reportedly over 9,000 episodes. After a brief sabbatical, Keeshan continued the program for six more years on public television until 1992, and the Captain lived on in videos and occasional public appearances.

By the example of his work, his life, and his vision, Keeshan redefined what was possible in children's programming, setting a high standard for those who followed in his footsteps, including the now-venerable *Sesame Street*, launched in 1968 by long-time *Captain Kangaroo* producer David Connell.

A statement issued by Keeshan's family in the wake of the man's passing said, "Our father, grandfather, and friend was as passionate for his family as he was for America's children. He was largely a private man living an often public life as an advocate for all that our nation's children deserve."

Keeshan's unceasing advocacy work included working with former VT Governor Howard Dean to enact the 1998 VT state income tax forms "children's checkoff," which steered financing to numerous children's programs.

Many 'urban legends' remain about Keeshan's life and TV career, almost all of which are apocryphal. TV, cartoon, and comics writer Mark Evanier dispelled many of them after Keeshan's death, noting "...there are a dozen different stories around about Lee Marvin and Bob Keeshan serving together in the Marines. In most, they served heroically in Iwo Jima and were awarded many medals. In truth, Keeshan did serve in the Marines but never saw combat and never saw Lee Marvin. There are also stories about Keeshan accidentally uttering a naughty word or doing the show with his fly open, but as far as I know, those things never happened."

At the time of Keeshan's death, Evanier wrote eloquently online about the man's career and legacy. With Mark's permission, we'll close with his words:

## *Mark Evanier on Bob Keeshan:*

I don't know if the formal obits will make it clear but Mr. Keeshan, with whom so many of us grew up, was an extraordinary individual. He had a capacity to talk to—not "down to"—children and to host a very difficult live TV show for a very long time...and this was a man who, when he first got into television, was by his own admission largely devoid of talent. As is probably well-known, his first role was as Clarabelle the Clown on the original *Howdy Doody* show. Less well-known is that he started there as a kind of go-fer/errand boy for the show's star, "Buffalo" Bob Smith. Among his duties was to herd the kids in and out of the show's Peanut Gallery and to get them to shut the hell up during the live broadcast. In this capacity, he occasionally got on camera and when some

NBC exec suggested it looked wrong to have a guy in a sport coat on the show, Keeshan was sent off to work up a clown costume. He started at the public library where he learned what he could about clowns, then he rummaged through the wardrobe and make-up departments and soon, Clarabelle was born.

Clarabelle (*right*) did not speak, partly because clowns were traditionally mute but mainly because Keeshan couldn't. By his own admission, he was too untrained and untalented to utter an on-camera word. By trial and error though, he managed to develop a pantomimed personality for his clown that the kids loved. It was mean, petulant and often quite nasty but it was Clarabelle. The only one who didn't love him was "Buffalo" Bob, who lived for the musical segments of his show and who was frustrated that the clown couldn't play an instrument. They tried giving Keeshan lessons but he had a tin ear and no sense of rhythm: He couldn't even play a triangle on the beat. At one point, Smith fired Keeshan and put a trained musician in the Clarabelle make-up... but the trained musician failed to capture the popular Clarabelle personality and they had to hire Keeshan back. That happened at least once, maybe twice.

After many years of Smith getting very wealthy off *Howdy Doody*, several cast members, led by Keeshan, made a stand and demanded better pay. They were fired and it looked like Bob Keeshan's TV career was over. But after failing in some non-television jobs, he made an amazing comeback with two different local shows on which he actually spoke. He had to, since he was the entire cast and mime wouldn't have worked. Eventually, it all led to *Captain Kangaroo*, which he did on CBS for thirty years. For much of that time, the show was live and it had to be done twice each morning, back to back. Keeshan and his small stock company (often, just Lumpy "Mr. Green Jeans" Brannum plus one puppeteer) would do an entire hour telecast live and then, after he said good-bye, they'd have sixty seconds to reset everything and do the entire show again for a different time zone. Somehow, it worked.

(In case you're interested in the chronology of Mr. Keeshan's shows: After being banned from Doodyville, he went off and took a job with his father-in-law but it didn't work out. He returned to television (local, in New York) in August of 1953 with a show called *Time for Fun*, in which the entire cast consisted of him as Corny the Clown, plus his dog. That was when he had to learn to speak on camera. Before '53 was out, he added a second show and a second character. On *Tinker's Workshop*, he played an old toymaker named Tinker. I've never seen any of these but Keeshan always told people that *Captain Kangaroo* was basically Tinker with more pockets in his coat.)

*Captain Kangaroo* started on October 3, 1955. Most folks don't know it but that wasn't Keeshan's final characterization. During the 1964-1965 season, he turned up on CBS Saturday morning with a show called *Mister Mayor*. Mister Mayor looked and sounded exactly like Cap'n Kangaroo but he was a different guy in a different outfit and with a different set and supporting cast. (The set had a wonderful, elaborate toy train layout.) At the time, I wondered why Bob Keeshan was playing one guy Monday through Friday and a different but similar character on Saturday. When I finally met him, it was one of the first things I asked about and he told me the following story...

It seems that when *Captain Kangaroo* was launched, Keeshan had an unwanted partner. I think—but am not sure—he said it was related to the fact that the Captain had evolved out of the Tinker character so someone who had a business interest in that show wound up with a percentage of *Captain Kangaroo*. As he explained it, Keeshan was having trouble with this partner and finally decided he wanted to have total ownership and control of his character. He tried to buy out the partner's interest but when the guy declined, Keeshan threatened to give up *Captain Kangaroo* and to create a new character...one in which the partner would not share. The partner said, "You wouldn't dare," and Keeshan decided to go ahead with his bluff. When CBS decided they wanted to add a Saturday morning installment of *Captain Kangaroo*, Keeshan insisted he would do it as *Mister Mayor*.

And he did. It was essentially a way to convince the partner that he was serious about abandoning *Captain Kangaroo*. "I was prepared to do that and continue as *Mister Mayor*," he told me. "But what

I really hoped was that it would convince him to sell out his interest in *Kangaroo*." That was how things played out. The partner sold out his share and the following season, the Saturday morning hour of *Mister Mayor* was replaced by an hour of *Captain Kangaroo*. I always thought this was a fascinating story...how close *Captain Kangaroo* came to disappearing due to a business dispute.

I actually watched the first telecast of *Captain Kangaroo* in October of '55. I was three and a half years old but I still remember it. A few years back when I worked with Mr. Keeshan, I of course told him this. He was very polite about it but I had the feeling that lots of people around my age told him that and he tended to not believe it. The project was a show called *CBS Storybreak*, which we taped over at Television City on Stage 33, the home of *The Price is Right*.

Keeshan had retired *Captain Kangaroo* by then and he hosted our show as Bob Keeshan. The network wanted him because of his enormous credibility in the area of children's programming and the fact that his hosting would help endorse a show they wished to have viewed as enriching. Mr. Keeshan, having learned well from "Buffalo" Bob, charged CBS what they felt was an exorbitant fee...but they paid it. One of the Business Affairs guys grumbled that the last few years *Captain Kangaroo* was on the network, as they kept cutting back his show and moving it to worse and worse time slots, he held the network up for vast amounts of cash. He kept threatening—they claimed—to go public and tell America that CBS didn't care about programming for children, and they essentially paid him off to let them phase out his show without a huge protest.

I don't know to what extent that's true but if it's completely true, it only adds to my respect for the man. Holding CBS up for money is an admirable skill, and I wish I was as good at it as he apparently was. Beyond that, I found him to be a genuinely kind, soft-spoken man who was everything you'd want Bob "*Captain Kangaroo*" Keeshan to be. He answered all my silly questions about his various TV endeavors, but he also kept asking everyone on the show about our backgrounds, particularly what kinds of training and education had led us to our present stations in life. He talked at length with the make-up lady about her family problems and joked with her about how, all the years he did *Captain Kangaroo*, he "grew into" the part and required less and less make-up. Eventually, he said, he reached the stage where they had to try and make him look younger than he really was. "That was a frightening moment," he said.

He said that despite turning into the kindly old man he played, he never got recognized in public by the visual. People, he said, only recognized him from his voice. It was a wonderful voice...warm and instantly friendly, and so much a part of so many lives for so many years. It's amazing to think that for so long, that man couldn't even use that voice in front of a camera. And it's sad to think of all the kids who won't grow up hearing it.

*Sources*:
"News From Me", an online journal by Mark Evanier, Jan. 23, 2004: "Keeshan Legends" (9:20 AM post) and "The Good Captain" (10:34 AM post); reprinted with Mark's kind permission. Go to:
http://www.newsfromme.com/archives/2004_01_23.html#003584
Brown, Les: *Les Brown's Encyclopedia of Television*, 3rd Edition (1977, 1982, 1992, Visible Ink Press, Detroit, MI), pp. 92, 267, 295.
Graff, Christopher: "Bob Keeshan Die at 76," Associated Press; *The Brattleboro Reformer*, Saturday-Sunday, January 24-25, 2004, pp. 1, 8.
Greenfield, Jeff: *Television: The First Fifty Years* (1977, Harry N. Abrams, NY; 1981 edition, Crescent Books/Crown Publishers, Inc., NY), pp. 226-227.
Poniewozik, James: "Appreciation: O Captain, My Captain," *Time*, February 2, 2004, Vol. 163, No. 5, pg. 70.
Shulman, Arthur and Youman, Roger: *How Sweet It Was: Television: A Pictorial Commentary with 1435 Photographs* (1966, Crown Publishers, Inc./Bonanza Books, NY), pp. 357-358.
Weiner, Ed: "Tributes: Bob Keeshan (1927-2004)," *TV Guide*, February 14, 2004, Vol. 52, No. 7, Issue #2655, pg. 15.

*Recommended Reading*:
Books by Bob Keeshan:
*Books to Grow By: Fun Children's Books* (Fairview Press, 1996)
*Captain Kangaroo: Tenth Anniversary* (self-published, 1965)
*Family Fun Activity Book: Playtimes and Activities to Bring Children and Grownups Together!* (Fairview Press/Deaconess Press, 1994)
*Good Morning, Captain: 50 Wonderful Years with Bob Keeshan, TV's Captain Kangaroo* (Doubleday, 1989; Fairview Press, 1996)
*Growing Up Happy: Captain Kangaroo Tells Yesterday's Children How to Nurture Their Own* (Doubleday & Company, 1989)
*Holiday Fun Activity Book* (Fairview Press, 1995)

Children's Books by Bob Keeshan:
*Alligator in the Basement* (Fairview Press, 1996)
*Captain Kangaroo's Get Well Elephant* (Robert B. Keeshan Associates/American Academy of Pediatrics, 1992)
*Hurry, Murray, Hurry!* (Fairview Press, 1996)
*Itty Bitty Kitty Makes a Big Splash: The Adventures of Itty Bitty Kitty* (Fairview Press, 1997)
*Just Right for Itty Bitty Kitty* (Fairview Press, 199?)

Listed as available from Books In, Books Out (Atascadero, CA) online at: http://dogbert.abebooks.com/servlet/SearchResults?an=Bob+Keeshan&imagefield.x=34&ph=2&bsi=90&imagefield.y=15

(information included here for archival purposes only):
"Captain Kangaroo *Scripts by Bob Keeshan and others*:
*The Captain Kangaroo Show: Television Scripts.* CBS Television 1963. Cloth. ...50 scripts in all! Bound volume of scripts from *The Captain Kangaroo Show*, [#1851-1900], dated February 4th, 1963 to April 12th, 1963... Only other copies in private collections or were donated to the NY Public Library and are on-line at New York Public Library Digital Library Collections (NYDPL copies may be viewed only by arrangement and photocopying is restricted). Books In Books Out copy belonged to music producer David Axlerod, his name in right hand corner on front of volume. Documention as follows: *Captain Kangaroo* Scripts: February 1, 1963 1 volume Bound typescripts [#1801-1850] are for the weekday show. Included with this rare volume of scripts, is rare original recording of the theme from *The Captain Kangaroo Show* (Puffin' Billy) by the CBS Orchestra, ca. 1954. transferred from reel to reel to CD (a gift to owner of Books In Books Out from a Hollywood publisher in the early 70's) in *sterling* condition! Theme originally used as theme for *Childrens' Favourites*, a British TV Show in 1952, written by Edward White. Theme sold only in Great Britain and only by Melodi Light Orchestra, not the CBS version (though it was copied almost note for note). This is *the* original theme song done by the CBS Orchestra for titles and endtitles of show when it debuted in 1954 until the theme music was changed in the early 70's."

Bob Keeshan, Bunny Rabbit and Bennye Gatteys on *Captain Kangaroo*

Stephen R. Bissette (right) with cartoonist James Sturm (left) in May, 2004.
Sturm is the founder of The Center for Cartoon Studies,
scheduled to open in White River Junction, VT, in the fall of 2005.
Bissette will be teaching there.
(*photo courtesy of James Sturm*)

## ABOUT THE EDITOR

**Stephen R. Bissette** earned kudos, awards, and scars working 24 years in the comicbook industry. He made his mark as a cartoonist, writer, editor, publisher, and co-publisher, and remains best-known for *Saga of the Swamp Thing, Taboo, 1963, Tyrant* and more. Bissette co-created the character of John Constantine played by Keanu Reeves in the upcoming feature film *Constantine* and worked briefly on Mirage Studios' *Teenage Mutant Ninja Turtles*; the character "Tokka" which appeared in the second *TMNT* feature film, *Teenage Mutant Ninja Turtles: Secret of the Ooze*, was based upon his drawings. He drew the world's second *24-Hour Comic*, invented by Scott McCloud as a challenge for Bissette. He retired from comics in 1999, but he's still a busy fellow. Since 1990, Bissette has illustrated numerous books by authors like Joe Citro, Neil Gaiman, Douglas Winter, Joe Lansdale, Rick Hautala, Christopher Golden, Nancy Collins, Matt Spencer and others, and painted the cover art for the Barrel Entertainment DVD *Last House on Dead End Street*.

As a writer, Bissette's fiction work includes the Bram Stoker Award-winning novella *Aliens: Tribes*, short fiction for *Words Without Pictures, Hellboy: Odd Jobs, Working for the Man* and more. His published non-fiction efforts include *We Are Going To Eat You! The Third World Cannibal Movies*, co-authoring *Comic Book Rebels* and *The Monster Book: Buffy the Vampire Slayer*, essays for *Cut: Horror Writers on Horror Films, Underground USA* and *Alan Moore: Portrait of an Extraordinary Gentleman*, articles for numerous film magazines and fanzines, and a two-year stint writing a weekly video review column for New England newspapers; he also wrote the liner notes for the Synapse DVD release of Radley Metzger's *The Image*. Stephen continues to write for *Video Watchdog* magazine; he edits, packages, and writes for *Green Mountain Cinema* and is currently at work on a book-length study of Vermont films and filmmakers. Bissette also works as a tutor, lecturer, and was a guest author at the prestigious Breadloaf Young Writers Workshop in Middlebury, VT.

He co-managed and remains an active partner in First Run Video in Brattleboro, VT, which won the national VSDA Award for Outstanding Independent Video Store of 2002. As a partner with Vermont author and folklorist Joe Citro and Take 2 Productions, he's currently co-producing their first feature.

Visit Bissette's website at http://www.comicon.com/bissette

Printed in the United States
23077LVS00001B/547-579